Corporate Strategy in Post-Communist Russia

Russian businesses in the post-Soviet period have been noted for their unusual, sometimes allegedly corrupt, business practices, and for their role in the enrichment of oligarchs. This book, which includes a wide range of case studies, and which draws on the author's first-hand experience of running a Russian company, argues that a key to understanding contemporary Russian business is the importance of arbitrage, that is, the ability to take advantage of price and cost differentials in different markets. The book argues that the conditions for such arbitrage advantages are often created by businesses that have special links to particular institutions; that arbitrage benefits are not available to all businesses in a sector, thereby providing unfair competitive advantages to some businesses; and that businesses' overall activities are often distorted by this system. The book includes an analysis of a wide range of different types of arbitrage activities in action.

Mikhail Glazunov is an independent consultant. He has worked as a Lecturer in the Department of Business Studies at the University of Hertfordshire, UK, and as a Chief Executive Officer of a Russian company.

Routledge Contemporary Russia and Eastern Europe Series

For a full list of titles in this series, please visit www.routledge.com.

Corporate Strategy in Post-Communist Russia

Mikhail Glazunov

Routledge
Taylor & Francis Group

LONDON AND NEW YORK

First published 2016
by Routledge

2 Park Square, Milton Park, Abingdon, Oxfordshire OX14 4RN
711 Third Avenue, New York, NY 10017

Routledge is an imprint of the Taylor & Francis Group, an informa business

First issued in paperback 2017

British Library Cataloguing in Publication Data
A catalogue record for this book is available from the British Library

Library of Congress Cataloging in Publication Data
Names: Glazunov, Mikhail, author.
Title: Corporate strategy in post-communist Russia / Mikhail Glazunov.
Description: Abingdon, Oxon ; New York, NY : Routledge, 2016. |
    Series: Routledge contemporary Russia and Eastern Europe series ; 69 |
    Includes bibliographical references and index.
Identifiers: LCCN 2015036974 | ISBN 9781138956704 (hardback) |
    ISBN 9781315665603 (ebook)
Subjects: LCSH: Management--Russia (Federation) | Corporations--Russia
    (Federation) | Arbitrage--Russia (Federation) | Competition--Russia
    (Federation) | Strategic planning--Russia (Federation)
Classification: LCC HD70.R9 G53 2016 | DDC 658.4/0120947--dc23
LC record available at http://lccn.loc.gov/2015036974

ISBN: 978-1-138-95670-4 (hbk)
ISBN: 978-1-138-47777-3 (pbk)

Typeset in Times New Roman
by Taylor & Francis Books

Contents

List of tables

Preface

This book develops a new perspective on corporate strategy as arbitrage between markets where various asymmetries are exploited by companies to increase profit. It reveals who creates the conditions for arbitrage and how it is accomplished. Different types of strategy as arbitrage, together with methods of how this strategy can be employed in the economy of Russia and the beneficiaries of arbitrage, are examined. The ability to create conditions for arbitrage is shown to be a valuable company resource, providing competitive advantage for owners.

The frameworks of research are enclosed by the borders of the post-Soviet space due to the fact that the Russian market provides excellent illustrations of this phenomenon. The book includes over 100 examples presented in the form of case studies, some of which are described in detail.

These detailed cases reveal how companies such as Gazprom, Avtovaz, Transneft, Norilsk Nickel and Yukos have competently used arbitrage as strategy, as well as describing why other companies have not succeeded at this challenge. The book reveals other generic strategies, apart from cost leadership and differentiation-arbitrage, which can be implemented by various firms in any industry or market to increase their performance.

This book is intended as a resource for academics and students of strategic management. Additionally, this study may benefit those who are interested in Russian modern history as well as those concerned with the analysis of new strategic models.

Acknowledgement

Numerous people, both Russian and British, helped to make this manuscript by sharing their stories, talking honestly about Russian business and helping me arrange my thinking about how to get it right.

I want to thank Peter Sowden, my editor at Routledge, with whom I have worked on both of my books. Peter's beneficial editorial experience has proved invaluable in enabling a Russian researcher to write beyond the limitations of the conventional approach. Many thanks are due to the staff at Routledge. I am thankful for the substantial advice that the anonymous advisers provided me and for their aid in configuring the chapters in order for the book to take its final shape and reach completion. I would like to thank my colleagues Elena Zhukova, Nicolas Anderson and the rest of the supportive team, who have been my day-by-day academic colleagues for the past three years.

I am grateful to everyone at the University of Hertfordshire Business School who have made this book possible. I would like to offer special thanks to Peter Ivanov, who read my book with admirable care and attention, making some especially valuable suggestions that I have incorporated.

I would like to especially show appreciation to my old friend Boris Demidov, who helped me in collecting information for my research. I am also deeply grateful to the people who took many hours to talk with me about their practice in Russian business and government organisations – Denis Kondratiev and Victor Ten – their ideas contributed to the creation of my vision of Russia. I am also deeply grateful to the businessmen, analysts and other thinkers with whom I have had a prolific dialogue about their practice in Russian business, including Lucy Demidova and Igor Kolesnikov.

I would like to express my special appreciation to Philip Cox for helping me, his attention to nuances was astonishing, he read every draft of this book and made every chapter better. Thank you to all those around the Russian Federation and the United Kingdom who have invited me to speak and contribute articles over the past few years – you know who you are.

Last, but undoubtedly not least, I want to thank my family for their love and support. Most of all, unquestionably, I must thank my son Mikhail, who could not play tennis with me as he wanted due to my writing the book, and my wife Maria, who surrounded me with love and assistance. I deeply appreciate her patience as she endured my writing.

Mikhail Glazunov
Bedfordshire, England
June 2015

Introduction

In the 1990s, as a somewhat naïve business consultant, I often discussed with my clients how they understood the strategy of their companies. In most cases, their vision of the strategy did not fit Porter's model, popular at that time. I tried to explain the focus strategy or cost leadership strategy; managers understood these approaches and the importance to their business. However, again and again I heard a simple explanation for success, which was expressed by everyone almost equally: the company needs to integrate into the system, it must have good relations with everyone and it should be able to buy cheaply and sell expensively. I was a little frustrated that their formulation of strategies was far from that accepted by academic science, and I attributed this to the fact that in 1990s Russia there was an initial accumulation of capital and the strategy was aimed at obtaining the maximum short-term profit in any way possible. Such methods as direct defaults on obligations, manipulation of taxes, and transfer of assets from a state or joint-stock company to the company where the sole owners are executives of the first company are widespread.

Generally, investment in companies was not commonplace and a strategic programme was implemented which consisted of four steps: buying assets, conducting the preparation and selling of assets and, last but not least, appropriating the revenues. As the medieval philosopher Witelo said, think about the end-game, about how to escape happily, rather than about how to enter. In the 2000s, with the continued accumulation of capital, this strategy changed to one of long-term presence, focused on sustained business growth. As a result, executives began to think about creating competitive advantage and reinvestment of profits in their own business.

A few years later, my research work in the University of Hertfordshire gave me the impetus to look at the strategy of companies 20 years after the beginning of the Russian reforms. Having read several hundred articles in Russian business magazines and carried out several dozen interviews with executives and experts, I undoubtedly saw new business, new methods and extensive opportunities. However, I sensed that sometimes I had studied such situations, but referring to the past in general rather than to specific companies. This was a state of *déjà vu* similar to re-reading a book first read 20 years ago. I could not remember what would happen on the next page, but analysed these events and the relationships between them in detail. Twenty years ago, many Russian companies which were analysed employed relatively similar approaches to corporate strategy.

Looking at the transformation of Russian companies over the past 20 years, of course, one can say that Russian companies have adopted different elements of the market economy. However, despite the dissolution of the post-soviet system of business, many operational elements of the Soviet system have not been eliminated. Many companies do not think about where the company should compete; how the company could achieve and maintain an advantage; or what capabilities, assets, structures and culture companies are needed to implement their strategy.

These companies used a simple strategy: buying cheaply and selling expensively, simultaneously creating barriers to prevent the entry of competitors to their respective segments of purchasing and sales by using a variety of approaches, from the creation of appropriate legislation to criminal methods. However, there has been a shift from brutal gangster methods to more elegant bureaucratic schemes with the same result. These strategies used a straightforward *modus operandi* and have been implemented by a large variety of firms in many industries and markets. The new strategy has universal applicability, does not depend on the company, and describes strategic positions at an uncomplicated and yet comprehensive level.

Along with the works of Ghemawat (2007), an article about arbitrage as strategy written by Professor Colin Haslam and co-workers from the University of Hertfordshire (Haslam *et al.* 2012) provides the missing element for a holistic understanding of this Russian phenomenon and creates a coherent theory which forms the basis for this book.

Arbitrage is one of the widespread concepts of modern economics, employing the law of one price and keeping markets efficient: if two assets have equivalent risk and return, they should sell at the same price. If the price of the same asset is different in two markets, there will be an arbitrager who will purchase the asset cheaply and sell in the market where it is expensive. Arbitrage involves the simultaneous purchase and sale of the same or analogous security in two different markets for profitably different prices and continues until prices in the two markets reach equilibrium; the object of arbitrage may be assets of a different nature, such as securities, currency, commodities or derivatives, in order to take advantage of differing prices.

Ghemawat (2003) proposes a new perspective on arbitrage as a component of corporate strategy. Here arbitrage is not cheap capital or labour, but rather the differences that continue among countries. Distance between countries impacts upon business in a new market because costs and risks are a result of barriers created by this distance. Ghemawat selects different forms of arbitrage, such as economic, cultural, administrative and geographical. In economic arbitrage, an arbitrager searches for price differences between similar goods and immediately takes the opportunity by buying the undervalued good and simultaneously selling the overvalued good. Other types of arbitrage take similar advantage of dissimilarities in human religions, attitudes and values (cultural arbitrage); the system of rules between states (administrative arbitrage); and geography (geographical arbitrage).

Haslam *et al.* (2012) propose a new look at corporate strategy as arbitrage between markets where different asymmetries are exploited by company managers to raise earnings capacity. They reveal three different types of strategy as arbitrage: product, which takes advantage of the variability in price structure between product markets; labour, exploiting social settlements governing employment; and thirdly capital market arbitrage, temporal price variations arising from asset appreciation in capital markets together with tax, interest and exchange-rate variations through transfer pricing.

Despite the growing number of publications devoted to corporate strategy as arbitrage, there is little empirical understanding of the critical issues involved – namely the creation of price asymmetries for arbitrage, and how purposeful human activity creates opportunities for arbitrage. From a development position, one can ask supplementary questions: Is this a new phenomenon in business practice? Is there another type of strategy as arbitrage? How can strategy as arbitrage be employed in the transitive economies of Russia? Also, what creates such asymmetries and opportunities for arbitrage in transitive economies? Is there a difference between technologies of arbitrage in the various industries of the Russian economy? Who is the major beneficiary of such arbitrage?

The framework of research here is narrowed down to the borders of the post-Soviet space due to the fact that Russia provides a lot of material for the study of this phenomenon, and studies within one country can slightly reduce cross-cultural and linguistic differences. This study of business in Russia from an arbitrage point of view also addresses those who are interested in Russian modern history, as well as those interested in the analysis of new strategic models.

The book reveals that the ability to create conditions for arbitrage is an important resource of a company, and in some situations it is a vital factor for success of the business. Conditions for arbitrage are valuable and relatively rare resources because they provide competitive advantage for owners, and there is a deficiency in their substitutability; if other firms can easily copy an arbitrage capability, it will not be a source of advantage. This book tries to find correlations between the ability to create conditions for arbitrage and insoluble relationships with authorities.

The book reveals different types of strategy as arbitrage and, where possible, demonstrates the specificity of Russia. As one example: the fundamental idea of labour arbitrage in Russia is production of value by considerably cutting remuneration and decreasing the qualification requirements of the labour force through replacing the domestic labour force by a foreign labour force, mainly from Central Asia. In contrast with modern trends, where Western entrepreneurs increase income by substituting the labour force with new equipment and technologies, their Russian counterparts substitute expensive labour with cheap labour.

Finally, migration gives a new impetus to Russian corruption and disruption of the law; employers prefer to employ migrants due to the absence of contracts or formal agreements, a *gastarbeiter* is not registered in Russian tax accounting and an employer does not pay tax. In addition, migrants, underprivileged in their countries, agree to live in inhuman environments that generate the conditions for the creation of large ghettos in the Russian megalopolises which are a source of unsanitary and delinquent behaviour. Moreover, the educational system is not ready to accept migrant children because of their lack of knowledge of the Russian language and due to the lack of school places. The actual economic impacts of an influx of cheap labour are an increase in revenues of companies that employ migrant workers and a consequent increase of unemployment among Russians, a significant reduction of wages in the Russian economy, deficit in pension funds and medical insurance funds, cash outflow from the Russian economy and impairment of Russian modernisation. Once again, this is an example from Russia, but the name could easily be changed to that of a dozen other European countries – which may indicate something about universal examples and theoretical concepts.

This book includes over 100 examples, presented in the form of case studies, some of which are described in detail while others are presented in outline. The case study method is widely adopted, and has a particular significance in this investigation because it offers the opportunity to study the phenomenon of arbitrage in its economic, geographic and social context. These cases were designed on the basis of analysis of personal experience, corporate and analytical reports and analysis of the mass media. Case studies are not only excellent illustrations of the theoretical constructs but, together with theory, encourage the reader to further reflection.

The book is designed to be understood by a broad range of readers: investors, entrepreneurs, business school lecturers and students who are interested in new business trends, or who want to escape from old-fashioned business models. Also, it may interest readers who are attracted to Russian politics and economics. The book provides a useful tool for understanding arbitrage prospects today, allowing the reader to realise arbitrage operations in any country.

The structure of the book

This book consists of nine chapters. Chapter 1 reviews the main perspectives on strategy, and considers the idea of corporate strategy as a process of arbitrage between markets where diverse types of asymmetry, including geographical, economic, social norms and values, cultural, and administrative, are exploited by corporate managers to increase income. The scope for arbitrage includes the differences that continue among countries and regions. Also, the chapter discusses arbitrage as generic strategies, distinct from traditional strategies such as cost leadership and differentiation.

Chapter 1 reveals different types of strategy as arbitrage: product, labour capital market and institutional arbitrage, which take advantage of the variability in price structure between product markets, social settlements governing employment, temporal price variations arising from asset appreciation in capital markets and tax, interest and exchange-rate variations through transfer pricing as well as institutional divergence. The chapter analyses of the use of arbitrage in Russia from a historical perspective, from Stalin's time to modern Russia. Historical illustrations from Russia disclose that arbitrage as an element of business performance is not a new phenomenon. Arbitrage was immanent within the Soviet system, and was one of the many regulators of economic life. However, in the Soviet Union, with strong central control and an authoritarian regime, price was regulated by the state and opportunity for arbitrage was minimal; in many cases arbitrage as a business operation was forbidden, and as an result was being carried out illegally. In the last years of the USSR, along with increasing political fluctuations and reducing state regulation in the economy there was exponential growth of opportunities for arbitrage.

In Chapter 2 an analysis of the possibility of implementing arbitrage, the matrix of price asymmetries and opportunity is proposed. Utilising a different level of price asymmetries and opportunity, the matrix reveals four possible options for arbitrage as well as different substrategies for managers. Examples from the Russian oil, financial and car businesses illustrate this theoretical model more precisely. Additionally, anti-arbitrage as a complementary generic strategy that is aimed at destroying price differentiation or the opportunities for arbitrage of competitors is analysed.

Chapter 3 shows that the regions of the Russian Federation have enormous variations, such as those seen between countries. Among the regions of the country there are Muslim and Orthodox areas, very traditional and modern areas, some mostly agricultural and others industrial, both subtropical and polar, highlands and plains. The chapter shows that the distance between two regions is a significant factor for businesses, which companies have to analyse thoroughly when they make decisions about regional expansion.

Chapter 3 goes on to show that it is more relevant for the analysis of arbitrage opportunities to use bilateral measures of distance, which include distance in culture, in the administrative and institutional context, geography and differences in economic attributes. Distance may have different dimensions, each of which create asymmetries, a key element for arbitrage as a strategy in Russia. The vastness of Russia and relatively weak transportation and communication links create variation between regions and form geographic distance between regions. Regional business culture reveals a number of examples of social norms and values which create distance between regions.

Chapter 4 analyses how institutions effect the implementation of arbitrage in the contexts of the associated transactions, and also of creating conditions for arbitrage utilising the theories of property rights, transaction costs, optimal contracts and public choice. The chapter reveals different types of transaction and institutional costs related to arbitrage contracts, and transformation costs of arbitrage associated with the creation of institutional change projects, the promotion of such projects, the creation and maintenance of intermediate institutions for project implementation, and the development of arbitrage or defence against attacks by rivals.

The chapter notes that arbitrage has become the dominant practice in business operations, evolving from a technical element to the dominant strategy, becoming a sustainable norm. The stability of arbitrage as strategy and as a norm of firms' behaviour is ensured by a stabilising mechanism with negative feedback. Domination of arbitrage generates a particular configuration of the organisational structure of the firm and its functionally oriented departments.

Chapter 5 attempts to answers the questions of by whom, and how, asymmetries are created; and investigates more deeply price asymmetries as opportunities for arbitrage, as well as causes of these asymmetries, particularly how purposeful human activity creates opportunities for arbitrage. This chapter reveals different technologies of forming conditions for arbitrage in the Russian economy by analysing various examples in the agro, food, oil, fish and construction industries. Case studies persuasively suggest that these conditions are being formed deliberately, and they show who the primary beneficiaries of arbitrage are.

The ability to create conditions for arbitrage is an important resource of a company and is often among the critical important factors for success of the business. Additionally, other aspects of conditions for arbitrage, such as access to the market infrastructure and relationships with authorities, are revealed as well as various nuances of competition in arbitrage. The chapter analyses how many conditions for arbitrage are valuable, rare, inimitable and nonsubstitutable resources of a company, and how they are a source of firms' competitive advantage.

Chapter 6 investigates goods arbitrage as a transaction of purchase and sale with settlements in the form of barter operations, and reveals how geographic differences, weak connections and administrative barriers create conditions for price asymmetries.

Companies affiliated with the establishment can hedge the market risk of adverse price changes in assets trading with the federal and regional authorities. Also, such companies can restrict the access of other companies to information and participation in tenders. Analysis of Gazprom business activity shows that the company widely uses arbitrage of product, by restricting access of independent gas producers to the Gazprom gas distribution network, supporting artificial quotas for gas consumers, and encouraging customers to buy gas at market prices from their subsidiaries which appear here as arbitrageurs.

Chapter 7 analyses labour arbitrage in Russia as a socio-economic phenomenon where Russian companies arbitrage labour costs by transferring operations to low-labour-cost regions to benefit from inter-regional differences in working hours and wages. There are two main paths in which higher-wage labour can be substituted for low-wage labour: the transfer of production processes to deprived regions with low salaries; and the transfer of the workforce from deprived Russian regions and from former Soviet Union Republics. In addition, the chapter investigates a third path: using the special closed zones, where it is possible to establish special conditions for working and have lower labour expenditures. Additionally, there are complementary advantages for companies moving to regions with low wages and emerging markets, exploiting asymmetries between high and low levels of labour safety cost, labour law cost, environmental pollution cost and knowledge cost in order to boost earning capacity.

The real social cost of labour arbitrage in Russia is explored: labour migration gives a new impetus to Russian corruption, and disruption of the law generates stipulations for the creation of large ghettos in the Russian megapolises with high levels of unsanitary and delinquent behaviour. The chapter discloses the central idea of labour arbitrage in Russia as an increase in economic value by dramatically cutting both wages and qualification requirements of the workforce through the replacement of the national labour force with foreign labour.

Chapter 8 investigates outsourcing – contracting with another party to perform a specific function which is not considered a core activity of the business and can provide cost savings. The chapter notes that outsourcing is not a new phenomenon in business; previously known as subcontracting, it was extensively employed in Japan, USA and USSR in the 1950s.

The most outsourced functions are information technology, accounting, payroll, administration, corporate property services, catering, office cleaning and security. The chapter analyses three types of outsourcing of personnel that prevail in Russia: staff leasing, temporary outsourcing and outstaffing. It notes that outsourcing of personnel generates serious problems, such as a lack of involvement in the organisation's business by workers and inattention of external staff to the reputation of their temporary employer.

Additionally, the chapter investigates tolling in sugar, ferrous metallurgy, aluminium and light industries, which is a relationship between two companies in which the ownership of the raw materials passes to the enterprise that manufactures from raw materials and returns finished products to the first company which, in turn, pays the manufacturing cost of processing and an agreed income.

Chapter 9 examines transfer price: the cost at which goods are relocated between related enterprises. A considerable proportion of transactions take place between related units within international corporations without transitions through the independent market, permitting corporations to manipulate internal prices of their goods to their benefit. These transfer prices do not represent real market prices and are often sham operations between related enterprises in order to reallocate business income or profit.

The chapter goes on to show that a firm's profit can be transferred to a Russian region that offers special conditions for business, such as internal offshore zones, permitting the firm to use a reduced corporate tax rate. Taking into account that Russia is a federation, the chapter investigates how domestic transfer pricing creates profit centres in regions, and how the distribution of revenue among different regions impacts on the sustainable development of territories.

The Conclusion presents an estimation of impact of arbitrage as strategy in the transformation of Russian business and economy for the past two decades and the fate of Russian business. I evaluate perspectives of more complicated models of arbitrage, and present my vision for development of the theory and practical application of arbitrage.

This book has many of the answers – but not all, as arbitrage and the business environment are continuously changing. Every second, entrepreneurs across the world create new opportunities for arbitrage. Life poses new questions for these entrepreneurs and there are new responses; some are successful, others are not. I hope my text will help to increase the number of favourable answers.

1 Demarcation of arbitrage

The chapter considers the idea of corporate strategy as a process of arbitrage between markets where diverse types of asymmetry – economic, cultural, administrative and geographical – are exploited by corporate managers. The scope for arbitrage includes the differences that exist between countries and regions. Also, the chapter considers arbitrage as strategy apart from traditional generic strategies such as cost leadership and differentiation.

Definition of strategy

According to the traditional definition, strategy is the direction and scope of an organisation over the long term, which achieves an advantage in a changing environment through its configuration of resources and competences with the aim of fulfilling stakeholder expectations (Johnson *et al.* 2013). In addition, strategy should help to the company to address the following questions: Where should the company compete? How could the company achieve and maintain an advantage? What capabilities, assets, structures and culture do companies need to implement the strategy? How can the company change?

Porter (1980) offers a strategy typology, and these strategic alternatives are labelled generic because theoretically any type of business can implement them, whether it is a mining company, a high-technology firm or a public organisation. According to Porter's approach, a company's positions itself in its industry relative to competitors, suppliers and customers, and as a result of positioning, presents a suitable choice of generic strategies of low-cost production, product differentiation or specific focus. In addition, firms' own choices of generic strategies have to bring them into line with all the other firms that operate along the value chain, as these initiatives impact on the company's performance.

Simplifying, the profit of a company is the difference between its revenues and the cost of units multiplied by the number of units sold. Consequently, companies can achieve high profitability (in Porter's terminology, competitive advantage) through attaining low costs and large quantity of sold units (cost leadership strategy) or by distinguishing their products from those of competitors (differentiation strategy). Later, Porter added a focus strategy, which suggests that a company may choose to focus on a narrow rather than a wide-ranging scope of products. By accepting and effectively realising one of these generic strategies, a company can produce higher earnings than the industry average (Porter 1985).

Porter notes that a company should select a strategy in order to operate in attractive industries, in which it can use its generic strategy and achieve higher profit than that of an average firm in the same industry. However, there is a problem with the determination of an industry average firm. It is quite difficult to identify the average firm in the car industry, for example, which includes Kia, Mercedes and Tesla Motors. Moreover, employing Porter's approach it is often impossible to find a single strategy for a large company. For example, the car manufacturer Mercedes produces the SLS AMG Roadster which costs £176,950 and this model competes with Ferrari; but on the other hand Mercedes also makes A and B class cars which compete against the mass products of VW or Ford, so it remains an open question as to which generic strategy will be optimal for Mercedes. The calculation of an average strategy from SLS AMG Roadster and A class is the same as the calculation of the average temperature of patients in a hospital: there is a lot of information, but not enough practical sense. Many companies are conglomerates and operate in different, unrelated industries or markets. As a result, a company needs to employ different generic strategies in one segment, where it uses a differentiation strategy, from those in another, where it uses a cost leadership strategy. This approach contradicts Porter's idea that a company has to employ one or other generic strategy across the area of the market served. Moreover, Porter's idea about one generic strategy for a company is inappropriate for highly diversified corporations.

Porter's concept of generic strategies also has other shortcomings. For example, the concepts of differentiation and cost leadership have many similarities: in the differentiation strategy we need to remember cost price; but in the cost leadership strategy we should not forget about quality standards. Also, cost leadership does not always bring more benefits than the second or third place in the industry, perhaps outperforming the leader in other parameters such as return on capital employed. In addition, there are difficulties because of the contradictory requirements for the organisation of activities, which includes each of the generic strategies.

Relatively similar generic frameworks for gaining competitive advantage have been offered by numerous researchers. For example, Treacy and Wiersema (1995) offer a framework where a company usually can choose to accentuate one of three strategies: product leadership, operational excellence or customer intimacy. Thompson and Strickland (2003) suggest a slightly different classification model from Porter, which comprises a strategy of cost leadership (cost reduction, which attracts a large number of buyers); a strategy of broad differentiation (giving goods specific features that attract a large number of buyers); a strategy of optimum cost (great value for customers through a combination of lower costs with broad differentiation); and a focused strategy based on low cost (low costs and a narrow segment of buyers).

Mintzberg (1988) offers a classification of generic strategies founded on differentiation by price; by image, which refers to generating an individual image for a product through marketing; by support, which suggests providing a unique service during or after the sale of the product; by design, offering products with exclusive features, design configurations and quality based on high reliability, durability and performance; and finally non-differentiation, in which a firm emphasises none of the differentiation dimensions. Analysis of the above papers allows the allocation of a series of generic business strategies: cost strategies, differentiation strategies, focus strategies, and a hybrid strategy which refers to the simultaneous aspiration of cost leadership and differentiation.

However, these models concentrate effort mainly on a company's external competitive environment and do not look inside the company context. As a result, supplementing Porter's work, resource-based theory has been created (Barney 1991). The resource-based approach considers a company as a set of tangible and intangible resources such as company assets, capabilities, organisational processes, knowledge and other elements. These resources allow it to develop and implement a competitive strategy. There are different types of company resources: financial, human, organisational, etc. The firm's task is to acquire the most important key resources that will be a source of sustainable competitive advantage. A company has a competitive advantage when it creates value for customers using a strategy that is not used by its competitors. Sustainable competitive advantage exists when none of these competitors can receive comparable benefits from existing policies.

The resource-based perspective highlights the need for a fit between the external market context in which a company operates and its internal capabilities. Resources are stocks of available factors, which belong to or are controlled by firms; capabilities are the capacity of firms to deploy these resources (Amit and Schoemaker 1993). This approach suggests that a company's unique resources and capabilities provide the foundation for strategy and permit a company to take advantage of its core competencies to exploit opportunities in the external environment.

Within the framework of this approach, Barney (1991) determines four characteristics ('VRIN characteristics') of key resources of a company. They must be valuable (the company's ability, using the resources, to realise opportunities and neutralise the threat of the environment); rare (the rarity of the resource is defined by the level of its employment among competitors); inimitable (resources must have several distinctive features that do not allow competitors to make similar use of them); and nonsubstitutable (no similar resources exist that could be used by competitors as an alternative).

Arbitrage

Arbitrage is one of the popular ideas of modern economics, implementing the law of one price and keeping markets efficient. According to the law of one price in a competitive market, if two assets have equivalent risk and return, they should sell at the same price. If the price of the same asset is different in two markets, there will be arbitrageurs who will buy the asset cheaply and sell in the market where it is expensive. In traditional meaning, arbitrage involves the simultaneous purchase and sale of the same or an analogous security in two different markets for profitably different prices, and continues until prices in the two markets reach equilibrium (Sharpe *et al.* 1998). Of course, an object of arbitrage may be assets of a different nature, such as securities, currency, commodities or derivative forms in order to take advantage of differing prices.

Miyazaki (2007) notes that arbitrage is a fundamental category of con-temporary economics and an ordinary trading strategy of investment banks. He describes the difference between arbitrage and speculation. Speculators gamble on the future movement of prices and take risks, whereas arbitrageurs profit by identifying current price differences and search to eliminate risk.

Presently, arbitrage is used relatively widely and it can be protracted to numerous markets and apparently mispriced assets, goods and services, as well as various kinds of transaction (Miyazaki 2013). For example, the financial crisis of 2008 was attributed to a practice known as ratings arbitrage (Nocera 2009). Nocera employs the example of the huge multinational insurance company AIG. The company was rated AAA, which meant ratings agencies such as Standard & Poor's (S&P) supposed its probability of defaulting was extremely small. Therefore the company was able to borrow more inexpen-sively than other companies with lower ratings. The London division sold credit default swaps (CDS).These exotic instruments acted as a form of insurance for the securities. As a result, the company mortgage-backed secu-rities were also rated AAA. The technique of using the rating was arbitrage. Nocera (2009) notes that Wall Street carried out these operations easily due to the transferred risk of default from banks to AIG, and the AAA rating made the securities attractive for the financial market. Certainly, AIG had profitable fees and it was naively thought that the market would grow forever. CDSs were not regulated and were not considered as a conventional insurance product; as a result money was not reserved for losses. When housing prices fell and there were losses, the company was in trouble. One can see that AIG arbitraged rating by employing a loophole in the regulations –in this case Nocera (2009) recommends that instead of the term 'loophole', one could use the less well mannered but possibly more accurate term 'scam'.

Ledyaeva *et al.* (2013) looked at the issue of why Russian companies invest in offshore jurisdictions and why these companies reinvest capital back to Russia, with its uncooperative institutional environment, instead of using it in more stable economies. In their study they utilised another concept, institu-tional arbitrage, which means a situation where a company is presented with opportunities to use dissimilarities between two institutional environments (Boisot and Meyer 2008).

Golikova *et al.* (2013) determined that the Russian institutional environment, which drives companies to escape to a foreign country, also makes available opportunities for institutional arbitrage. This is demonstrated by possibilities to establish in foreign jurisdictions, which are targeted by Russian customers seeking a secure location for their capital abroad or support services for their international trade. As a result, understanding of the Russian institutional environment together with the opportunity to run one's business within the European regulatory framework gives a competitive advantage for Russian-owned companies.

Huang (2003) also notes that institutional arbitrage is used where companies from emerging economies search for institutions capable of maintaining global operations, establishing particular parts of their operations in developed economies. He offers the example of an institutional arbitrage operation where Chinese local companies transfer assets out of China and then return, assuming the likeness of foreign investors. A similar strategy was realised by South Africa's companies SAB-Miller and Anglo American, which relocated their headquarters to London, fearing the uncertainties associated with changing authorities in the 1990s (ibid.).

In the case of Russia, the protection of property rights in EU countries, and the benefits given to foreign companies in Russia beyond those with Russian owners, can reduce the exit costs of business. Therefore one can use the term 'institutional arbitrage' for Russian companies taking advantage of inexpensive institutions outside Russia; in other words, Russian business exploits the differences between various institutional arrangements functioning in different states.

A cycle from Russia offshore and back to Russia is example of an institutional arbitrage operation. Travelling in a foreign country may amplify a company's business capability when returning to Russia, as the company can capture benefits of the same legal and economic protections outside Russia enjoyed by foreign companies operating there. Also, the round-trip company has the ability to protect against the deviant behaviour of government and domestic business partners. Therefore round-tripping can be a considered a global business strategy (Ledyaeva *et al.* 2013).

Initially arbitrage as a concept was seen as a purely economic phenomenon rather than a technical method, but currently the concept of arbitrage is used comparatively extensively. It has become a more complex phenomenon, capturing the areas of culture, law and politics. For example, in late 2013 the Russian government decided to invest $15 billion in Ukraine's sovereign Eurobonds, and shortly afterwards the government purchased the first Ukrainian Eurobond tranche valued at $3 billion with a two-year maturity, a coupon rate of 5 per cent annually and coupon payments twice per year (TASS 2015). Russia could not invest the other $12 billion in Ukraine's bonds due to a change of power in Kiev. The Ukrainian Eurobond issue prospectus includes covenants providing that Ukraine must meet all obligations on its sovereign debt. Moreover, one covenant says the Ukraine should not permit its debt-to-GDP ratio to rise beyond 60 per cent (ibid.).

However, after the crisis of the Ukrainian economy in 2014, the Russian government received an opportunity to use this debt as a tool for causing the collapse of the Ukrainian economy. Gelpern (2014) termed this contract arbitrage. She notes that Russia is the principal holder of Ukrainian bonds due for repayment in the period of the term of the newly approved International Monetary Fund programme, and these Russian bonds can be used to apply political power over Ukraine and give it additional influence in any debt negotiations. One can see that buying assets (in this example bonds) can give additional future political benefits which can be transferred, under certain circumstances, to arbitrage profit.

Arbitrage as strategy

Recently, a new prospect of corporate strategy as a process of arbitrage between markets has been shaped. Ghemawat (2003) suggests a new perspective on arbitrage as an element of corporate strategy, where arbitrage is not cheap capital or labour; rather the scope for arbitrage is the differences that persist among countries. Distance between countries impacts on doing business in a new market because costs and risks result from barriers created by distance.

Arbitrage benefit from the influence of physical distance on transportation and communication costs. It has been the essence of trading throughout history – buy or produce goods in a place where they are very inexpensive and sell them in another place where there is a high willingness to pay. A good example of such geographic arbitrageurs is the Honourable East India Company, which took advantage of huge international variations in prices for a range of different products by delivering them from the East Indies to the markets of Western Europe in the seventeenth to nineteenth centuries.

Another historical example of arbitrage is the trade route from the Varangians to the Greeks, which connected the Byzantine, Scandinavia and Kievan Rus. The route was established in the ninth century when Varangians (hired professional soldiers) searched for plunder and also for slaves and other lucrative goods. The route utilised a long-distance waterway including the Baltic Sea, rivers flowing into the Baltic Sea and rivers of the Dnieper River system. From Scandinavia merchants exported iron, amber, ivory, whaleskin products, weapons, artworks and objects looted by the Vikings in Western Europe (French wines, jewellery, silk, cambric fabric and silver utensils). From the Byzantine Empire came wines, spices, jewellery, glassware, expensive fabrics, icons and books.

Despite the dramatic fall in costs of communication and air transportation in the past 20 years, the scope of geographic arbitrage strategies has not significantly diminished. Moreover, the political and economic transformation in many countries in recent decades has generated a new opportunity for geographic arbitrage. For instance, in Russia the relative cost of transportation has dramatically increased, destroying the close relationship between the western and eastern parts of Russia. As a result, the Russian East has been trading with China more actively than the European part of Russia and this creates conditions for arbitrage.

The traditional understanding of distance is geographical distance. However, as noted by Ghemawat (2003), distance does not only indicate geographic separation. He offers a four-dimensional framework for measuring distance between countries that includes differences in culture, the administrative and institutional context, geography, and economic attributes. As a result, the types of distance influence businesses in various ways, and these differences from country to country launch a mass of strategic arbitrage opportunities.

According to Ghemawat (2003), administrative arbitrage is legal, institutional and political differences from country to country, and tax differentials are a comprehensible example. In general, administrative arbitrage is prevalent in legal tax avoidance: in 1990, many Russian businessmen had holding firms in Cyprus, which was a tax haven. Another example is a large share of foreign direct investment in Russia in fact originating within Russia, for reasons of tax concessions and improved legal protection.

Arbitrage as strategy has an economic element due to its intention to add value to business. Economic arbitrage strategies exploit cross-border differences in economic factors such as cost of labour. Ghemawat (2003) offers economic arbitrage, which employs specific economic factors such as differences in the costs of labour and capital, and dissimilarities in knowledge technologies or infrastructures; these factors are not obtained directly from the geographical and administrative context. A commonplace type of economic arbitrage is the exploitation of cheap labour in textile manufacturing in China and Vietnam.

Cultural arbitrage takes advantage of differences in culture among countries and regions (ibid.). For example, Italian culture has long underpinned the international success of Italian architecture, cuisine, couture and shoes, and the extraordinary dominance of Italian shoes in the Russian upper market, which during the first decade of the twenty-first century accounted for over 60 per cent of the Russian shoe market. However, many of these shoes were in fact made in China and were counterfeit products.

In modern years, cultural and administrative distance has become more important because transportation and communication costs have dropped sharply, reducing the effect of physical distance. International enterprises have benefited from arbitraging capital and labour. Ghemawat (2007) notes that differences between countries are opportunities and not limitations, and it is possible to employ these differences to increase a company's corporate performance.

Multinationals' global operations consistently underperform in their internal operations because these companies' strategies concentrate on similarities across their markets: whenever achievable, international companies standardise their business models to achieve economies of scale. As a result, they consider regional differences as obstacles to be overcome, not as opportunities to be leveraged. Ghemawat (2007) notes that this perspective blinds companies to an opposition strategy: arbitrage, the exploitation of differences (in culture, administrative practices, geographic distance, and labour or capital costs) across markets. First-class firms take advantage of such differences while also leveraging similarities that create scale.

Ghemawat (2007) presented his approach in three principal concepts that can help a company to receive an advantage when operating on the global market: adaptation, aggregation and arbitrage ('AAA triangle'). The three As symbolise the three different types of global strategy. Adaptation is aimed at increasing income and market share by adapting the company's products and services based on local conditions. Aggregation tries to bring economies of scale by generating regional and global operations. Aggregation includes homogenising the product or service offering, combining activities such as development, production and marketing at a regional level or by languages. Arbitrage, as noted above, is the use of distinction between national or regional markets, frequently by localising separate parts of the supply chain in dissimilar residences.

Haslam *et al.* (2012) offer a new look at corporate strategy as a 'process of arbitrage between markets where physical, financial and temporal asymmetries are exploited by corporate managers to boost earnings-capacity'. They propose that arbitrage is a process consisting of buying and selling on different markets with the intention of taking advantage of the differentiation in the price quoted. Also, they reveal three different types of strategy as arbitrage: product, labour and capital market arbitrage, which take advantage of the variability in price structure between product markets, social settlements governing employment, temporal price variations arising from asset appreciation in capital markets and tax, interest and exchange-rate variations through transfer pricing. In addition, arbitrage offers companies opportunities to rebuild their value chain across national and international borders. Changing the design of value chains allows global corporations to arbitrage between domestic products, labour and capital markets and their foreign equivalents to increase earnings capacity (ibid.).

Arbitrage in Russia from a historical perspective

As noted above, arbitrage is the exploitation of differences between national or regional markets. Traditionally, the analysis of arbitrage focuses on differences between national markets; arbitrage does exist within local and regional markets, but the variation of prices will be less than in global trade. It is important to note that, historically, arbitrage was developed in local markets, and has become global only after the creation of international transport communications.

Usually arbitrage is associated with the market economy, where there are opportunities to exploit differences between markets. In the planning economy, strong regulation of economic behaviour limited activities above the permitted standard levels. In general, entrepreneurial activities were not encouraged and indeed were punished. On the other hand, existing imbalances in the Soviet economy generated strong demand for different goods and consequently created asymmetries between regions. These differentiations created motivation for arbitrageurs, despite huge risks of arbitrage operations not coordinated with the authorities. To paraphrase Marx, one can say that with a 20 per cent profit margin an arbitrageur will agree to any normal transaction; with 50 per cent profit he is ready to engage in unethical behaviour; at 100 per cent he will be willing to break the law; and at 300 per cent he is willing to do anything, even under pain of death.

An over-centralised economy was established in the Soviet Union, which focused on defence and heavy industries. It could not satisfy the varied needs of the Soviet citizens. Partially, the deficit in a wide range of important goods and foods was made up through speculation and through illegal production and distribution of goods. Simplifying, in our context, speculation is deriving income from the difference between the bidding and asking prices, and is relatively similar to arbitrage. Speculation became a characteristic of everyday life in Soviet cities and rural areas throughout the Soviet period.

Even in the early post-war Stalinist regime, as Bogdanov (2010) notes, police reports from the field recorded a steady growth in speculation. The Ministry of Internal Affairs for the last three months of 1946 reported 66,793 arrests in the markets of the country for the purchase and sale of ration cards, of which 10,063 resulted in prison sentences. In that time the ban on the grain trade unavoidably produced a rise in prices on *kolkhoz* (collective farm) markets and increased speculation. Traders were in collusion with the chairmen of the *kolkhoz* and sold grain and flour in deprived regions (ibid.). This arbitrage was strictly forbidden but it managed to save millions of citizens from starvation.

It is a trivial fact that the Soviet economy was managed through the State Planning Commission (Gosplan), which had a poor quality of planning and insignificant reliable feedback; industrial goods and military industry were permanently the focus of the Soviet authority and the production of consumer goods was disproportionately low. Consequently, there was a scarcity of many consumer goods leading to a widespread black market. Some black market goods were sold by arbitrageurs (officially called speculators and prosecuted by the state) who exploited price asymmetries. Generally, arbitrage and speculation were immanent within the Soviet system because they were one of many regulators of economic life.

In the USSR, speculation was considered as illegal income and was a criminal offence. According to the Criminal Code, speculation – purchase and resale of goods with the intention of making money – was punishable by imprisonment for a term not exceeding two years with or without confiscation of property; speculation in the form of business was punishable by imprisonment for a term of two to seven years with confiscation of property (Criminal Code 1960). Moreover, in some cases the Soviet authorities were extremely cruel, as in the Rokotov–Faybischenko case, described below.

In the Khrushchev epoch (1960s), the country became more open and some Soviet citizens began to be able to visit foreign countries; consequently demand arose for foreign currency and dealing in foreign currency started taking place, although such operations were illegal. Fedoseev (1997) notes that in the early 1960s, the Moscow black market in currency was not much different from the bazaars of the Arab East. In general, currency and gold were delivered by employees of several embassies in Moscow and Arab students of military academies. Rokotov, Faybishenko and Yakovlev were among the leaders of the currency black market. In 1961, the KGB broke their group, composed of nine people, and the case was tried in the Moscow Court. The trial lasted two weeks and was attended by the mass media. Rokotov and Faybishenko were sentenced to 15 years in a correctional camp and confiscation of all property.

The General Secretary Nikita Khrushchev was informed about the court decision and was outraged by the soft punishment, expressing himself on this point quite clearly: 'Let the strict punishment for what he did make a deterrent effect on others and serve as a warning that this could result in the same for them. Otherwise it may become of horrible size. If we do not stop it, will grow irreversibly, like a cancer.' (ibid.).

On 1 July 1961, the decree 'On strengthening the criminal liability for violation of the rules on foreign exchange transactions' was signed, which allowed the death penalty (Decree 1961). Immediately after this, General Prosecutor Rudenko blocked the city court solution of this case and the Russian Soviet Federative Socialist Republic (RSFSR) Supreme Court accepted the new case for trial. In two days the case was retried by the Supreme Court and, according to the latest law, they were sentenced to death by shooting with confiscation of all their assets; soon afterwards they were shot. The fact that in this case the law was retrospective did not trouble Khrushchev (Fedoseev 1997).

The Rokotov–Faybischenko case prompted the leader of the Soviet state to take extremely tough measures against illegal business activities, currency exchange, speculation and theft of state property. However, more importantly, it was an attempt to control the Soviet nomenclature and demonstrate that any non-normative activity would be strictly punished.

In 1985, Gorbachev announced the start of the reforms in the Soviet economy which were called acceleration, liberalisation and *perestroika* (restructuring), and arbitrage was legalised. Generally, between 1987 and 1992, nobody understood for how long *perestroika* would exist and businesses had no experience of strategy planning, therefore arbitrage was the dominant strategy for new companies. During that time, government policy and regulation gave a huge opportunity for strategy as arbitrage.

In May 1985, the Soviet authority started the struggle against drunkenness, alcoholism and brewing by using different methods including administrative and criminal penalties. Trade unions, the system of education and health, and all social organisations were participating in the unprecedented struggle against alcoholism (Decree 1985). The state decreased revenues from alcohol which were a significant part of the budget and cut the production of alcohol sharply. A lot of stores selling alcoholic drinks were closed. Prices of alcohol were raised, many wineries were destroyed and sales of alcohol were restricted. Simultaneously there was a large disparity between regions of the country in alcohol supply and demand that created price asymmetries and lucky break arbitrage.

Official data showed that alcohol sales per capita during the years of the anti-alcohol campaign fell by more than 60 per cent. Additionally, the country had strong social results such as an increase in male life expectancy, rising birth rates, reduced mortality and an overall decrease in the crime rate. On the other hand, the actual reduction in alcohol consumption was less significant, mainly due to illicit brewing and the illegal production of alcoholic beverages in state enterprises. Moreover, large-scale home brewing had led to shortages in the retail of moonshine's raw materials such as sugar, cheap candy, tomato paste, peas and cereals. Despite the decline in the total number of alcohol poisonings, there was an increase in the number of poisonings from alcohol substitutes and non-alcoholic intoxication (Back-in-USSR 2012). Vodka and other products became items for arbitrage. There were disparities of alcohol distribution between regions of the country which created an imbalance between demand and supply and consequently differences in price.

Speculation in alcohol reached unimaginable dimensions: often the production of a large distillery was completely bought up by grey traders who obtained 100–200 per cent profit (Back-in-USSR 2012). Reducing alcohol sales caused a harsh blow to the Soviet economy as retail turnover fell dramatically: before 1985 the share of alcohol was approximately 25 per cent of total retail revenues. Losses from the sale of alcohol were not compensated, and by the end of 1986 the budget collapsed (Pushkarev 2005).

During the *perestroika* of 1985–90, encouragement of entrepreneurship and cooperatives by the state gave a new impulse for arbitrage. Generally this was a major type of entrepreneurial activity due to production assets belonging to the state, and almost all goods were produced and distributed according to Gosplan and Gosnab prescriptions. Therefore arbitrage operations as well as private trading were often connected with criminal activity because it was practically impossible to take goods for business operations legally.

At the end of the 1980s and beginning of the 1990s, arbitrage became the main instrument of initial accumulation of capital; as a result, huge private assets began to form in Russia. The most profitable arbitrage was formed in commodities, especially in the energy sector of the Russian economy, due to a large discrepancy between internal and external prices. For instance, domestic oil prices in Russia were cheaper than the world price in December of 1990, 1992 and 1993 by 0.6, 25 and 37 per cent, respectively; and there was a similar relationship in prices of natural gas, in 1990, 1992 and 1993, 0.2, 3 and 22 per cent, respectively (Mulyukov 1997).

Mulyukov (1997) notes that in the early 1990s the problem of the liberalisation of prices for oil and other energy was one of the central issues in the debate around the strategy of Russian market reform. Supporters of free pricing argued that such a measure would give the oil and gas industry funds for self-financing, increased budget revenues from taxes and rent payments for royalties, and would create incentives for energy savings and structural changes in the economy.

Critics of free pricing argued that free oil and gas prices would cause high inflation and would lead to a chain of bankruptcies in the power consuming industries, which would not be able to adapt to the new price over a short period. In addition, they argued that cheap energy is a natural competitive advantage of domestic manufacturing; therefore it was necessary to support it, at least for a transitional period, to keep energy prices at a level significantly below global. As a result, at the beginning of 1992 the Russian government chose the compromise decision, replacing the one-time energy price liberalisation by its regulated gradual increase of the price (ibid.).

This solution opened the doors for extremely profitable arbitrage on the oil and gas markets and gave substantial possibilities for wealth accumulation before the upcoming privatisation of the Soviet inheritance. Distribution of state assets was realised mainly to those who previously were able to accumulate starting capital. Someone who was poor before mass privatisation could not accumulate large capital – unless, of course, he could organise a gangster group.

Arbitrage with Soviet money

Basically, money in the Soviet economy was divided into cash and non-cash shares. Non-cash money in such a system was primarily a method of accounting. In principle, this is not money but rather accounting units, through which the distribution of material assets was organised. Cash served as a means of distribution of wealth in the Soviet economic system, often regardless of the actual performance of a company or an individual employee. In addition, the consumer sector and other parts of the economy (capital goods, military sectors and infrastructure) were, as a rule, almost unrelated. The flow of finance between these parts was generally prevented. The Soviet system rigidly separated the two sectors of the financial system and distributed cash and non-cash flows by directives of the State Planning Commission. In the USSR, cash could not be freely exchanged for other currencies or invested in production.

The above scheme created arbitrage potential due to there being different values of cash and non-cash money. In other words, there was incentive to swap virtual (non-cash) money for real cash. These swaps could be implemented in the agricultural business and cooperatives in gold mining. The financial state authorities strictly regulated exchange of non-cash roubles that existed in the accounts of public enterprises to real cash. However, Soviet *perestroika* and new economic policy opened the door for uncontrolled transactions between cash and non-cash roubles.

Berezkin (2006) notes that from the beginning of the reform in the USSR, swaps between cash and non-cash roubles became effectively legal. Initially, schemes were built according to the principle of transfer of non-cash money from business accounts to other accounts from which it was possible to get the roubles in cash. In order to have the opportunity of building a shadow financial scheme to access non-cash accounts of the enterprise, it was almost enough to find a suitable company that would have the legal right of lawful removal of large sums of cash roubles; to agree with the company management about the terms of the transaction; then to prepare and submit the documents for it to perform some kind of work; transfer a certain amount of non-cash roubles with one company to the cash account of the arbitrageur company; and, in accordance with the agreement, pass cash back to the company. Of course, in Soviet times the scheme was undoubtedly illegal and therefore could not become a mass phenomenon of economic life.

However, after 1987 certain non-state enterprises, such as centres of scientific and technical creativity of youth (*Nauchno-Tekhnicheskoe Tvorchestvo Molodezhi*, NTTM centres), youth housing cooperatives and other cooperatives, were officially allowed to conduct this operation. NTTM centres were established for development of innovation in accordance with the Government, Council of Trade Unions and the Komsomol (Young Communist League) in March 1987 (Resolution 1987), but they quickly moved away from this initial orientation, having been engaged in various forms of commercial activity. It was revealed that youth centres did not justify their brand name: only 17 per cent of organisations were engaged in production and research activities; the rest specialised in the simple resale of raw materials (Tulskiy 2004), which can be regarded as *perestroika* arbitrage.

NTTM centres were active participants in the exchange of non-cash roubles for real cash, and did it quite openly and broadly. However, as noted by Berezkin (2006), new legislation was introduced removing the distinction between non-cash and cash accounts. Consequently arbitrage of roubles ceased to be interesting for NTTM centres, but soon they occupied a new business direction.

They arbitraged the difference between the price of buying (often they purchased at a fixed state price) and the market price of selling. The buyers were production cooperatives, which were widespread at that time and produced low-cost consumer goods. The most advanced NTTM centres carried out barter exchanges with foreign countries. In this case profits could be astronomical due to the purchase of consumer goods in the West for pennies and sale of them in the hungry Soviet market.

By the early 1990s in the USSR, as noted by Tulskiy (2004), there were already more than 600 NTTM centres. They had tremendous privileges: they did not pay any taxes, but they deducted 3 per cent of income to the union fund of NTTM and 27 per cent to local funds of NTTM. The state did not receive anything at all.

Having the right to arbitrage money, NTTM centres become the cradle of the Russian business elite. On the other hand, they were also the engines of inflation, and Komsomol capital grew by leaps and bounds. Very quickly the country was covered by a network of commodity exchanges that were based on NTTM centres and commercial banks with capital from NTTM centres. One example might be the bank Menatep, owned by Khodorkovsky (see the case of Yukos in Chapter 9).

Is arbitrage generic strategy?

Porter (1980, 1985) supposes that generic strategy is a fundamental approach to the creation of strategy that can be adopted by a large range of companies in any industry and market to increase their performance. They have universal applicability and are derived from basic postulates. Porter's generic strategies are universal because they do not depend on the company and they describe strategic positions at an uncomplicated and comprehensive level.

The above analysis of the fundamental works (Mintzberg 1988; Thompson and Strickland 2003; Treacy and Wiersema 1995; Porter 1980, 1985; Hitt *et al.* 2007; Kim 2005) allows allocation of a series of generic business strategies: cost strategies, differentiation strategies, focus strategies, and hybrid strategies which refers to the simultaneous aspiration of cost leadership and differentiation. In connection with the discussion of generic strategies, it is reasonable to ask whether there are other generic strategies apart from these. A quick answer is yes – there are types of business strategy that can be described as undetermined strategy, in which a firm does not have a definite and consistent strategy or does not spend time explicating strategy. The absence of strategy is also a sort of generic strategy.

However, there is one more type of generic strategy – arbitrage. The short view signifies that arbitrage uses a simple *modus operandi* in the formation of strategy, and can be implemented by large firms in any industry or market to increase their performance. It has universal applicability and so does not depend on the company, and it fulfils the criterion of describing strategic positions at an uncomplicated and comprehensive level.

As a result, the company's comparative position in the market is set by its choice of generic strategy: cost leadership, differentiation, arbitrage or their symbiosis, and choice of competitive opportunity. Competitive opportunity differentiates between companies targeting broad market segments and those focusing on a narrow segment.

Companies may have different levels of strategic management, and various authors (Collis and Montgomery 2005; Johnson *et al.* 2013; Wit and Meyer 2010) describe these levels of strategy differently, but the critical problems can be resolved using three levels: corporate-level, business-unit and functional (operational) strategies.

Corporate strategy includes decisions made regarding the direction of a group of firms as a whole, without regard to the specific development of participating business units. This strategy defines configuration and coordination of the company's multimarket activities (Collis and Montgomery 2005).

Corporate strategic choices define extension into recently developed markets, diversification, vertical integration, acquisitions and creation of new businesses, optimal resource allocation between different activities of the company and evaluating the value of a business unit in the total portfolio of activities. Corporate strategy is established at the highest levels of the group and usually is focused on a long-range time horizon (Johnson *et al.* 2013). The purpose and content of corporate strategy of a firm answer the question: In which sectors of business should the company operate?

A business strategy is concerned with the direction of a particular, semi-autonomous corporate unit which competes in a specific industry. Decisions at the business strategy level relate to matters such as marketing, manufacturing effectiveness and increasing business value for the corporate stakeholders (Wit and Meyer 2010). Business strategy answers the question: How does a company need to compete in a particular industry? This level of strategy is focused on a particular business unit and is concerned with real difficulties.

The task of corporate strategy is selection of spheres of activity, but the task of business strategy is monitoring and controlling the movement of a firm in these spheres. Usually, corporate strategy is established by executives and it is more constant and should not be transformed repeatedly; whereas business strategy can be made by line managers and can be changed regularly in order to respond to changes in the operating environment (Johnson *et al.* 2013).

Business strategies are developed and implemented as functional strategies in terms of production, R&D, marketing, human resources and finance. For that reason, functional strategy takes into account the specific functions of procurement, production, resource management and others. Thus all levels of strategic planning are interrelated and are aimed at implementation of the chosen strategy.

Functional strategy is a management plan of a key functional area within a certain business unit, such as production, marketing, customer service, distribution, finance and human resources (Wit and Meyer 2010). For example, the marketing strategy of a company may be a management plan to capture part of a new market. Functional strategy is narrower than business strategy, and specifies some details in general organisational development by identifying practical steps to provide management of individual departments or business functions. Functional strategy is exceptionally important in determining the realisation of other strategies by way of transmitting strategic decisions into strategic actions (ibid.).

This book takes an integrated approach to company strategy: considering all the different levels of strategic management, it is possible to use arbitrage as a strategy at corporate, business and functional levels of strategy. Moreover, within one company arbitrage as a strategy can be used contemporaneously at different levels of strategy. For example, the leading Russian automaker Avtotor realises its arbitrage corporate strategy by developing the special economic zone in Kaliningrad and lobbying special tax legislation for its companies. For the realisation of business strategies of the corporate units, such as assembling BMW cars, the company has developed business programmes that use arbitrage approaches for competition in specific segments of the car industry. The functional level of Avtotor arbitrage strategy employs a foreign labour force and so is an example of labour arbitrage (the case of Avtotor is examined in detail in Chapter 2). The main focus of this book is on business and functional strategy, because the diversification of large corporations in Russia is severely limited and their corporate strategies are poorly developed.

In this book, the inductive approach, which is a process of logical inference on the basis of the transition from a particular position to the total, has been useful for developing a theory of arbitrage. Indeed, the inductive reasoning employed connects prerequisites with the conclusion, not strictly through the laws of logic but rather through some actual representations. We will use the middle-range theory as a solution to the problem of the gap between theory and empirical evidence, which can be defined, according to Merton (1968), as a collection of techniques to examine reality and allow for the creation of theoretical explanations.

In addition, a case study method is adopted. Yin (2003) defines the case study research method as 'an empirical investigation that examines an existing phenomenon within its real-life context when the boundaries between phenomenon and context are not clearly evident' and in which numerous sources of evidence are used. This method has particular significance in this research because it offers the opportunity to study the phenomenon of arbitrage in context, both within its industry and in the wider economy, therefore helping to clarify the correlations between these factors. The case study method is a common way to carry out qualitative investigation to bring us to an understanding of a composite problem, and emphasises comprehensive contextual analysis of a limited number of events and their connections.

In the following chapters, nuances and practical applications of this strategy are disclosed and described by way of hundreds of examples taken from current Russian business practices and economic history. I have deliberately limited the theatre of operations to Russia because the narrowing of the space analysis helps to present the material in a more systematic and compact manner. Also, numerous cases and their analysis allow for a better understanding of modern Russia.

Conclusion

Conventional arbitrage exploits price asymmetries where these are bountiful to generate a profit, but recently a new viewpoint on arbitrage as an element of corporate strategy has developed, where the scope for arbitrage is the differences that continue between countries. Traditionally these are included in the sphere of arbitrage; nevertheless, the opportunity for arbitrage could develop due to discrepancies that exist between separate regions within one country; the extent depends on the size of the country, the political system, the institutional context of variation in culture and the geography of the country.

There are four forms of arbitrage: economic, cultural, administrative and geographical. In economic arbitrage, an arbitrageur searches for price differences between similar goods and immediately takes the opportunity by buying the undervalued good and simultaneously selling the overvalued good. In this way, the arbitrageur has made profit that is the difference between the selling and buying prices. The other types of arbitrage take similar advantage of dissimilarities in religions, attitudes and values (cultural arbitrage); the system of rules between states (administrative arbitrage); and geography (geographical arbitrage).

We can distinguish a key type of strategy as arbitrage: product, labour and capital market arbitrage, which takes advantage of the variability in price structure between product markets, social settlements governing employment, temporal price variations arising from asset appreciation in capital markets and tax, interest and exchange rate variations through transfer pricing.

Historical examples from Russia disclose that arbitrage as a component of business practice is not an innovative phenomenon. Arbitrage was immanent within the Soviet system and was one of many regulators of economic life. However, with strong state regulation under the authoritarian regime of the Soviet Union, price was regulated by the state, therefore the opportunity for arbitrage was minimal. Moreover, in many cases arbitrage as a business operation was forbidden and as a result was being carried out illegally. Only in the last years of the USSR, with increasing political fluctuations and reduction of state regulation in the economy, was there exponential growth of opportunities for arbitrage

There are other generic strategies apart from cost leadership and differentiation. Arbitrage as strategy can be implemented by firms in any industry or market to increase their performance. It has universal applicability and it does not depend on the company. It is possible to employ arbitrage as a strategy at corporate, business and functional levels; furthermore, within one company arbitrage as a strategy can be used at only one level, or simultaneously at different levels of strategy.

2 Models of strategy as arbitrage

A matrix of price asymmetries and opportunity is proposed to analyse the possibility of implementing arbitrage. Utilising a different level of price asymmetries and opportunity, the matrix reveals four possible options for arbitrage as well as a different substrategy for managers. Three cases – Roman Abramovich and cold Chukotka; Browder, Magnitsky and Kalmykia; and Avtotor, which assembles Russian BMW – elucidate the theoretical model. Additionally, anti-arbitrage as a complementary generic strategy that is aimed destroying price differentiation or opportunities for arbitrage of competitors is analysed.

Model of price asymmetries and opportunity

Imagine a treasure hunter who sometimes has successful and sometimes unsuccessful business. In addition, he can experience different situations in search of treasure. In one case the hunter has both a good team and plenty of money, but does not know where the treasure is. In another case, despite all his activity he does not have any idea where the treasure can be, half his team run away to another adventure seeker, and the other half are married, raising children and under the heels of their grumpy wives. Sometimes our hunter knows where treasure is, but nobody believes him, potential lenders roar with laughter at him, and as a result he cannot organise the expedition. And last but not least, he has everything he needs: a chest of coins, dozens of desperate guys and a ship, and consequently the treasure is acquired.

A similar situation arises when a company or a person tries to organise arbitrage.

Option 1 describes a situation where the opportunity exists for carrying out operations required for arbitrage, but where there are few price asymmetries to exploit. The hunter has both a team and money, but he does not know where the treasure is.

Option 2 is the standard case of arbitrage where there is opportunity for implementation operations required for arbitrage and there are strong price asymmetries. In this case the treasure can be acquired because the hunter has everything he needs.

Table 2.1 Matrix of price asymmetries and opportunity

	Absent price asymmetries	*Strong price asymmetries*
Strong opportunity for arbitrage	**Option 1** Absent price asymmetries and strong opportunity for arbitrage	**Option 2** Strong price asymmetries and strong opportunity for arbitrage
Weak opportunity for arbitrage	**Option 3** Absent price asymmetries and weak opportunity for arbitrage	**Option 4** Strong price asymmetries and weak opportunity for arbitrage

Option 3 cannot lead to arbitrage as neither asymmetries nor opportunity exist, as when the hunter does not have a team, money or any idea where the treasure is.

Option 4 – strong price asymmetries and weak opportunity for arbitrage – is the typical case that determines state and regional regulation, bureaucratic barriers and limitation of infrastructure of the country and region. Often these determinants are positive because they protect the ecological and economic interests of the country, but often they have strongly negative intentions. This case is similar to when the hunter knows where treasure is, but nobody believes him and consequently he cannot organise the expedition.

At first glance, only Option 2 (strong price asymmetries and robust opportunity for arbitrage) is interesting for business strategy, as without price asymmetries or opportunity the operations could not be profitable or realised. From a purely technical standpoint this is absolutely correct; but from a position of strategic business development, one may obtain arbitrage from any starting position. It could be argued that arbitrage strategic planning is the alignment of the route from Option 3 to Option 2, and in favourable situations is the alignment of the routes from Options 1 and 4 to Option 2, with subsequent saving and retaining of Option 2. The ability to hold strong price asymmetries and a robust opportunity for arbitrage will be the competitive advantage of the company in its specific business segment. The history of the Russian oligarch and a big fan of British football, Roman Abramovich, is an illustration of the model.

Roman Abramovich and cold Chukotka

In August 1995, Presidential Decree 872 united the oil producer Noyabrsknef-tegas with the country's largest and most up-to-date Omsk oil refinery to form the backbone of a new company, Siberian Oil Company (Sibneft). In addition, rolled into Sibneft were a few large companies dealing in oil geology and the distribution of oil products. All the businesses were allocated from the Russian Rosneft (Presidential Decree 1995). The company was in a difficult situation because its oil production had been falling gradually through the 1990s.

In December 1995, the Finance Oil Corporation (FNK) gained control of Sibneft, in exchange for a $100.3 million loan. FNK was controlled by business tycoon Boris Berezovsky and his young business partner Roman Abramovich.

Later, in 2011, Abramovich said in a London court, under oath, that in fact this auction was fictitious: the Berezovsky group conspired with other bidders and allowed them to avoid competition and buy the company for the starting price (Overchenko and Dmitrienko 2011).

In 1996, 19 and 15 per cent of company shares were transferred under control of the Berezovsky group for a symbolic price of around $25 million and a promise to invest a further $80 million. In May 1997, FNK officially gained total control of Sibneft. In late summer 1997, Sibneft became the first Russian company to issue a Eurobond. The $150 million bond was the first in a series of Russian corporate debt issues. Money was used as payment for loans which were taken for buying company shares (NGFR 2008b).

In 1998 Sibneft wanted to merge with Yukos, the largest Russian oil company controlled by Mikhail Khodorkovsky. In terms of reserves, the merged company would be the largest private sector oil company in the world. The merger would definitely create advantages connected to productivity because Sibneft had surplus refining capacity which would offset surplus crude extraction of Yukos. However, there were considerable disagreements over strategy between the owners of Sibneft and Yukos, and consequently the merger was decisively stopped after four months' negotiation (ibid).

In the 2000s Sibneft had the fifth position in oil production in Russia. In the end of 2002, the company's reserves, according to Miller and Lents, reached 4,575 million barrels (MMbbl) of oil and 0.86 billion cubic feet of natural gas, and total reserves were 4,718 MMbbl. The company owned Omsk oil refinery with capacity of 145 MMbbl per year and large shares in the Moscow and Mozyr oil refineries (Olma 2004). In 2000 the company came under the control of Abramovich.

In 2002 the Russian Chamber audited Sibneft and its subsidiaries (Sibneft–NNG, Sibneft-Omsk Refinery and JSC Sibneft-Omsknefteproduct) to determine how correctly these companies calculated taxes and other obligatory payments to the federal budget. The report shows that in 2001, Sibneft and its subsidiaries produced 20,593 million tonnes of crude oil. The main volume of crude oil (98.4 per cent) was produced by JSC Sibneft–NNG which was a subsidiary of the company (Accounts Chamber 2002).

Crude oil was sold to small companies (Olivesta, Vester and so on) which were registered in the Republic of Kalmykia zone with tax benefits (an internal offshore of the Russian Federation which was created for development of the weak regional economy). These companies were completely exempt from the regional and local parts of the income tax, which accounted for 24 per cent of profit. Also, to reduce the remaining 11 per cent payable to the federal budget, the companies used the labour of the disabled, due to income tax being reduced by 50 per cent if the total number of the company's employees with disabilities were 50 per cent or more. For example, of the seven full-time employees of the company LLC Olivesta which in 2001 resold 4.47 million tonnes of oil, six were disabled. As a result, profits from these operations were subject to a tax rate of 5.5 per cent (Accounts Chamber 2002).

According to the inspection report of the Accounts Chamber, the price of crude oil for these mediators was 1,300 roubles per tonne (ibid.). After that, these small companies sold crude oil to Sibneft at price from 2,200 to 3,800 roubles per tonne (average price 3,160 roubles per tonne). Additionally, these companies sent crude oil for refining at the Omsk oil refinery on a give-and-take basis. The agent for the transportation of crude oil from the oil metering unit of Sibneft–NNG to the oil metering unit of the Omsk oil refinery was Sibneft. The crude oil was processed at the Omsk oil refinery then petroleum products were sold in the market.

Almost at the same time, in 2001, Roman Abramovich was elected Governor of the Chukotka region. He gained not only a political position but also an opportunity to create a tax haven for himself. Abramovich has built up trading companies, which allowed him to reduce taxation of his business including the major asset, Sibneft. In Abramovich's first years in the post of Governor, Sibneft surpassed all of its previous achievements: his companies could reduce corporate tax by more than $2 billion (Belkovsky *et al.* 2006). Already in the third quarter of 2001, Sibneft was operating through Terra and other small companies which were similar to the previously mentioned offshore companies in Kalmykia, but registered in Anadyr (Chukotka).

Abramovich and his partners used a similar model of business. The limited company Terra bought crude oil on the site of registration, Sibneft–NNG, at the price of 1,300 roubles per tonne, then this crude oil was resold on the same site to Sibneft at a price of 3,800 roubles per tonne without incurring any significant expenditure. From a legal point of view, the owners of the oil were mediators; however, the organisation of export deliveries, payment of customs duties, and payment for transportation and refining in Russia were carried out by Sibneft. Thus the production process and the associated costs were being paid by Sibneft, whereas mediators only accumulated profits without functional operations. If there was a direct relation between subsidiaries of Sibneft (without mediators), taxable income of Sibneft in 2001 was theoretically 45.4 billion roubles and tax could be paid of 16.1 billion roubles. In reality, taxation received in 2001 was just 5.8 billion roubles (including taxes paid by affiliates of Sibneft). Thus the company saved 10.3 billion roubles (around $350 million) and so the government did not receive these 10.3 billion roubles; but in the same year the shareholders of Sibneft received 29 billion roubles in dividends (Accounts Chamber 2002).

Paying tax at a rate of one-sixth of the maximum, these small companies with their profits were added to Sibneft, which is registered in Moscow. Consequently, Sibneft profit before tax in 2001 (prior to these mergers) was only 1.75 billion roubles. After joining with the mediators, Sibneft's profit was 29.79 billion roubles, all of which was available for dividends.

According to Tsaregorodtsev (cited in Makeev and Romanova 2004), Sibneft's profit before taxes in 2000 was $753 million. From this amount Sibneft paid $78 million to the state treasury at a rate of 10.35 per cent. In 2001, Sibneft's income rose to $3.57 billion. However, the company paid taxes at a rate of

9.3 per cent, just $134 million. In 2002 Sibneft earned $1.34 billion. In this case, the company paid taxes at a rate of 12.3 per cent, $163 million. In 2003 Sibneft's tax payments were even less. For the first half of the year, profit was $1.449 billion. Taxation Sibneft actually paid to the state was at an effective rate of 4.8 per cent and total taxes amounted to $70 million (Makeev and Romanova 2004).

The main factors reducing the income tax were established by the legislation of the regions of the Russian Federation where companies are registered, often using a zero rate of taxation. As a result, the huge company Sibneft paid only symbolic payments to the local authorities. Also, a 50 per cent reduction in income tax rate was achieved due to the special condition of the federal legislation on incentives for companies where more than half of the employees are disabled. As a result, six disabled people with an average annual salary of around $1,000 had saved the company around $10 million.

Article 277 of the Tax Code of the Russian Federation indicates exemption from taxation of income earned as a result of the reorganisation (merger) of companies. That allowed Sibneft in 2001 to assimilate the companies with assets worth 28.8 billion roubles in exchange for 2207 Sibneft shares worth $4,400 (Accounts Chamber 2002).

The imperfection of the Russian legislation in 2001 allowed the company to generate profits of 29.79 billion roubles, mostly (97 per cent) the profits of a company which were merged. The profit obtained was almost fully used to pay dividends to the nominal owners of Sibneft which were registered in the offshore zone in the Republic of Cyprus and the British Virgin Islands. Dividends of 28.9 billion roubles transferred to the accounts of the companies: Gemini Holdings Ltd, Carbonrow Investments Ltd, Martachello Co. Ltd, White Pearl Investments and Kravin Investments Ltd (Accounts Chamber 2002). In early 2003, Sibneft sold to TNK shares in Orenburgneft and ONAKO worth about $850 million. Sellers and buyers were offshore companies, so profit was formed outside Russia and the taxes were not paid (Belkovsky *et al.* 2006).

In March 2004, the Ministry of Taxes and Levies woke up, like a brown bear from winter hibernation, and filed a tax claim in the amount of $1 billion against Sibneft. Then S&P downgraded the rating of Sibneft from B+ to B and set a long-term rating to the list of Credit Watch, with negative implications (Olma 2004). However, Sibneft rapidly managed to find a common language with the tax authorities and get rid of the problem quite easily: the company paid about $300 million extra instead of $1 billion in additional accruals (Egorova and Grozovskiy 2005). In August 2005, President Putin subordinated the Russian Accounts Chamber to himself, and its chairman Stepashin immediately withdrew all claims to the Russian joint venture of Abramovich and Sibneft (Belkovsky and Golishev 2006).

In the West, Sibneft had a reputation as the most opaque of Russian companies and it had no chance of being sold at market price. The negotiations between Sibneft and ChevronTexaco on the sale of shares of Sibneft, which were conducted in the summer of 2003, had no success (Belkovsky *et al.*

2006). However, the Russian authorities and executives of Gazprom had their own vision of the development of the company. The miracle happened – in September–November 2005 Gazprom bought 75 per cent of Sibneft for $13.7 billion from Millhouse Capital, which is considered to belong to Roman Abramovich although the real owners are unknown (Nemtsov and Milov 2008a). It is interesting that before the agreement between Gazprom and Sibneft, the company was released of all claims under the Federal Tax Service.

The General Prosecutor's Office had the mass of facts which could lay much more serious charges upon the management of Sibneft and Abramovich than those that have been brought against persons involved in the Yukos investigation (see Chapter 9). In this case, shares of the company could legitimately return to state ownership for free, but they were bought for dramatically more than their fair market value. Therefore the purchase of shares of Sibneft can be regarded as an unjustified waste of public funds (Belkovsky and Golishev 2006).

Now, almost three years after the transaction with Sibneft, it is safe to say that the management of Gazprom in the business was a failure. Average daily oil production of Sibneft fell from 95,800 tonnes per day in September 2005, when the company was bought, to 84,700 tonnes in June 2008 – 11.5 per cent less than three years previously. Gazprom has invested $13.7 billion in a failed project from the point of view of output and obviously overpaid the structures of Roman Abramovich (Nemtsov and Milov 2008a). Sibneft was the one Russian oil company that had reduced its oil production from 34.1 million tonnes in 2005 to 30.48 million tonnes in 2008 due to, as supposed by Belkovsky *et al.* (2006), the depreciation of company fixed assets and the exhaustion of oil deposits.

One can see that Abramovich's companies arbitrage differences which arise between oil prices in different parts of Russia and between the external and domestic oil markets. But, more importantly for our analysis, Abramovich's companies employed transfer pricing which operates as an instrument for the allocation of costs, income and profits between numerous linked companies in different regions, reducing the effective tax rate of Sibneft. His companies sold oil and petroleum products to subsidiaries at below-market prices. Then these mediators sold products to the final buyers at market prices which generated profit. This scheme was widely employed by shell companies which were registered in internal or external offshore zones, and many of them evaporated after they had done the required number of transactions.

Also, one can note that there were different trajectories to achieve Option 2. Initially, when the business of Abramovich and Berezovsky was started, there were some tax asymmetries between regions but their company had weak opportunity for arbitrage (Option 3). However, relatively quickly offshore companies were created and financial schemes and good relationships with authorities were established that made arbitrage possible (Option 2). Later, when Abramovich was elected Governor of Chukotka, he took the position of Option 1, creating the tax regime giving opportunities for his companies which he regarded as necessary and sufficient to obtain extraordinary profit.

One can say that the Abramovich arbitrage strategic planning was the alignment of the route from Option 3 to Option 2 via Option 1 (creating its own offshore zone), with subsequent saving and retention of Option 2. The ability to hold strong price asymmetries (favourable taxation and weak tax administration) was the competitive advantage of the company in the oil segment. For several years, until Sibneft was sold to the government, Governor Abramovich created special taxation for his business and supported it in the difficult struggle for tax arbitrage with the federal tax authorities. Of course, Abramovich was not the only one who used arbitrage between different taxation zones – similar schemes in some combination were used by all Russian oil corporations – but only Abramovich managed to create his own offshore zone.

The next case reveals strong price asymmetries and robust opportunity for arbitrage (Option 2).

Browder, Magnitsky and Kalmykia

Hermitage Capital Management (Hermitage) was founded by Bill Browder and Edmond Safra in 1996 for the purpose of investing capital in Russia. The business was extremely fruitful, making money from trading Russian blue chips which were considerably undervalued. In Russia, Hermitage is widely known in the context of the tragic history of Sergei Magnitsky who was murdered or, according to the prison official's version, died due to a rupture to the abdominal membrane, in the Moscow prison Butyrka in November 2008.

At the end of the 1990s the company was one of the leading foreign investors in Russia (Dyck 2002) and operated in different segments of the Russian economy. It was an exceptional shareholder in Gazprom (ibid.) due to its vigorous anticorruption activity. The largest and most influential Russian gas goliath, Gazprom, was a zone of special interest of many foreign investment funds including Hermitage due to its huge size and good perspective for growth of capitalisation.

The Presidential Decree (1997) established that during the privatisation of the Russian company Gazprom there was a limit for the combined share of foreign participants in the authorised capital of the company to the amount of 9 per cent. Later, in 1999, it was increased to 20 per cent (Bushueva 2001). The decree prohibited the acquisition and holding of shares of Gazprom companies by residents of the Russian Federation which have mutual participation in each other's capital, if the share of the direct participation of non-residents in their authorised capital exceeded 50 per cent. The decree was lobbied by the Russian national elite, including executives of the company who aspired to consolidate shares of the company. As a result of this state regulation, there was a large difference between the internal and external price of Gazprom's shares due to existing domestic and foreign market shares of the company.

Shares of Gazprom were divided into two parts: local shares and those traded on foreign exchanges (American depositary shares, ADS). Because of the limited supply of foreign depositary shares they were traded twice as much and sometimes the gap was even more significant (Kudinov and Nikolsky 2013). Strong demand from foreign investors ensured that the external shares were quickly traded at a substantial premium over the price of the internal shares, generating a motivation for potential external buyers to create schemes to purchase shares which traded at internal prices. Consequently, foreign investors needed to use different arrangements for holding Gazprom shares, including through holding companies incorporated in Russia (ibid.).

For example, Hermitage created a special construction consisting of two Russian companies (which were registered in the Russian internal offshore zone Kalmykia) and a third company registered in Cyprus. The Cypriot company had a 49 per cent holding of the first Russian company, which in turn owned 51 per cent of the second Russian company. This second Russian company also owned the remaining 51 per cent of the first Russian company. The Cypriot company's shares in the other companies were preferred stock. Both Russian companies had three employees: a General Manager who was an official from non-Russian investor and two additional disabled workers who were Kalmyk. The Russian companies had Moscow bank accounts and held Gazprom shares in the Moscow depositary (Gross 2013).

This construction, from a formal point of view, did not contravene legislation and it allowed Hermitage to conceal the real owners of Gazprom shares as well as dramatically reducing the tax liability. Hermitage's approach was not unique; it is believed that United Financial Group (UFG) was one of the first to come up with the grey ownership scheme of Gazprom as early as 1997 (Kudinov and Nikolsky 2013). And in the period from 1997 to 2005, shares of Gazprom were acquired in a similar way at the prices of the domestic market by many other foreign companies, such as Vostok Nafta, Pharos Gas, Noviy Neft and Charlemagne Capital, Rengas Holding, Gasinvest Capital and others (Chelischeva 2013). Moreover, at that time Gazprom organised a joint venture with German energy company Ruhrgas, which had a similar pattern of possession of Gazprom shares. A service of acquisition and holding of Gazprom shares for nonresidents of the Russian Federation was carried out by many operators of the Russian securities market such as UFG, Renaissance Capital, Troika Dialog, Alfa-Bank, Aton, Deutsche Bank, Gazprombank, JP Morgan and many others (ibid.).

In 2002, Dmitry Medvedev (who later became Russian President), when he was the Chairman of Gazprom, said that Gazprom is aware of the fact that the company's shares are purchased by nonresidents at the prices of the domestic market, but does not challenge the legality of such acquisition. Therefore investors would not be penalised for using these schemes because they became possible as a result of the gaps in the Russian legislation and the government's mistake (ibid.).

Hermitage did not disclose the size of its Gazprom shareholding, but in 2002 Browder enlisted the voices of the owners of more than 3 per cent of shares for nomination to the Board of Directors. However, he was unable to be elected

Director (Kudinov and Nikolsky 2013). Also, according to the Russian investigators, Browder managed to purchase 131 million shares of Gazprom (0.55 per cent) (ibid.).

In 2001, foreigners officially owned 11.5 per cent of Gazprom shares (6.02 per cent were owned by the Gazprom Dutch subsidiary Gazprom Finance B.V., 1.98 per cent by the Western market in the form of ADS; 3.5 per cent by the German gas company Ruhrgas). But in reality the share of nonresidents in the share capital of Gazprom was much higher (Bushueva 2001).

After all, the management came up with, and has always supported, the division of markets of shares (Bushueva 2001). Restrictions on transactions in shares of Gazprom were lobbied for by Gazprom itself, and one can suppose companies such as Troika and UFG and other undercover Gazprom executives.

For a long time there was a price discrepancy between the internal and external markets of Gazprom shares and the external shares traded at a substantial premium over the price of the internal shares, generating motivation for arbitrage. This price discrepancy was maintained by the company executives because of their desire to privatise Gazprom shares for less than the real market price. Also, they had a lack of funds for the fast purchase of shares so it was impossible to put in a bag all the money from the Gazprom finance department and yet not stop gas extraction. However, on the other hand, there were other solid participants in the privatisation race who wanted to make money immediately. Therefore the confrontation lasted for a long while, with the passionate rhetoric of Gazprom managers about the preservation of the national heritage and the ardent anticorruption speeches of their opponents. And, of course, both opponents could not harvest Gazprom assets until 2005, when the controlling stake was taken under state control and all restrictions on foreign ownership of Gazprom shares were abolished.

Trading of Gazprom shares by Hermitage on the internal and external markets reveals the example of Option 2, where there is strong price asymmetry between markets and robust opportunity for arbitrage. When speaking of an opportunity for arbitrage, we mean that the company prior to the project had almost all the necessary intellectual and financial resources and those barriers to arbitrage are not significant.

Also, it is necessary emphasise that arbitrage of Gazprom shares had different risks in comparison with traditional share dealing on the open market: in the first case there was risk of recognition by the state of illegal operations with shares of Gazprom and the subsequent confiscation of shares; whereas in the second case there was traditional price risk. Developing a theory of arbitrage (in Russia particularly) one may add a new component into the model in Table 2.1 – the opportunity to exit without problems upon successful arbitrage. This case, and others analysed in this book, confirm the importance of this idea.

Let go back to our protagonist, who employed a large spectrum of arbitrage methods, some of which we can try to reveal. As noted above, Hermitage arbitraged the Gazprom shares market and employed two Russian companies which were registered in the internal offshore zone of Kalmykia and employed disabled persons.

The Kalmyk special economic zone (SEZ) was opened in 1995 in one of the most pure regions of the Russian Federation. The regional tax exemptions were based on Federal Law and Kalmyk tax laws of 1995 and 1999 (Law of Kalmykia 1995, 1999) which effectively reduce the federal tax rate from 35 to 11 per cent and swap municipal and regional taxes set at 5 and 19 per cent, respectively, to a negotiated payment. To obtain tax incentives, according to the Kalmyk tax laws (ibid.), the company had to hold a tax benefit certificate issued by the Kalmyk authorities and make an agreement with the regional government on a contribution to an investment project listed in a public offer issued by the government. In addition, after the official registration the company had to make established payments. In response to these incentives, many large Russian companies such as TNK BP and Hermitage registered their business in Kalmykia.

In addition, Hermitage employed disabled persons due to the possibility of using tax incentives. After the start of the Russian reforms the government had a huge budget deficit and could not pay acceptable pensions and social benefit payments for handicapped persons. Consequently, the parliament passed the Law on Corporate Tax of Enterprises, allowing companies to reduce the tax rate from 11 to 5.5 per cent on condition that at least 50 per cent of the company's staff were disabled (Gross 2013). The authorities, in preference to subsidising such essential expenditures by recognised tax revenue, the collection of which was difficult due to the weakness of the Russian tax institutes at that time, actually attempted to privatise support to the disabled by gifting tax advantages to companies paying them living remunerations (ibid.).

As a result, employment of disabled labour was a usual approach for tax optimisation. Beneficiaries of this arbitrage were not only businesses, however; it was also profitable for disabled people who were employed in many companies and as a result had additional money for living. Also, it created jobs for recruitment agencies (suppliers of labour force with special conditions), for doctors who could sell invalidity certificates and for tax consultants who sold ready-made small businesses with disabled workers. Small companies were used extensively for transfer pricing and tax optimisation. The Russian law did not identify any job qualifications which were required from the handicapped employees. As a result, one could enrol in an investment company that has, say, three traders and three disabled cleaners, and the company would benefit from tax reductions.

The two Kalmyk subsidiaries of Hermitage employed six persons. The companies had an insignificant workforce, therefore it was not problematic to achieve the 50 per cent limit of disabled employees needed to be eligible for the tax benefits. The six people were given a job title in accordance with the main activities of the companies. They were given objectively unsophisticated responsibilities corresponding with their severe invalidity, including following the regional mass media and reporting on applicable developments to the

Hermitage office in Moscow (Gross 2013). It is quite difficult to understand how the Hermitage office in Moscow was going to employ this information, but wages to these staff were paid regularly.

The total profit amounted to the equivalent of about $17 million, of which $14 million concerned exemptions from Kalmyk local and regional taxes and $3 million corresponded to a reduction of the federal tax rate foreseen by law as an incentive for the employment of disabled employees (Gross 2013). In the case of Hermitage's Kalmyk subsidiaries, it cost the state $3 million in tax reductions to obtain the payment of wages to five handicapped persons and one director for one year, which cost Hermitage around $6,000.

It is important to understand that high profitability of business in Russia can carry extraordinary risks. Unsurprisingly (because loopholes for buying Gazprom shares were not made for Hermitage), in 2004 a criminal case was opened against Hermitage. However, as noted by Gessen (2011), the company's documentation and audits carried out by experienced tax authorities could not confirm the law violation by Hermitage and the criminal case was closed. Nonetheless, the Hermitage business in Russia was wound up in 2005, and a little later came the tragic finale: the death of Sergei Magnitsky (Gessen 2011).

When the business of Hermitage started, there were established tax asymmetries between the Kalmyk SEZ and other Russian regions and reduced tax for disabled workers. In addition, there were no difficulties in opening companies with tax privileges that consequently made arbitrage (Option 2). Relatively quickly, offshore companies were created and respectable relationships with the authorities were established that made it possible to arbitrage (Option 2). However, the cases of Kalmyk SEZ and the employment of disabled workers for reduction of tax again risks recognition by the state of operations for tax reduction. Here the problem arises of easy entry into arbitrage and heavy exit after realisation (this problem is discussed in more detail in Chapter 4).

Avtotor assembles BMW and GM

Movement from Option 4 to Option 2 is the typical situation, when the agent wants to realise arbitrage but there are different types of barriers, such as state and regional rules and regulations, deprived infrastructure of the region and lack of starting capital. However, it is important to note that conditions do not remain stable due to the variability of the economic and social environment. Therefore, to obtain the long-term competitive advantage that is the long-term use of arbitrage, a company should be able to maintain these conditions. The following case shows a car company that for 15 years created and supported the conditions for arbitrage and implemented the arbitrage itself.

After the disintegration of the USSR, unstable economic situations resulted in a decline of car manufacturing. From 1990 to 1995, Russian car production fell sharply from 1,074,000 to 834,000 cars per annum (Russia in Figures 1997). The automotive industry was affected by new state boundaries and lost markets in the far east of Russia and in the Kaliningrad enclave. These lucrative markets were taken over by Japan and Germany, respectively (AvtoVAZ 1996, 1998).

Between 1991 and 1995, Russia had a comparatively underdeveloped car market and, according to official statistics, car market penetration was at 83 cars per 1,000 people, considerably lower than in other European markets. For example, in Germany for every 1,000 inhabitants there were approximately 500 cars (ASM 1995). This factor created a huge demand for cars because national manufacturers did not have adequate capacity and the quality of cars could not satisfy consumers. The basic disadvantages of the Russian auto industry were poor quality of cars, old fashioned models and scarcity of intellectual resources for making new models.

In November 1991, the Soviet government issued a decree that allowed individuals to import one car duty-free, and for the first time imported cars faced real competition; globalisation had begun to impact on Russian industry. The underdeveloped Russian car market created a huge demand for cars and price asymmetries between domestic and external markets. Consequently, numerous entrepreneurs employed opportunities for arbitrage. The market share for foreign cars grew from 2 to 18 per cent (ASM 1995) and in 1996 growth in foreign second-hand motor vehicles rose to 457,000 (about 50 per cent of the market) (ASM 1997). Second-hand cars were a serious threat to the domestic automotive industry. In order to stop the significant growth of used car imports, car manufacturers (mainly Avtovaz) lobbied the increasing tariffs on used and new imported cars. Throughout the history of the Russian automotive industry, one of the most important measures to support it has been the high duties on imported cars.

In June 1992, import duties were imposed at 15 per cent of the customs value of new cars and 25 per cent for second-hand cars. The customs value was determined on the basis of the car manufacturers and foreign merchants. In November 1993, the Russian government once again raised the fees for the import of all cars in Russia. For engine volumes up to 1,500 ccm the fee was 35 per cent of the customs value of the car; up to 3000 ccm it was 50 per cent, and over 3000 ccm, 70 per cent (Kozichev 2009).

In January 1994, a new rate of customs duty was introduced for individuals, including VAT and excise duty of $6 per ccm. The aggregate amount of fees was from 80 to 130 per cent of the declared price. In July 1999 the accrual system of fees for used (over three years) cars was slightly modified. They had a dependence on engine size: up to 2.5 litres, €0.85 per 1 ccm, more than 2.5 litres, €1.4. The new machines have continued to take shape at the rate of 30 per cent of the cost (Kozichev 2009).

One can see how the Russian car producers held off a massive offering of low-cost foreign cars and this offer, together with price asymmetries, created conditions for arbitrage operations. There was only one problem: how to find an opportunity for arbitrage, how to jump from a field of strong price asymmetries and weak opportunity to a happy field of arbitrage where one can gather a good crop of money. Of course, cars could be imported through holes in the border, and thousands of imports have been made in that way. But in the following stories our hero and his team managed to create arbitrage opportunities using only their own experience, relatively little money and good relations with the authorities.

Avtotor was established in 1996 by the international fund Interprivatizatsiya, led by the current principal owner and Chairman of the Board of Directors of the company, Vladimir Shcherbakov (Morzharetto 2011). He was the first Vice-Premier of the Soviet government, a member of the Central Committee of the Communist Party, one of the youngest senior officials of the Soviet Union (he was then 42) and a favourite of the first Soviet President Mikhail Gorbachev (Popov 2013).

In October 1991, Gorbachev signed a decree on the establishment of 'the international fund for privatization and foreign investment in the USSR (Interprivatizatsiya)' and Shcherbakov was elected the President of the foundation. Interprivatizatsiya had very serious money. Shcherbakov's first team of the fund included six former Soviet ministers. In the late 1980s, according to the order of the Central Committee, money of the Communist Party was siphoned into joint ventures and it is possible that this money was put into the fund (ibid.).

Soon the fund Interprivatizatsiya was merged with another venture – the Soviet–Austrian joint venture Nordex, which exported metals and oil products in 1991 and had a turnover of $900 million. In total, Interprivatizatsiya raised on the markets in the West $600 million to fund projects in Kazakhstan, Uzbekistan and Belorussia. Shcherbakov had a friendship with the Russian Prime Minister Viktor Chernomyrdin, and his support opened the door for customs exemptions for the Kaliningrad region and the creation of car manufacturing (ibid.).

The federal act 'On special economic zone in the Kaliningrad region' of 1996 was the principal document behind regulation of economic activity in the Kaliningrad region over ten years, and a preferential regime of a special economic zone was opened which allowed duty-free import parts and components if a manufacturer added 30 per cent to the cost of selling cars in Russia (Federal Law 1996). The Shcherbakov team created the programme of development of car manufacturing in the region and it managed to lobby for Government Resolution of the Russian Federation N 524 of 23 April 'On measures of state support for the creation of modern assembly production of passenger cars in the Kaliningrad region' (Government Resolution 1996). Moreover, the Ministry of Finance provided an investment loan for the project (Popov 2013).

Kaliningrad was also chosen as a place of car assembly because the Kaliningrad region had a large number of empty machinery and shipbuilding plants which were easy to transform into an automotive company. Additionally, the city has a sea port with suitable infrastructure and the region had a surplus of well educated labour. On 30 July 1996, the 'Agreement on cooperation in the development of industrial production in the special economic zone of the Kaliningrad region, between KIA Group and the International Fund' was signed (Autostat 2010).

In 1996–97, partial conversion was made at Yantar shipyard; several old buildings were reconstructed where the assembly line was installed. A high-quality assembly line was bought from Nissan in Greece for $18 million in instalments. The design capacity of the shop was 50,000 cars per year (Lubnin 1997). Total investment in the project was approximately $130 million including credit from Swiss and Austrian banks (Gubskiy and Shtanov 2012).

At that time Kia was an unknown company that wanted to penetrate the Russian market, so an agreement was quickly signed. The Korean company supplied kits on credit terms such that payment was made after the sale of assembled cars (Popov 2013). The speed of construction and installation was very fast: in December 1996 the equipment arrived and in May 1997 the new plant began assembling budget models of Kia (Gubskiy and Shtanov 2012). The first car of the new company KIA-Baltic entered the market in 1997. This was one of the first production models of foreign design and Russian assembly.

In the end of 1997, the car plant had two sites: a huge workshop at Kaliningradbummash and the production area at Yantar shipyard. For assembling cars, it used the slipway technology (without a conveyor). Bodies of cars with all elements (seats, dashboard and even mirrors), but without engines, transmission and wheels, were shipped from Korea. When the car came into the shop, identification numbers corresponding to the Russian standard were attached to the body and engine, then the car was driven onto a lift, where workers assembled transmission components and matching engine and wheels. Then, using special equipment, wheels, brakes, adjustable headlights, engine performance and toxicity levels were checked. That was all that was done and the cars were ready for distribution. On average, during one working day, two workers assembled two cars. The designed capacity of the plant was to produce 25,000 cars a year. The company had only 18 assembly operations, but it promised to organise the production of 65 per cent of KIA parts in Russia (Lubnin 1997).

The first car were Kia Avella Delta and Kia Sephia with an engine capacity of 1,500 ccm, which are relatively similar to the Russian Lada cars (9 and 10 series) but more comfortable than their domestic counterparts. Using this arbitrage scheme, Avtotor was able to offer these models for around $8,500 and $14,500, respectively. This was $1500–2000 less than the cost of the cars assembled in Korea (Lubnin 1997). In May 1997, Avtotor and KIA Motors signed an agreement to assemble new models of cars: Avella, Roxta, Clarus, Sportage and van Besta. Their assembly began in 1999; as a result the monthly volume of production in 2003 for the first time exceeded 1,000 cars (Autostat 2010; Popov 2013)

The company continuously expanded its business, and in October 1999 serial production of BMW 5 and 7 series cars was launched. Later in 2001, the production of 7 series BMW was stopped but assembly of 3- and updated

5-series were established, as well as off-road vehicles BMW X3, BMW X5 and BMW X6 (Autostat 2010).

Working with BMW, the company employed a relatively simple business model: off-road BMW X5 and X6 were produced in factories in the USA, then the vehicles sailed on ferries to the shop of one of the largest logistics operators in the automotive industry, BLG Logistics in the port of Bremerhaven. In BLG Logistics the engine, transmission, mirrors, headlights, bumpers and wheels were removed from the cars, then the cars were sent to Kaliningrad where they were reassembled (Popov 2013). Using only 19 assembling operations (Gubskiy and Shtanov 2012), Avtotor bypasses the need to pay the customs duty on imported cars. For 12 years Avtotor assembled over 50,000 BMW sedans and sport utility vehicles (Morzharetto 2011).

Lobbyist activity did not stop, and in February 2000, in order to attract more investment, the Law of the Kaliningrad region 'On state support of investment project for the production of cars, motorcycles and bikes in the Special Economic Zone Yantar and providing tax breaks to companies participating in the project' was passed (Autostat 2010). In August 2003, the company signed agreements with General Motors to organise the production of GM cars (Hummer, Trail Blazer and Tahoe) in Kaliningrad. The main building of 10,000 square metres allowing the production 6,000 cars was built with the assistance of GM. In the next year, 842 cars were assembled (Avtotor 2013).

During the first 10 years, the two basic operations of disassembling the finished car abroad and its reassembling in Kaliningrad allowed Avtotor to avoid customs duties on the import of foreign cars in Russia thanks to the benefits of the Kaliningrad SEZ, because auto components can be imported free of duty. However, using customs facilities of the Kaliningrad SEZ has not been a privilege only of Avtotor. For example, the company Maxik was able to dismantle used cars in Lithuania and the parts were brought into Kaliningrad, assembled, recorded and sent into Russia. Also, televisions are assembled from five components; and pellets of frozen meat from Europe are split using a heat gun, becoming Russian meat products, and are sent to retailers across the country (Popov 2013).

However, Prihodko *et al.* (2007) note that Kaliningrad SEZ contributed to the collapse of manufacturing production because, unable to resist competition with imports, numerous local manufacturers went bankrupt. Despite this, the region has been a frontrunner in the dynamic of industrial production and the SEZ made the region favourable to placement of enterprises that deliver to Russia goods made from import duty-free raw materials and assembly parts. The region has an artificial structure of the local economy and it is unable to coexist with other regions when identical economic rules are introduced (ibid.).

In 2006, Avtotor started assembling Chinese Chery (Tiggo and Amulet) and Chinese commercial trucks (YUEJIN). However, in April 2008, under pressure from the Russian authorities, Avtotor terminated production of Chery cars and broke off relations with the Chinese automaker in exchange for keeping the zero customs exemptions on import of components for semi-knocked-down (SKD) assembly of vehicles, which the company enjoys under the law on the special economic zone of the Kaliningrad region (Autostat 2010). Also, in the 2000s, foreign automakers coming to Russia were forced to enter into agreements with the government for industrial assembly, including the gradual localisation of production. Nevertheless, Avtotor was not concerned because in the special economic zone it was enough to add 30 per cent of the cost.

In November 2008, Avtotor and GM opened a new production with capacity of 50,000 cars a year. GM investment was €80 million. The first model produced in Kaliningrad on a full cycle was the Chevrolet Lacetti, one of the most popular Avtotor models. The model has Russian battery, wheels, tyres, glass, floor mats and interior details, but there is no further localisation as parts from European contractors are cheaper. At the end of October 2009, Avtotor launched SKD assembly of Opel Astra cars and the Zafira minivan (Autostat 2010).

The company, together with Magna, wants to build an automotive cluster in Kaliningrad to the total value of 100 billion roubles. In partnership with BMW, General Motors and others will set up six factories with capacity of 350,000 vehicles per year. To increase localisation from the current 15 per cent to 50 per cent, 15 automotive component productions will be opened (Gubskiy and Shtanov 2012). However, the agreement between Avtotor and Magna is the last chance to stay afloat, because from 2016 the SKD car assembly technology will be ceased, causing a major loss of income.

In 2010–12, Avtotor assembled 26 models of five brands: BMW, Cadillac, Kia, Opel and Chevrolet. Some models were made in dozens, others in the tens of thousands. The assembly of vehicles has been an impressive success. In 2000, Avtotor produced around 3,000 cars; in 2011, 222,000 were produced. Presently, the company ranks second after Avtovaz in the list of automakers (Avtotor 2013). Currently Avtotor produces more than 40 per cent of the gross regional product and in 2015 contributed about 50 per cent of all taxes in the region (Gubskiy and Shtanov 2012).

In 2012, Avtotor saved tens of billions of roubles on customs duty, and the legality of these actions was upheld in dozens of court cases (Popov 2013). With the growth of the company, claims against it by the federal and regional authorities increased. Avtotor was accused of failing to pay taxes and customs duties, and of importing smuggled automotive components (Gubskiy and Shtanov 2012). Nine billion roubles of claims by the Federal Customs Service against Avtotor regarding the classification of imported completely knocked down (CKD) cars did not find support in the courts.

According to the Avtotor position, the plant categorises these as a collection of parts but not as a disassembled car. However, professionals such as the former Soviet Minister of the Automotive Industry Nikolai Pugin evaluate the business of the company simply: 'Avtotor is not a full-fledged production, it simply bypasses duty' (Popov 2013). Shcherbakov is a highly skilled executive, but for the success of the company it was more important that he was able to keep the benefits for his companies in the region. Using friends in the Russian government he actively lobbied for the right solutions for the special economic zone, not only for his business but for others, thus the special economic zone survived for so many years (ibid.).

Despite the financial crisis, unstable legislative system and often unfriendly environment, the company made great achievements. It successfully arbitraged the Russian market for over 15 years. There were strong price asymmetries between the Russian and foreign car markets due to active lobbying by the industry leader, Avtovaz, thanks to which the government regularly increased tax duties. One can say that Avtovaz tirelessly battling for protection of the market against imported Western vehicles created conditions for Avtotor. However, the lobbying success of Avtovaz provided only half of Avtotor's success; the other part of it was created by the company itself, constantly generating opportunities for arbitrage.

When Avtotor had just started its business in the region, it had the position of Option 4 because in the car market there was robust dissimilarity between domestic and external prices. However, very shortly Shcherbakov was able to form conditions (special tax legislation) which allowed movement from Option 4 to Option 2 and realised arbitrage. Also, the case shows the struggle of the company to preserve the position in Option 2: despite constant attempts by competitors to block the special customs regime and thereby destroy this robust opportunity for arbitrage, Avtotor was able to preserve it.

Anti-arbitrage strategy

In previous sections it was shown that employing arbitrage in different business situations and arbitrage as strategy can be efficient for achieving companies' aims. But often, beyond the analysis, competitors have remained, and the reader may have been given an impression of the invulnerability of this strategy. If arbitrage is a kind of strategy, how can competitors fight? The answer is simple: if the train to the destination has no free places, one can take a jet; if there is no jet, one can ruin the railway and get ahead of competitors on foot. That is, competitors can use the strategy of destroying either price differentiation or opportunities for arbitrage, or both. Examples from Russia can help us to understand the concept more precisely.

Destroying of price differentiation

As a beginning, examine the approach which destroys the price differentiation. Consider the possible case of a medium-sized business in a suburb of Moscow. The company uses around 100 Vietnamese people, who were being forced to work up to 18 hours a day without weekends or holidays (for more information about labour arbitrage of Vietnamese workers see Chapter 6). The workers were poorly fed, frequently beaten up and forbidden to leave the workshop buildings. Also, the company was producing counterfeit products, did not pay taxes, and used slave labour that gave a significant competitive advantage on the Russian consumer market but with a relatively insignificant market share. However, when the company dramatically increased production capacity and its market share became significant, it would have to undergo a considerably increased number of inspections: fiscal, fire department and sanitary inspections every week tormented the company.

It is important to note that the activity of inspectors increased dramatically after the production of the company became larger than was traditional for the market. Surprisingly, nobody wanted to shut down the business but everybody wanted money. It can be assumed that in the new market competitors showed resistance to a new player and, using their connections with the authorities, began to create problems for the company.

As a result, transaction costs of production, such as shady institutional expenditures (kickbacks and bribes), costs of monitoring the performance of personnel, costs of compliance with regulations and standards, and costs of safety were considerably increased. Also the cost of labour was raised. All these diminished the price differentiation and made arbitrage impossible. That is, the company did not have the ability to hold strong price asymmetries and it was forced to move along the route from Option 2 (strong price asymmetries and robust opportunity for arbitrage) to Option 1 (absent price asymmetries and strong potential for arbitrage), and eventually the business was liquidated.

Destroying opportunities for arbitrage

Destroying opportunities for arbitrage may be demonstrated by the example of the Russian car industry. As noted above in the case of Avtotor, in the 1990s there was a huge demand for cars and price asymmetry between domestic and external markets. In that time, Avtovaz was the largest Russian firm that built and assembled approximately 750,000 cars per year and held off a massive offer of low-cost foreign cars. In theory, the target of Avtovaz was clear: domestic traders did not have to find an opportunity for arbitrage and any attempt to jump from a field of strong price asymmetries and weak opportunity to a successful field of arbitrage where one can harvest a good crop of money should be strictly suppressed.

To implement the strategy, Avtovaz constantly lobbied in the government to establish high customs duties on imported cars and for the customs service and the traffic police to carry out strict administration duties. Of course, one could import cars via holes in the border and holes in the law. Nevertheless, Avtovaz did not relax and constantly blocked the appearance of new opportunities for arbitrage. For example, in May 1996 the government introduced privileges on the import of foreign cars for diplomats, sailors, fishermen and flight crews, as well as for those who were abroad for more than six months. Each of them could import a car into Russia and register it at a discounted rate. Soon preferential foreign cars accounted for about 20 per cent of imported cars (Kozichev 2009). Implementing its strategy, Avtovaz managed to terminate customs benefits to Russians who worked abroad for more than six months and imported cars for themselves. Moreover, the government made the decision that future owners must deposit into a special account 80 per cent of the import duties on foreign cars before delivering a car to Russia, which complicated car import for citizens.

After the default of 1998, the price of imported cars climbed and Avtovaz was increasingly competitive. However, after three years the market was saturated by national cars; the auto industry faced new challenges and the president of Avtovaz began a new round of struggle for the rise of duties. To support the car industry, it was decided to effect an increase in duty on second-hand foreign cars, import of which cost three times as much as in the previous year. Consequently, in 2002 the government increased the duties for vehicles older than seven years, the prices of which were established as equal to the prices of new cars. For example, the fee for vehicles older than seven years with an engine up to 2500 ccm increased to €2 per ccm (a 2.3-fold increase), and for engines over 2500 ccm went up to €3 per ccm (a 2.1-fold increase).

For a few years this measure helped the company to be profitable. However, despite high duties which reduced demand for second-hand foreign-made cars, Avtovaz could not save its position due to the growth of the national economy that shifted consumer preferences toward new foreign-made cars of low and average cost.

The Russian new car market steadily posted solid rates of growth throughout the 2003–07 period. Additionally, after years of protecting the domestic car industry through prohibitive tariffs, the government reduced the duty on imported auto components to virtually zero. This motivated the world's car producers to significantly increase production facilities in Russia. Foreign companies using wide, aggressive marketing and improved and developed dealer networks took 70 per cent of the total sales of new passenger cars in 2007 (ASM 2007). Generally, Avtovaz maintained its volume of production, which fluctuated between 600,000 and 700,000, but the company dramatically decreased market share from 50 to 24 per cent. It managed to maintain position only in the cheapest market niche and therefore, despite the fact that the company increased annual sales from $3.3 billion to $5.1 billion, its share of the total financial volume of the market decreased from 32 to 20 per cent (ASM 2007).

The financial crisis of 2008 practically buried the company's hopes of existing as an independent producer, and in 2009 sales decreased by more than 40 per cent. However, the major elements of its salvation were similar to previous years: lobbied protectionist measures were obtained and the government increased customs duties on imported cars older than five years to €5.8 per ccm, which practically closed the market for them (Kozichev 2009).

This case reveals a strategy of defence against the arbitrage approach and it clearly discloses the Avtovaz anti-arbitrage strategy – raising the trade barrier for foreign competitors. In the context of matrix 'price asymmetries – opportunity', the strategy of the company was the relocation of the opponents' position from Option 2 (strong price asymmetries and robust opportunity for arbitrage) to Option 4 (strong price asymmetries and weak opportunity for arbitrage), and as a result of this movement it had decreasing opportunities for arbitrage. Moreover, the problem facing Avtovaz was its increasingly weak finances driven by wealth extraction, poor operating finances and weak strategy where the anti-arbitrage struggle against foreign manufacturers of new and used cars was the central component of corporate strategy. The case discloses a limitation of employing anti-arbitrage strategy if this strategy is employed independently from alternative strategies and is not supported by supplementary elements of corporate management.

Conclusion

This chapter has shown that arbitrage is possible when there are two conditions: the same asset does not trade at the same price on all markets and there is a technical opportunity of realisation arbitrage; as a result it is possible to create a matrix of opportunity and price differentiation. This matrix reveals four possible options for arbitrage as well as a different strategy for managers of companies.

Option 1 describes a situation where the opportunity for carrying out operations required for arbitrage exists, but where there are few price asymmetries to exploit. Option 2 is the standard case of arbitrage, where the opportunity for implementation operations required for arbitrage exists and there are strong price asymmetries. Option 3 cannot give arbitrage as neither asymmetries nor opportunity exist. Option 4 is strong price asymmetries and weak opportunity for arbitrage; this option is the typical case that determines state and regional regulation, bureaucratic barriers and limitations of infrastructure of the country and region.

Examples from the Russian oil, financial and car businesses reveal how executives getting competitive advantage may create price asymmetries and opportunities for arbitrage.

The case of Governor of Chukotka Abramovich discloses how Abramovich's companies arbitraged differences that arose between oil prices in different parts of Russia as well as on the external oil markets. Also, they employed transfer pricing which operates as an instrument for the allocation of costs, income and profits between numerous linked companies in different regions, reducing the effective tax rate of his main company, Sibneft. This scheme was widely employed by shell companies which were registered in internal or external offshore zones and many of them evaporated after they had done the required number of transactions. The ability to hold strong price asymmetries (favourable taxation and weak tax administration) was the competitive advantage of the Abramovich company. For several years, Governor Abramovich created special taxation for his business for tax arbitrage with the federal tax authorities.

The case of Magnitsky and Hermitage reveals the trading of Gazprom shares by Hermitage on the internal and external markets and the example of Option 2 where there is strong price asymmetry between markets and robust opportunity for arbitrage. Additionally, the case shows that the high profitability of business in Russia can carry extraordinary risks if an arbitrageur does not have a close relationship with the Russian authorities.

The complementary generic strategy of anti-arbitrage is aimed at destroying price differentiation or opportunities for arbitrage of competitors. The case reveals an anti-arbitrage defence strategy against the arbitrage approach of competitors in the Russian car market. In the matrix framework the firm's strategy can be seen as the relocation of the opponents' position from Option 2 to Option 3 (absent price asymmetries and opportunity for arbitrage) or Option 4 (absent opportunity for arbitrage), and the consequence of this movement is decreased opportunities for arbitrage. However, the case reveals a limitation of employing anti-arbitrage strategy if this strategy is employed independently of alternative strategies and is not supported by other elements of corporate management.

3 Asymmetries

The regions of the Russian Federation have enormous variations such as that typically seen between countries. Among the regions of the country there are Muslim and Orthodox areas, very traditional and modern areas, some mostly agricultural and others industrial, both subtropical and polar, highlands and plains, and so on. This chapter shows that distance between two regions is a significant factor of businesses, which companies have to analyse thoroughly when they make decisions about regional expansion. Distance may have different dimensions and they each create asymmetries, which is a key element for arbitrage as a strategy.

Rating and evaluation

Geographically, Russia has highly uneven economic development. This unevenness is determined largely by the availability of natural resources, infrastructure, climate, mentality of the population and other factors. Much in the current regional development has been determined by historical aspects such as the creation of industrial towns in the 1930s and 1950s, and geographically, for example by the regions producing oil and gas. In addition to objective factors influencing the development of a region, there are economic policies of local authorities. The degree of difference of a region from others may depend on how efficiently the authority uses regional advantages and how effectively it compensates for disadvantages through its own unique initiatives. Moreover, the impressions of the regional advantages, disadvantages and policies can differ between the authority and the external investor, which can create tension between them and impact on the realisation of investment projects. As a result, there are many examples where a successful business has been transferred from the original region where it was started to other regions of Russia, where it experienced a fiasco. One example is the Segezha Pulp and Paper Mill (SPPM) case. SPPM is Russia's largest producer of kraft paper and paper sacks, located in the Republic of Karelia, 700 km to the north of Saint Petersburg. In 1992 SPPM was turned into an open joint-stock company (SCBK 2012). In 1996, 57.3 per cent of shares of SPPM were bought by the American company Stratton Group, which, since 1997, was wholly owned by the Swedish concern AssiDomän. The Swedish team of managers with CEO Soren Oberg ruled SPPM, and AssiDomän promised to invest $100 million in the company over three years and turn the company into one of the leading suppliers of packaging paper, paper bags and cardboard on the world market. Nevertheless, before they invested, AssiDomän and lenders to the project made a number of demands to the government of Karelia: transfer of a 20 per cent stake of SPPM to AssiDomän, which was the Republic's property; AssiDomän also asked for land for a logging concession, but instead the government offered to participate in the development of Karelia timber companies. AssiDomän also demanded the restructuring of SPPM's debts inherited from the previous owners. The regional government could not accept these requirements and, as a result, in March 1997 the company was mothballed (Cheberko and Rozhkova 1997).

According to AssiDomän, this occurred because of the reluctance of the authorities to fulfil the obligations of Karelia to reduce the company's debt. In addition, the Moscow Arbitration Court decision made it possible to realise external project financing of the investment programme in SPPM (AssiDomän 1998). According to the authority, the project was stopped because of reluctance to develop the company since it created competition for AssiDomän plants in Europe (Ionov and Sapozhnikov 1998). The struggle lasted until March 1998, when the management of AssiDomän finally ceased work on SPPM and Swiss personnel left the company. CEO Lennart Ahlgren notes that when AssiDomän entered into this project it observed enormous opportunities on the market and the potential to develop sack paper production in Russia; on the other hand, the company underestimated the troubles with Russian bureaucracy and the problems inherited from the previous management (AssiDomän 1998).

In addition, AssiDomän requested that the government buy back its shares; in the same year as the company was declared bankrupt, it was put under external management and shares belonging to AssiDomän were sold to Segezha Management Company, set up by Russian managers of SPPM. By November 1999, SPPM's production managed to grow by an average 50 per cent. In 2000, the bankruptcy procedure was completed and the creditors signed a settlement agreement (SCBK 2012).

Of course, there are many explanations for the AssiDomän failure. However, the overriding cause of failure lies in poor regional conditions and a lack of understanding of these conditions. AssiDomän supposed that investment-making in the period of the Russian transformation and the solid title of the company would hold the doors of bureaucrats' offices open forever, whereas the regional authority held that the company was sold inexpensively and the owner must develop the business much more quickly, pay more tax, and actively participate in regional social programmes which might include projects such as building a new hospital or funding the local football team. This case reveals that there is a risk of fiasco when a successful business moves from the original country or region where it was started to another country or region.

As noted in Chapter 1, distance (both cultural and geographical) between regions is an important factor of business, so for evaluating a region's attractiveness and risk it is conventional to use different ratings and an expert's evaluation. For evaluation of the influence of region it would be practical to use the observations of Porter (1990, 1996). Porter notes a correlation between the competitiveness of a country or region and market conditions, both macroeconomic and microeconomic. He offers the model of analysis of national competitiveness ('diamond of national advantages'). His model suggests four interrelated aspects, each of which demonstrates a determinant of regional advantage: corporate strategy, structure and rivalry; demand conditions; factor conditions; and related and supporting industries. 'Chance' and 'the government' are two factors that influence these four determinants, but are not considered separately within the model. Together these six factors make up a system that differs from region to region, explaining why some firms or industries succeed in a particular location. Not all six factors need to be optimal for a firm or industry to be successful.

The methodology proposed by Porter has become the basis of the *Global Competitiveness Report* (Lopez-Claros 2006). Competitiveness is summarised in the Report using nine factors: institutions, infrastructure, macroeconomy, health and primary education, higher education and training, market efficiency, technological readiness, business sophistication and innovation.

Ratings of the socio-economic status of subjects of the Russian Federation by the experts of rating agency RIA Rating, based on the aggregation of key indicators of regional development, answers the question of a region's position on the economic map of Russia. The rating is based on objective measures of the Ministry of Finance and the official Russian statistics which are available for a wide range of interested users. However, the rating does not use expert estimates that diminish the set of indicators (RIA Rating 2013).

The Russian national ratings agency Expert RA produces ratings of the investment climate in Russia's regions (Expert 2012). It uses two parameters as the major components of the investment attractiveness of Russian regions: investment risk and investment potential. Investment potential takes into account macroeconomic characteristics such as the geographical concentration of industrial facilities, consumer demand, and other factors. The aggregate investment potential of a region consists of eight individual potential factors: natural resources, institutional, financial, innovative, production, infrastructure, consumer and labour. The ranking of a region depends on a quantitative estimate of its potential as a share of the sum of potentials of each individual region. The 'investment potential' of a national agency is very similar to the factor conditions of Porter's model. The degree of investment risk typifies the probability of a loss of investment or return. This risk is made up of five different risks: political, social, economic, ecological and criminal. The ranking of regional risks is calculated by the investment risk index: the relative deviation from the average Russian risk. The fundamental indicator of potential risk is calculated as the weighted sum of special potentials or risks. Indicators are added together with an assigned weight. The influence of the input of each component to the aggregate potential or integral risk is evaluated by interviewing a number of experts from investment and consulting companies.

In general, ratings are used for monitoring the current situation in the regions on specific parameters, for demonstrating their capacity, and for assessment of regional policy. To define the goal of regional policies and primary objectives, it is more relevant to use classifications.

Classifying regions is carried out by the government to formulate the priorities of the regional policy of Russia when there is a need to justify a list of regions that are to become targets of government support. Classification of regions can also show territories with a higher and lower level of business development.

Grigoriev *et al.* (2008) note that Russian national classifications use mainly economic indicators, but the social indicators complement them. Also, differences between Russian and international approaches to the classification of regions, due to incomplete statistics published by the municipalities, limit the ability to build classifications at several territorial levels.

INDEM (2004) offers classification on the basis of more than 230 indicators combined in complex indices. These indices characterise a variety of conditions and factors of socio-economic development: natural resources, geographical location, infrastructure, standard of living, quality of labour, specialisation and economic potential of the regions, the development of foreign economic relations, fiscal potential, institutional climate and political environment.

The Ministry for Regional Development (Minregion 2010) offers a classification where a group of Russian regions are allocated depending on the degree of involvement of territories in the global development processes: globalisation, urbanisation and neo-industrialisation. The separation of groups of regions was carried out by experts, based on the analysis of data on socio-economic development.

Four basic groups of regions were identified: 'locomotive of growth', characterised by a high level of socio-economic development and the presence of centres of science and high technology as well as strategic initiatives relevant to the whole country; 'supportive', faced with more problems than the locomotives of growth and showing a lack of product competitiveness, low standard of living and lack of realistic development projects; and 'depressive' (which constitute more than half of the subjects of the Russian Federation), for which the main challenges are low living standards, outdated and uncompetitive technological base, and lack of training and investment. The least developed regions of the European part of the country, as well as Siberia and the Far North, form a fourth group due to the adverse natural conditions of human life relating to the critically depressed regions. Typical problems of this type of region are more acute: unemployment, high levels of social conflict and lack of infrastructure. Notable amongst such territories are the Republic of Chechnya and Ingushetia, where economic backwardness and social problems are increased exponentially by the criminal situation.

However, these models focusing on the unilateral characteristics of regions cannot consider the effects of distance; therefore it is more relevant to use bilateral measures of distance. As noted in Chapter 1, Ghemawat (2007) offers a four-dimensional 'CAGE' framework for measuring distance between countries which includes distance in culture, in the administrative and institutional context, in geography and in economic attributes. The types of distance influence businesses in various ways, and one can use this framework for analysis of distances between Russian regions. Initially, however, it is important to discuss certain specific, peculiar properties of Russia. In the following sections these variations are examined in the context of arbitrage.

Geography

The Russian Federation is a federal republic comprising 83 federal subjects. Russia occupies a huge area of around 17 million square kilometres (Blinnikov 2011). The country extends across the whole of northern Asia: the extent of the territory of Russia from west to east is close to 10,000 km; and from north to south more than 4,000 km. It spans nine time zones and includes a broad range of environments and landforms. However, the Russian population is just 143 million people (CIA 2012). Russia's average population density is about 8.36 persons per square kilometre, one-fifth of the world's population density. The population is distributed unevenly: 48 per cent of the population are concentrated in two federal districts – the Central and the Volga regions – and 75 per cent of Russia's population lives in 48 regions, covering an area of around 15 per cent of the territory of Russia (Petrov and Titkov 2012). The urban population in 2010 was 73 per cent (Census 2010).

Russian cities play a special role in supporting the frame of settlement, as centres for the development and maintenance of the surrounding area. The cities' availability and their network density are extremely important for the national economy. In the European part, which holds 77 per cent of all cities in the country, the average distance between cities is more than 70 km. For comparison, in Western Europe the figure is 20–30 km. In the eastern parts of Russia the average distance between cities is greater than 225 km, including the most developed southern zone of Western Siberia – 114 km, and the vast Far East – 300 km. The small number of cities and the large distances between them have obvious social consequences. Firstly, there is low territorial mobility of the population, and poor commuting infrastructure even within agglomerations (with the exception of the capital, Moscow), which does not allow people to find the best places of employment and to realise their full potential without significant expenditure to change their place of residence. Secondly, there is slow modernisation of lifestyle and much worse adaptation to reforms in the vast spaces outside agglomeration (Petrov and Titkov 2012).

The huge dimensions of Russia and relatively weak transportation and communication links form a geographical distance between regions. However, geography is not the only factor which establishes the distance between regions in Russia. New economic centres such as China and South Korea create new opportunities for Russian business, and they diminish the economic attractiveness of the European part of the country in favour of the Russian Far East. Nevertheless, the gap between the Russian East and West is increasing. The government tries to fix this situation by supporting the transport industry, as the large size and the relatively expensive and unreliable transport systems create asymmetries in Russia.

The Russian Federation is divided into 83 federal subjects and each federal state is a constituent part of the Federation. The average area of the federal subjects is 191,900 square kilometres, but there are enormous differences between the regions in size: the largest region is Yakutia (around 3.1 million square kilometres) and the smallest is Moscow (around 2,500 square kilometres). There are huge differences in the number of residents of Russian regions, the biggest is Moscow (10.3 million people) and the lowest is Chukotka (53,800) (Census 2010).

Zubarevich (2011) describes four different Russias. The first Russia is the country of big cities: there are 14 cities with a population around 1 million and above, in which more than 21 per cent of the country's population lives. Most of them have been de-industrialised in the past 20 years, and only in Ufa, Perm, Omsk, Chelyabinsk and Volgograd do Soviet industrial enterprises still dominate the regional economy. In this group of large cities, the share of the population of qualified 'white-collar' workers and those employed in small businesses is growing. Big cities have quickly adopted a Western European model of consumer behaviour. Also, migration in Russia is directed toward the largest cities, their share of the population of the country is growing. The only difference is that the agglomeration of the two federal cities pulls together workers from across the country, concentrating 80 per cent of the total net migration of Russia, and other major cities attract workforce mostly from their own region.

The second Russia is a country of 334 single-industry towns with a population, in general, of 20,000 to 250,000 people. About 25 per cent of the population lives in the second Russia. The population of these industrial towns is rapidly declining due to young people moving to regional centres (ibid.).

The third Russia consists of the inhabitants of villages and small towns, with their total share of 38 per cent of the population. Depopulated towns and villages with a very elderly population are scattered across the country, but there are especially many in Central Russia, the North-West and the industrial regions of the Urals and Siberia. The fourth Russia is the North Caucasus and southern Siberia (Tuva, Altai), which has fewer than 6 per cent of the population. They include both large and small cities, but almost no industry. For the fourth Russia, which has a mainly rural, poorly educated population, support from the federal budget is important (ibid.).

Culture

Culture is a set of codes, 'inheritable genetic information in the sphere of human behaviour', that dictates the behaviour of a person with certain inherent feelings and thoughts (Lotman 1992). Cultural code defines a set of images that are associated with a particular set of stereotypes in our minds. This is a sort of cultural unconscious, which is hidden even from our own understanding, but is seen in our actions. The cultural code of a nation enables one to understand behavioural responses (Kononenko 2003). Culture establishes how persons perform together and are expressed in different religions, languages, ethnic groups, social norms and values.

Ethnic groups

The Russian Federation is a multinational state and has over 185 ethnic groups designated as nationalities; ethnic Russians make up 81 per cent of the total population. Their dominance is in Central Russia, the main part of the North, the Volga region, the Urals and the South, the most populated areas of Siberia and the Far East (Census 2010). There are a large number of smaller nations that have, as a rule, small areas of compact residence. Five relatively large ethnicities have a population exceeding 1 per cent: Tatars (3.9 per cent), Ukrainians (1.4 per cent), Bashkir (1.1 per cent), Chuvash (1 per cent) and Chechens (1 per cent) (Census 2010).

The territory of Russia can be divided into five areas of residence of other nationalities. In the North Caucasian area (the Greater Caucasus Mountain Range, South of European Russia) the largest group is the people of the North Caucasian language family. In the Volga-Ural area (regions of the Middle Volga, Kama) live the people of the Turkic and Finno-Ugric groups. The South Siberian area (the southern parts of Western and Eastern Siberia) is settled by representatives of the Altai family (Turkic and Mongolian group). In the North-west area (north of the European part of Russia) are representatives of the Finno-Ugric group. The North area (northern Siberia and the Far East) is a vast area characterised by highly dispersed settlement of minority northern people (Turovsky 2006).

Languages

Russian is the official language, but some republics declare other official languages. In reality, in many republics the second or third official languages often have a decorative character because citizens and officials use Russian. Russian is the fundamental language of education; nevertheless around 10 per cent of schools provide teaching in a total of 38 minority languages (GKS 2003). However, in the past 20 years migration of poorly educated workers from Central Asia republics and other Asian countries added around 10 million people who cannot speak Russian fluently.

Religions

In the Soviet time, as a rule, religious activity was not publicised and often was limited. Atheism was an element of the state ideology and practical politics. Religion is, to a certain extent, a new factor which creates differences in Russia. As noted by Sreda (2012), there are no exact figures on the distribution of citizens between the faiths, but according to a poll the main religions represented in Russia are Christianity (mainly Orthodox) (41 per cent), Islam (6.5 per cent), other religions (14.5 per cent), and around 40 per cent are non-religious. Tarusin (2010) notes that according to the polls, about 60 per cent of respondents are not truly of the Orthodox faith. However, a few times a year many will go to church, for some public services such as cake consecration, baptismal water, and so on. Some of them may not even believe in God, but still call themselves Orthodox Christians (VCIOM 2010).

There is a different distribution of the faiths between regions. The majority of the Muslim population is in seven regions of the Russian Federation: Ingushetia (98 per cent), Chechnya (96 per cent), Dagestan (94 per cent), Kabardino-Balkaria (70 per cent), Karachay-Cherkessia (63 per cent), Bashkortostan (54.5 per cent) and Tatarstan (54 per cent) (Census 2010). The number of Muslims continues to rise due to natural growth, especially among the peoples of the North Caucasus, as well as increasing migration, mostly from Central Asia and Azerbaijan. Along with the reduction of the population of Russians, this leads to a significant rate of increase in the proportion of Muslims in the population of the Russian Federation. Currently there is a process of spiritual reunification of the Russian Muslims with their coreligionists abroad. In the past 20 years, tensions between ethnic Russians and Muslims in Caucasus regions increased due to the Chechen wars, growth of ethnic criminality in the Slavonic areas and internal migration of Muslims from Caucasus to the Slavonic areas.

Turovsky (2006) notes that belonging to the same fraternity in Russia remains an important factor uniting elites. This creates spheres of influence centred on the principle of regional origin; typically they are composed of people who were born and grew up in a region. Another incentive for consolidation is the fact of belonging to the same ethnic group which facilitates communication processes, creating a close, trusting relationship.

Social norms and values

Social norms and values play critical roles in the economic development of regions. Stiglitz (1999) notes that without some minimal quantity of social credence and norms, public relations would be diminished to a minimum of tentative and suspicious bargains. Institutional conditions (rules, norms and values) play their role in underwriting or frustrating performance of regional businesses.

Regional business cultures reveal a number of examples of social norms and values which create distance between regions, such as rituals, legal nihilism, nepotism, and the style of relationship of business with authority and non-state institutions.

Ritual is symbolic behaviour that is socially standardised and repetitive (Kertzer 1988). Rappaport (1999) identifies characteristics of a ritual: the ritual's acts and expressions are determined by orders, which firstly had to be set up by others, not by the actors themselves; ritual includes deliberate, not accidental, devotion to form; rituals have to include some unvaried recurrence. In addition, a ritual must involve both participants and audience, as the aura surrounding the ritual plays a crucial role.

Rituals of Russian regions are different from each other, although many have common authoritarian characteristics. Regional authorities employ many rituals, which maintain functions of control, pressure, creating an atmosphere of mistrust to avoid undesired political alliances, enhancing the authority and expansion of the region leaders, and disciplinary actions.

Through ritual, the regional authority emphasises what is particularly valuable since it can be included in different activities, such as parties and business gatherings, festivals and celebrations, as well as informal meetings. The utilisation of regional rituals by companies may have implications for their embeddedness in localities. One of the key functions of rituals is to establish quickly the suitability of counterparties and to determine their bearing and range, in a way that is relatively similar to the military identification system 'identification: friend or foe'.

Cultural distance increases when there is a lack of connective ethnic or social networks. Cultural differences between regions frequently decrease business interactions between them. Paradoxically, the growth of national self-consciousness in the Russian autonomies creates bigger cultural distance between regions. Analysis of language and religion shows that there is not a large distance in language and religious aspects between Russian regions, with few exceptions, notably the Caucasus republics. However, there is cultural distance between Russian regions which is determined by different social norms and values.

The administrative context

As noted above, the Russian Federation is divided into 83 federal subjects. Each federal state is a constituent part of the Federation, and there are different types of federal states. There are 21 republics within the Federation that enjoy a high degree of autonomy on most issues, and these correspond to some of Russia's numerous ethnic minorities. The other types include 46 provinces; nine territories, essentially the same as provinces; four autonomous districts, originally autonomous entities within regions created for ethnic minorities; and one autonomous province. In addition, there are two cities of federal importance: Moscow and St Petersburg (Constitution 2013). The Russian Federation has inter-regional ties which depend on many factors, mostly geographical distance between regions.

It is important to note that republics and national–territorial autonomies are a product of the Soviet epoch, with a legacy of shortcomings and unsolved problems. The Constitution of 1993 declared that the subjects of the Russian Federation are equal but there are asymmetries between subjects. The Federal Constitution provides that only the republics have the Constitution of the Republic, the regions have a regional Charter. The Constitution of the Republic declares that the republics have their citizenship, which is not typical for other subjects. Also, their constitutions, which proclaim them as sovereign states, provide that the land and other natural resources are the property only of the people of the republic (Constitutional Law 2013).

A certain asymmetry is visible in a number of bilateral agreements between the Republics and the Russian Federation on the division of powers; these documents transferred certain powers which, according to the Federal Constitution, are the responsibility of the Russian Federation, but other subjects do not have such devolved powers. Some subjects have some advantages not enjoyed by others. For example, all are equal in the transfer of duties collected on their territory, taxes to the federal budget and receiving payments on their share of the latter. Some subjects are administered in such a way that a substantial part of the taxes collected are not remitted to the federal budget, and instead are left at regional disposal (Constitutional Law 2013). The central government supports certain regions mainly based on the principle of regional aid, which manifests itself in faster growth of incomes of the population. Therefore the political factor has a significant impact on administrative distance between regions.

It is important to differentiate between structures of power, which are built according to Russian law, and real power structures. As noted by Turovsky (2006), regional differences in formal legal norms are small. What is crucial is who fills the power structures, in other words; who are the powerful elite? It is clear that the formal configuration of authority often does not reflect the real balance of power, because in reality various power structures can be controlled from one centre of power. Also, on the contrary, even within the regional administration what is usually presented as a well knit team may have serious internal contradictions.

In general, the centre of power in the region is the governor (senior official of the region), but there can also be other centres of power which can be crystallised around senior officials of the federation, influential officials in the regional administration, a speaker of the Regional Legislative Assembly, Mayor of the regional centre, strong federal politicians with interests in the region or law enforcement authorities (ibid.).

Officially, federal subjects have neutral relationships with each other; however there is some tension which is determined by the competition for federal resources and some unregulated relations. Relatively common in Russia are territorial disputes between the subjects of the Federation due to ethno-political problems. Sometimes this generates ethno-political conflict, which can evolve into armed conflict.

An example is the border dispute between North Ossetia and Ingushetia in 1992, which escalated into armed conflict. As a result, in Ingushetia around 64,000 Ingush refugees from Vladikavkaz, part of the former Chechen-Ingush Autonomy, were resettled (Human Rights Watch 1996).

There is inter-regional competition due to regions competing with each other for commodity resources (electricity, gas and water), trade quotas and subsidies. However, for a particular business, administrative distance between two regions is determined mostly by differences in personal relationship with the authorities (the level of authority depends on the scale and ambitions of the business) and to a lesser extent by legislation.

A regional authority protects local industries, and the desire to protect domestic industries often increases administrative distance. Regional governments try to build some special conditions for loyal regional businesses and raise a wall for external companies. In general, these protection barriers are most likely to be built if a domestic industry meets one or more of the following criteria: authorities are given financial incentives by the business, the business belongs to a high regional authority, the business is a large employer of a region and its closing will create unemployment, or the business is a significant supporter of the government.

Kharitonova (2010) notes not only that entrepreneurs need connections with the government, but also that the authority has a particular interest in supporting financial and industrial groups. These links give regional leaders the opportunity to enrich themselves and, most importantly, allow them to pursue their own, quite independent policy. The assistance provided by commercial entities to a governor's team may be very different in nature: first of all, the friendly business supports the administration, allocating funds for the elected campaign in the region. Secondly, in exchange for the benefits and support, regional businesses give the administration various types of services. Thirdly, with the support of a number of companies, special development programmes are financed (ibid.). As a result of these interactions, regional businesses can form administrative rules for the regional government, that is to say they can be rule-makers instead of just being rule-takers.

Institutional context

Russian regions as well as the Russian Federation have formal and informal systems of governance. The constitution, different codes, laws, and so on present formal systems, whereas the implicit and unwritten agreements present informal systems. These informal systems reflect norms, values and models of the interactions between people, classes and ethnic groups. As noted by Hodgson (2006), institutions are systems of conventional social rules that organise social interactions and they include formal rules, informal conventions, habits, norms and values.

Weakness of formal and informal systems of governance (an institutional weakness) frustrates inter-regional activity. Numerous companies avoid doing business in regions recognised for higher than typical levels of corruption, erratic enforcement practices and zones with a high level of criminal or ethnic conflicts. However, corruption is immanent within the Russian regions because it is one of the significant regulators of economic and social life. Navalny (2011) notes that corruption in Russia is the basis of state power and the basic idea of the elite's consensus. The consensus is that all the heads of regions and districts delegate their political rights to the central government. Consequently, the highest state authority delegates the economic power right down to the regional authority level.

Rulers of Russian regions have two tasks: they have to guarantee that, on their territory, there are no protest rallies and that Putin and his political party get, as an absolute minimum, a majority of the electorate's votes. In exchange, regional leaders would be able to enrich themselves as much as necessary without fearing criminal prosecution, provided they are carrying out such enrichment reasonably discreetly and intelligently. Corruption in Russia impedes sustainable economic growth and the development of institutions.

Corruption is also connected with a lack of transparency in the regional judicial and law-enforcement systems. This amounts to system-wide corruption. Putin (2012) notes that businessmen have to find protection and come to some sort of an agreement with authorities, rather than abiding with the law. An absence of developed institutions does not motivate Russian businesspeople to facilitate effective performance; it motivates them to overwhelm their competitors and establish the market position for themselves by tapping the potential of affiliated bureaucrats from the law enforcement and judicial systems (ibid.).

A huge role in regional management is played by the informal structure of the regional elite leading the struggle for power and economic resources. Informal groups were formed on the basis of interpersonal relationships between regional rulers and subordinates, pursuing the personal aims of the leaders. Often, in such groups, informal norms and agreements infuse all aspects of regional administration.

In sociology this type of relationship is named clientelism, which is the distribution of discriminatory benefits to individuals or groups in exchange for political support. Clientelism is a form of personal exchange generally marked by a sense of commitment and frequently by an asymmetrical balance of power among participants of the exchange. Originally the concept was used as a descriptor of hierarchical exchange characteristic of feudal society or hierarchical patron–client relationships in traditional rural societies (Hopkin 2006).

Brinkerhoff and Goldsmith (2002) also note that clientelism refers to a complex chain of personal ties between political benefactors and their clients. These ties are founded on common material benefit: benefactors provide excludable resources to dependents and accomplices in return for their support.

Using the ideas of Brinkerhoff and Goldsmith, one can build the basic characteristics of the Russian clientelism: personal enrichment and aggrandisement are core values; leaders tend to monopolise power and are not accountable for their actions; leaders' relationships to followers are opaque and often unreliable; no regular procedures exist regarding the replacement of leaders; power is cemented by providing personal favours that secure the loyalty of key followers; decisions are taken in secret without public discussion; civil society is fragmented and characterised by vertical links; supporters' interests guide decisions and extensive scope exists for patronage. Of course, these are not exclusively Russian characteristics; many other authoritarian regimes in the world have similar characteristics. Afanasev (2000) notes that clientelism exists in almost every organisation. It grows on the basis of family relations, friendship or alliances. The heart of clientelism is personal connections, the system of informal compromises and agreements existing on top of the formal structure.

The typical Russian region is a system of patron–client ties that bind leaders and followers in relationships of reciprocal assistance with recognised and accepted inequality between boss and supporter. In Russia there are regional pyramids of patrons and clients, usually culminating with the regional ruler and using clientelism as a permanent mechanism of control in society. There are political alliances of local government and regional economic elites in order to establish control over regional resources. Lapin (1998) gives an example where, in Primorsky region, Governor Nazdratenko has set low electricity prices for companies belonging to his economic group PACT, which pushed him into power. This situation granted structures close to the regional authority an opportunity to create unequal conditions for local manufacturers, which was the cause of the deep energy crisis in the region in the winter and summer of 1997.

To describe the situation with regional management, one can employ some ideas of Weber's (1947) model of patrimonialism, which is relatively similar to the feudal system of lords and liegemen. However, the patrimonialism is less ritualised and regularised than a feudal relationship. In our context, patrimonialism is where the regional rulers are appointed by the President and bear responsibility to him. The Governor of the region is delegated jurisdiction over the region and set key agreements and tasks.

In Russian regions, the bouquet of patrimonialism and clientelism, with added fraternity and ethnic groups, generates a large administrative distance between regions, providing good prospects for arbitrage.

Differences in economic attributes

Russia has historically formed differences between regions in economic development, which had a significant impact on the political system, economic structure and economic efficiency. Large differences between regions obstruct realisation of the federal policy and the formation of a national market, increasing the probability of inter-regional conflicts and damaging the national economy. The government tries to reduce disparities in economic development of the regions, but after the beginning of market reforms differences in socio-economic development of the regions were amplified, which can be explained by the significant weakening of the regulatory role of the state. Simplifying, the Soviet system was broken but a new system was not formed.

In the Soviet planned economy, new cities and enterprises were created without considering the particularities of the territory. During the transition period, many of them became unsustainable: mono-industrial city-factories, which did not really become cities with diversified employment and an urban lifestyle, were degraded and many enterprises were set up without taking into consideration the real costs (transport costs, infrastructure, quality of the labour force); these were not able to adapt to new conditions and have been halted (Petrov and Titkov 2012). Modern spatial patterns of socio-economic development have become extremely mosaic: earlier-developed industrial regions, newly developed resource-extraction areas and the southern agro-industrial regions were divided into regions open and closed to the global economy (ibid.).

A persistent feature of the post-Soviet period of development is the increasing concentration of special benefits in the strongest economic regions in Russia: the Moscow and Tyumen regions. Since 1994, their share in the total gross regional product (GRP) of the country has doubled from 16.5 to 35 per cent in 2006 (ibid.).

The government declares reducing disparities in economic development as a key task because it creates favourable conditions for the development of the internal market, optimising social and economic reforms, and strengthening the unity of the Russian state (Government Decree 2001). The government notes that every federal district has unfortunate regions and the Siberian, Far Eastern and Southern Federal Districts have the worst situations. In general, socio-economic development of the Southern Federal District remains well below the average level, including the share of the GRP per capita and the volume of foreign trade turnover per capita (ibid.).

Over the past decade, the differences between the subjects of the Russian Federation and the size of social spending from the federal budget and budgets of other levels have increased, which leads to an increase in regional disparities in the provision of social benefits, services, education, health, culture and art (ibid.).

At present, differences in the development of the Russian Federation according to the basic socio-economic indicators have reached a critical level. This sharp inter-regional differentiation has the inevitable consequences of increasing the number of regions lagging behind, weakening of the mechanisms of inter-regional economic cooperation and increasing inter-regional conflicts (Government Decree 2001).

The inability of the Russian government to provide a strong state regional policy aimed at smoothing the differences in socio-economic development of the regions of the Russian Federation has increased differences in the living conditions of the population between the centre and the periphery, violating the principles of social justice and increasing separatism.

There are huge regional differences of per capita GRP. In 2006, the maximum difference was presented between the centre of the Russian oil industry Yamalo-Nenets Autonomous District and the underdeveloped Republic of Ingushetia, where the ratio was 81:1. In addition, this gap between the federal subjects is widening: the minimum and maximum values of GDP per capita in the Russian Federation in 2008 increased to 272 (Ignatov 2009).

Other comparisons show analogous differences: the ratio of retail trade turnover per capita between Kalmykia and Moscow is 34:1; distinctions in the ratio of regional budgetary income per capita between Dagestan and Tyumen Region is more than 50:1; and a factor of 29 exists between the registered unemployment rate of the Ingush Republic and the Orenburg Region (Government Decree 2001). The level of poverty in 2008 between the regions differed greatly, from 3.1 to 55.6 per cent of the population (Ignatov 2009).

In the North Caucasus republics, the unemployment rate is several times higher than the average in Russia. For example, on 1 January 2009 the total number of unemployed as a percentage of the economically active population in the regions of Russia differed from 0.9 per cent in Moscow to 55 per cent in Ingushetia, while the average in Russia was 6.3 per cent (Grigoriev *et al.* 2008).

There are considerable differences between the subjects of the Russian Federation in innovation, in terms of the number of employees in research and development per 10,000 people; the difference between the subjects of the Russian Federation in 2001–02 was tenfold, from 400–500 people in Moscow and St Petersburg regions to 5–15 people in Altai, Khakassia, Lipetsk and Pskov regions. By share of domestic expenditure on research and development in the GRP, the ratio was 143:48, about 43 of 1,000 roubles of GRP in St Petersburg and Moscow regions and 0.3–0.9 of 1,000 roubles of GRP in Altai, Khakassia and Lipetsk regions (Granberg and Valentey 2006).

Ignatov (2009) notes that there are significant disparities in personal income between regions, which has stabilised in the past 20 years. In 1995, in the most disadvantaged regions of Russia, the average income was 250 roubles per month and in the richest regions 1,250 roubles per month. In 2008 the highest average monthly salary was in the Yamal-Nenets Autonomous District (43,600 roubles) and the lowest was in the Republic of Dagestan (7,500 roubles). The average monthly wage in 2008 in the Southern Federal District (11,800 roubles) was around two-thirds of the national average (17,200 roubles). In that time, practically all the republics of the North Caucasus had much higher than the Russian average infant mortality (Grigoriev *et al.* 2008).

The most sensitive component of economic distance is income of population (Zubarevich 2008). In Russia there are two complementary mechanisms to reduce regional income inequality: government policies aimed at increasing employment; and remunerations in the undeveloped regions and social transfers to low-income groups, the share of which in the depressive regions is always higher (ibid.). The second sensitive component of economic distance is the impact of demographic factors: the shift of the many regions in the area of low unemployment, but also the reduction in the number of young people entering the labour market, and the large number of employees who have reached retirement age exiting it. In the less developed republics of North Caucasus, the situation is completely different: there is a growing entry of young people to the labour market, but there are a small number of new jobs created in the regional economy because of numerous institutional barriers (ibid.).

Gusev (2011), exploring statistical data about inter-regional trade of food and household consumer goods, reveals that trade in goods of domestic production between regions of Russia is a reflection of the demand for the domestic market. The trade turnover of consumer goods between Russian regions (excluding sales of own-region production) in 2009 amounted to 2.76 trillion roubles (7.12 per cent of GDP). These figures show a minimum amount of regional production, demand on the local market of other regions of the Russian Federation and the absence of significant economic ties between them. In this context, many regions appear as autonomous feudal estates, effectively independent of each other.

Gusev (2011) notes that there are two clearly defined commodity donors: North West and Volga federal districts, which have a volume of goods export two times higher than the volume of imports. The Central Federal District is the largest market which generates the largest outgoing and incoming trade flows. The Far Eastern Federal District is practically separated from the economic life of the country.

Comparative analysis of the proportion of export–import operations in the GRP of federal districts and the degree of trade integration of the regions shows that the federal district as an administrative unit is ten times more dependent on foreign markets than on economic interaction between districts. In this sense, the territorial integrity of the country is devoid of a strong economic base. The probability of failure of internal economic space will not be a major problem for people in many Russian regions, as their economic relations with other areas of the country are insignificant (ibid.).

Economic distance is maintained by a weak flow of population between regions. Immobility of the population makes migration as a response to changes in regional condition impossible. A large low-income population creates an excessive concentration of low-cost jobs. Instability, strong fluctuations in the regional economy (such as booms and recessions), and overdependence by a region on the performance of an individual industry or business, also increase distance.

Economic distance is attributed to differences that influence inter-regional business through economic mechanisms. According to Ghemawat (2003), economic distance marks specific economic factors such as economic size, per capita incomes, differences in the cost or quality of labour, natural resources and capital, dissimilarities in knowledge of technologies, and infrastructure, and these factors are not obtained directly from the geographical and administrative context. He notes that interactions between rich and poor countries often implicate arbitrage, in which companies agree supply and demand not within domestic markets, but across borders.

There are different types of sensitivity to each component of distance and this naturally poses a question about which distance has most influence on the business. One can suppose that cultural distance in Russia is important when products are important to ethnic identity, such as food, health care and social services, services for the household and hospitality.

Administrative distance is important when regional governments are involved in regulation and create special rules. Typical examples are exploiters of natural resources (forestry, mining and fishing), production and distribution of electricity, gas, water, transport and communications, and key regional retail trades. Geographical distance in Russia is important when products have a low value-to-weight ratio, such as the oil and gas industries, mining and production of building materials. Economic distance has the biggest impact when the character of needs changes with the welfare of the citizen, as is the case with health care, social services and consumer goods.

Russian industry is dominated by gigantic physical production facilities, and development of small and medium enterprises is insubstantial. Restructuring in the industrial sector did not include the downsizing of overconcentrated production facilities of the Russian economy.

Globalisation gave an impetus to the Russian economy by integrating it into world production and capital flows. The growth of the economy after 1999 has been pushing up demand for commodities and devaluating the national currency. At the same time, the disparities between Russian regions have been increasing. In addition, income differences between rich and poor increased. However, it is important to note that distance in large vertical integration companies, which have strong maintenance from the country's high authority, have less sensitivity to distance because they can break administrative and economic distance.

Conclusion

There are widely utilised unilateral characteristics of regions: ratings which are used for monitoring the current situation of specific parameters for demonstrating regions' capacity and for the assessment of both regional policy and classification of regions. These ratings are employed to define the goal of regional policies and primary objectives, and to formulate the priorities of regional policy. Russian national classifications mainly use economic indicators, but social indicators complement them. Classification of regions can also show territories with higher and lower levels of business development.

However, it is more relevant for analysis of arbitrage opportunities to use bilateral measures of distance, such as a four-dimensional CAGE framework, which includes difference in culture, in the administrative and institutional context, in geography and in economic attributes.

The huge dimensions of Russia, together with relatively weak transportation and communication links, create variation between regions and constitute a geographical distance between regions. Russian cities play a special role in supporting the frame of settlement, as centres for the development and maintenance of the surrounding area. The cities' availability and their network density are extremely important for the national economy. However, the small number of cities and the large distances between them decrease the territorial mobility of the population.

The degree of difference of one region from another depends on how efficiently the authorities use regional advantages, and how effectively they compensate for disadvantages through their own unique initiatives. A region's business culture reveals a number of examples of social norms and values which create distance between regions. With few exceptions, there is not a large distance in language and religious aspects between Russian regions, but cultural distance increases when there is a lack of connective ethnic or social networks. Growth of national self-consciousness in the Russian autonomies and undeveloped cultural cooperation between regions create bigger cultural distances between regions.

Russia has inter-regional ties which depend on many factors, mostly geographical distance between regions. Also, there is inter-regional competition due to regions competing with each other for commodities, trade quotas and preferences for local participants in the form of subsidies.

For a particular business, administrative distance between two regions is determined mostly by differences in personal relationships with authorities and, to a lesser extent, by legislation. A regional authority protects local industries, and the desire to protect domestic industries often increases administrative distance. Regional governments try to build special conditions for loyal regional businesses and raise a wall against external companies.

Large differences between regions obstruct realisation of the federal policy and the formation of a national market; they also increase the probability of inter-regional conflicts and disintegration of the national economy. Modern spatial patterns of socio-economic development have become extremely mosaic: earlier-developed industrial regions, newly developed resource extraction areas, and the southern agro-industrial regions were divided into regions open to the global economy and closed, economically isolated regions.

The differences between the subjects of the Russian Federation and the size of social spending from the federal budget and regional budgets have increased, increasing regional disparities in the provision of social benefits, services, education, health, culture and art. There are huge regional differences in socio-economic development of the regions and in the living conditions of the population, as well as differences in turnover and GRP per capita, in the level of poverty and the unemployment rate, in innovation, and in domestic expenditure on research and development.

Economic distance is maintained by weak flow of population between regions. Immobility of the population makes migration as a response to changes in regional conditions impossible. A large low-income population creates an excessive concentration of low-cost jobs. Instability, strong fluctuations in the regional economy, and overdependence on a region upon the performance of an individual industry or business also increase distance.

Thus distance may have different dimensions, each of which creates asymmetries, which is a key element for arbitrage as strategy in Russia. However, it is important answer the questions: Who creates asymmetry? And how is it accomplished? Chapter 4 offers answers to these questions.

4 Arbitrage and institutions

This chapter offers a definition of institution, and reveals how institutions affect the implementation of arbitrage in the context of arbitrage transactions and creating conditions for arbitrage. It describes different types of transaction and institutional costs as well as transformation costs of arbitrage. It notes that arbitrage has become the dominant practices in business operations and has evolved from a technical element to the dominant strategy.

Definition of institution

Before starting to analyse the relationship of arbitrage and institutions, we need to discuss the key concept – the institution. According to Veblen (1994), an institution is a common way of thinking about the relationships between society and the individual, and the functions they perform. Later Rawls (1971) defined institutions as public systems of rules that define the situation with regard to respective rights and obligations, power and immunity. These rules specify certain particular forms of action as permissible and others as prohibited, and therefore one type of action being punished and others being protected when violence occurs. As examples, he discusses the games, rituals, trials, parliaments, markets and systems of property.

Currently, within the framework of modern institutionalism the interpretation of North (1989) is widespread. Institutions are human-made formal rules (constitutions, laws, property rights) and informal restraints (sanctions, customs, taboos, traditions, codes of conduct) that structure political, economic and social interactions.

Hodgson (2006) offers a similar definition of institutions as 'systems of established and prevalent social rules that structure social interactions'; he adds a list of institutions including language, money, law, systems of weights and measures, firms, rules, table manners, norms of behaviour and social conventions.

However, it should be pointed out that there are no established and prevalent social rules that would not structure social interactions, as all established social rules were originally created for the structuring of social interactions of people and groups. That is, in this definition there is no differentiation from non-institutions and therefore the author is forced to enumerate examples of institutions. Here it is appropriate to recall the principle of Ockham's razor: 'plurality must never be posited without necessity' (Ariew 1976).

Within the framework of another approach, 'new institutional economics', institutions are seen as mechanisms for managing the contractual relationship. Therefore the most important economic institutions are firms, markets and relational contracting. This approach focuses attention on individual transactions mediated by institutions (Williamson 1985).

The concept of the institution in modern literature seems quite blurred in that, in general, it reflects the diversity of the academic community's views about its definition. We can see the continuous evolution of the term 'institution', which changes constantly depending on the position of the authors, varying from the scale of a social system to routine individual action. There is a fuzziness of the category 'institution', which can be identified with virtually any phenomenon of objective reality. If we take institutions as meaning any existing within the economy and societal norms, it would be logical to refer to institutions such as the bus schedule in London, time norms for the production of one car, norms of radiation safety and microbial contamination in hospital, and norms of internal rate of return for business.

Most definitions of an institution, which is a cornerstone concept of institutional economics, use a nominal definition, that is, the condition or agreement regarding the use of a given symbolic form, and which can be explained in terms of what a particular thing is called, or that it will be referred to using a given term. In contrast to the nominal definition, the real definition (explication) describes the content of the concepts, that is, the defined subject stands out from a class of similar objects according to this hallmark.

The result of this type of determination is a propositioned characteristic of subjects denoted by a given term that is, as a rule, more heuristic. The most common form of explicit definition is the definition by genus and specific difference – a definition in which the defined concepts are introduced within the scope of a broader concept and thus distinctive features (specific difference) are distinguished among the objects of this broader concept.

It should be also noted that the word 'institution' is used in language to refer to two essentially different realities. On one hand, the institution is the accepted rules and standards of behaviour enshrined in laws or in the systems of morality and ethics. On the other hand, institutions are stable social structures such as family, the company and the state. In everyday speech there is no clear distinction between the concepts of institutions and organisations. For example, it is possible to use the term 'special economic zone' as an economic institution, when we are interested in how to define the objectives of this institution (organisation) and its position in the market. It is possible that a special economic and legal regime, as a set of rules and regulations, is an institution. If we are interested in what the impact of the legal construction of the economic zone will be on the results of its activities, we talk about it as an institution.

For the purposes of the subsequent exposition, a working definition is used: institutions are systems of formal and informal rules that define the relationships of people in society. Additionally, we can add that the institution is a systemic social feature, acquired by a group (firm) in a joint activity that determines the level and quality of social relations in this group.

An institution is considered as a system of relatively stable traits and outwardly manifested characteristics of an organisation, which are recorded in the judgments of the organisation itself, as well as judgments about it by other organisations or people. The institution is a specifically human or social formation, produced by social relations, in which an organisation carries out its activities. If the institution (as an organisation) is indivisible, with its integral characteristics forming its nature, the institution as a set of rules is also an integral structure, but created as a result of the activities of various individuals. That is, regarding the activities of an institution as the unit of analysis can be a fundamentally new theoretical postulate.

Institutional characteristics of the Russian economy

Each country has its own specific institutional system and therefore one can consider some features of the institutional system of Russia that distinguish that institutional system from, for example, that of the European Union. Since the beginning of Russian reforms in the 1990s and the transformation of the Russian political and economic system, there have been a considerable number of people and groups in society that break the bounds of formal and informal, new and long-established norms, rules and behavioural stereotypes.

At the same time there was a sequential weakening of positions of the state, which was encumbered with a wide range of commitments and challenges. The new bureaucracy was not quite ready to rule the country under these changed conditions and was forced to learn from its mistakes in real time.

New Russian business had a basic strategy of tight integration with the state in order to obtain from the government special preferences and privileges, to implement desired laws and to lobby for personal interests, while seeking to distance itself from the state in the distribution of profits. Also, in Russia there was no effective external control (state, proprietors and workforce) over the activities of corporate executives.

There is a widespread opinion that Russia has bad institutions that hamper economic reforms. It seems that to discuss institutions in terms of good or bad is counterproductive to understanding these processes, because these institutions reflect the prevailing attitude in society and they are relevant to the level of economic development of the country. When someone describes the Roman or Tudor times, no-one talks about the underdeveloped institutions of the Roman Empire, or the institutional vacuum of the era of the Tudor dynasty. One can say that Russia has enough institutions, and they are relevant to the tasks of the post-Soviet feudal–capitalist system.

After the collapse of the Soviet system, Russia actively borrowed management experience from the economies of developed countries, including the import of institutions that were often borrowed without proper analysis of their suitability for the specific conditions of the Russian economy. As a result, many developed countries' institutions were atrophied, degenerated or completely rejected within an inadequate institutional environment. The major social groups interested in importing institutions were primarily the new political and economic elite, seeking to consolidate their power.

In Russia, importing market economy institutions was additionally determined by the process of primary capital accumulation, which in reality was a transfer of capital from depersonalised public ownership into private property. To ensure these processes were appropriate, institutions were created that provided speedy implementation of privatisation, and which were often cancelled or scaled back after reaching the goal of privatisation.

When talking about the implementation of formal laws, the first thing to note is that Russia is a country of legal nihilism, with a level of disregard for the law that is the highest in Europe (nihilism is an absolute rejection of all systems of authority, morals and social convention which, as a significant political and philosophical movement, was created in Russia in the nineteenth century; Rosen 2000). Legal nihilism is one of the forms of justice and social behaviour of individuals or groups, characterised by a negative or sceptical attitude towards the law and the values of law. Expressed as contempt or conscious disregard of legal requirements in practice, it serves as one of the causes of delinquent behaviour (Academic Dictionary 2009).

North (1992) notes that life in the modern world economy is ordered by laws and property rights. However, formal rules establish only a small part of the constraints that shape choices. In day-by-day interactions, the governing structure is strongly defined by codes of conduct, norms and conventions. The Soviet Union as well as post-communist Russia never suffered from a lack of formal rules in the economy. Nevertheless, despite Russia having numerous formal rules that are sometimes very detailed, these rules frequently leave occasion for uncertainty that encourages arbitrage on their actual significance. Moreover, formal rules create supplementary uncertainty and are mainly substituted by informal rules (Radaev 2000).

Russians like to say that, in Russia, there is life not by the law but according to unwritten rules. However, these unwritten rules also are institutions that are formed and maintained by the community. Formal institutions have a mechanism of enforcement that comes down to the fact that there are some specially trained people, such as tax inspectors, prison guards, police and military, who are engaged in coercion. But within the framework of informal institutions, coercion is provided by the whole society. One can see that in Russia often there is a replacement of formal institutions by informal ones, which carry sanctions for violation of the formal rules. For example, a fire inspector or sanitary control officer may take money from an offender and often may pocket the proceeds. The society agrees with the punishment and the fact that this money will not be transferred to the budget of a country or region. As a result, the sanction for violation of the rules has occurred and triggered an informal institution that replaced the formal one; furthermore, a legal institution has been supplanted by illegal one.

In the USSR, natural resources did not receive adequate market evaluation, and ownership of resources and business income belonged to the state. After the transition to a market economy, a new system of allocation and assignment of natural resources arose. In terms of vagueness of institutional environment, the mechanism of formation of natural resource rents became opaque; proprietary rights for natural resources became uncertain, thus making possible the assignment of rental income by owners of capital. Blurring and contradictions of property rights led to the creation of inefficient institutions which blocked the stable economic development of Russia.

The sluggish and inconsequential economic reforms in Russia created narrow groups who were able to modify government policy to meet their own interests, concentrating their economic power. Additionally, deficiency of democracy reduced the transparency of government actions that created opportunities for rent-seeking (Åslund 2007). Consequently, rent-seeking as an alternative to non-discriminatory and open competition became the key source of business success. Rent-seeking activity is a complex phenomenon and there has some clear consequences: raised transaction costs and uncertainty in transition countries; unproductive economic results; inhibited foreign and domestic investment; increased corruption and underground economic activity; and destabilised state legality (Tache and Lixandroiu 2006).

Corporate executives have developed a personalised communication system to obtain favourable economic conditions from government officials. Corporation executives' networks with the authorities play an essential role in Russian business. Informal relationships of high-ranking company authorities give inside information about new projects and contracts. They have different preferences and competitive advantages over underembedded executives. Often, authority uses the contradictory application of laws and regulations on a non-transparent foundation; nevertheless, informal relationships with authority permit firms to mitigate this problem, influencing the embedding and com petiveness of a company. However, formal inclusion of executives into authorities can create enormous business opportunities and dramatically reduce political risks. Therefore oligarchs, executives or people affiliated with them frequently aim to become involved with the authority. Numerous examples show that many oligarchs and executives of large corporations have become federal ministers, regional governors and members of the Russian parliament.

Oligarchic networks lobby their own interests and play an important role in Russia. Informal interactions perform essential functions, such as the transfer of confidential information and reduction of transaction costs. The Russian oligarch system is characterised by prevalent alliances between bureaucrats and business, the participation of relatives and friends in management of state assets and unexplainable allocation of budget funds, and the creation of opaque state management and its stagnation and deterioration (Nemtsov and Milov 2008b).

Nepotism is a widespread accusation in Russian business and politics when the relatives of executives or powerful figures climb to comparable power, apparently without suitable qualifications or experience. Aron (2008) suggests that the Russian regime is 'sultanistic', summarising the tendency for Putin's friends to rule most of the state corporations. Additionally, he notes that political and personal allies of the President headed companies which jointly accounted for 40 per cent of the national economy (ibid.). Similar tendencies have been transmitted to regional and corporation levels: by the use of authorities' relatives, friends or former colleagues, a company may embed more deeply into the region's environment.

The embedding of a quasi-democratic system into the global capitalist economy forms in the country an oligarchy closely connected with a corrupt bureaucracy. This alliance, for the purpose of maintaining position, requires stability that can be realised by authoritarian power. One can say that oligarchy creates authoritarianism, then authoritarianism itself preserves oligarchy, and so they become inseparable. The alliance of the authority and the oligarchy does not provide substantial growth and modernisation of the economy. Moreover, it consistently demands the regulation of public life, repression of political opposition and direct electoral fraud.

The opportunities available to an organisation are established by the composition of arm's-length and embedded ties making up the network with which it transacts. Strong, dominating, embedded ties could create overembeddedness and an inability for a company to access information circulating in the market and test new trading partners. One can presume that in Russia, companies have a positive attitude towards maximal political embeddedness and try to increase this by setting solidly embedded ties with authorities. The extent of the embeddedness of Russian companies in the regional environment depends on extensive relationships and networks with whichever authorities play an essential role in those environments. Moreover, the quality of networks often has more impact on embeddedness, and influences accessed resources and personal familiarity.

Many non-state institutions, such as financial institutions, training agencies, trade associations, local chambers of commerce, innovation centres, unions, government agencies providing premises and land, business service organisations and marketing boards, were created at the start of Russian reforms in the late 1980s, but many of them are ineffective and do not influence the embeddedness of companies. This result confirms the suggestion of Hardy *et al.* (2005) that the existence of non-state institutions is an essential but not sufficient condition to embed firms, and these institutions need to be linked by collaboration, regular interactions, confidence and cohesion.

According to Radaev (2000), there are many recognised business unions and societies in Russia but many of them are not powerful because their directors prefer to lobby independently or join minor, unofficial groups. These groups and individuals establish primary-level networks which usually include durable business companions that connect directly with companies' operations.

Participants in primary-level networks use a combination of formal and informal rules and regulations, and these institutions are linked by collaboration, regular interactions and cohesion.

Radaev also notes that networks play a vital role in Russian business, and unofficial relationships carry out essential functions such as the transfer of confidential information, the evaluation of business partners, the shape of reputations, creation of confidence and reduction of transaction costs. Likewise, networks offer some privileges to business partners on an exclusive basis, often including price reductions, cancellation of pre-payment obligations, flexibility of payment and delivery terms, additional free services, and so on (Radaev 2000).

There is a fairly widespread perception in Russia that theft and bribery of officials is a generic tradition which has existed since ancient times, and only in conditions of totalitarianism, for example Stalin's epoch, may there be some order in the country. It was noted in earlier chapters of this book how Russian history shows that, even in a harsh dictatorship, corruption did not disappear; it just acquired a specific character, and retribution in the event of crime often was part of life. Using the concept of arbitrage, we can consider that the cause of corruption lies in the fact that society gives the bureaucracy an opportunity to organise a system of institutions that allow them to receive a part of arbitrage income.

Moreover, do not think that corruption offences in Russia feature only Russian companies. The institutional environment can generate attitudes for the delinquent behaviour of companies regardless of the location of their company headquarters. An example is the history of Hewlett Packard (HP) in Russia. In 1999, the Russian government announced a project to automate the computer and telecommunications infrastructure of its Office of the Prosecutor General (PGO). The potential value of the order reached $100 million (FBI 2014). This would be the biggest deal by HP in Eastern Europe. To secure victory in the first tender with a value of €35 million, leaders of HP Russia enlisted the support of number of intermediaries, who had connections with officials who were responsible for the tender. In April 2003, various dummy companies received transfers of €8,000,000 (ibid.).

In order to hide these illegal payments, Russian HP employees maintained two parallel systems of accounts: one for internal use – where the recipients of bribes were detailed; another cleansed of suspicious payments for outsiders. In its secret version of the file was a column 'Other expenses', where corrupt payments were transferred through a German mediator. The corrupt scheme worked as follows: HP Russia sold computer equipment, intended for the PGO, to its partner at the usual prices. Then HP bought back the same products from an intermediary at a large premium. Finally, the same equipment was supplied to the PGO at the overestimated cost. One can say that it was a virtuoso arbitrage scheme between PGO and HP that allowed the beneficiaries to receive income of €8 million (ibid.).

However, the idyll was ruined by the US Department of Justice. It noted that the subsidiaries of HP created a fund for bribes, organised an elaborate network of dummy firms and bank accounts for money laundering, carried out parallel bookkeeping, and used anonymous email accounts for the organisation of secret meetings. However, the company reached an agreement with the Ministry of Justice and the Securities and Exchange Commission on extrajudicial settlement of the case and paid $108 million to US authorities for corruption in Russia (Krajewski and Viswanatha 2014).

The impact of institutions on arbitrage

Institutions directly and indirectly affect the implementation of arbitrage in the context of arbitrage transactions and in the context of creating conditions for arbitrage. In order to assess the impact of institutions for arbitrage, it is possible to use a variety of approaches including the theory of property rights, the theory of transaction costs, the theory of optimal contracts and the theory of public choice.

The system of property rights in neo-institutional theory refers to the whole set of rules regulating access to resources, which are established and protected by state and other social mechanisms such as manners, rules and moral attitudes (Demsetz 2008). Property rights have a behavioural meaning: they encourage some forms of action, whereas others are suppressed through bans or inflating the cost and thereby influence the choice of individuals. Property rights act as rules of the game which bring order to relations between individual agents (Eggertsson 1990).

From the perspective of individual agents, property rights are seen as 'bundles of powers' to make decisions about a particular resource. Each bundle may be split so that one part of these powers belongs to one person and another part belongs to the other person. Honoré (1987) proposed a classification of property rights to distinguish the right to use the good, the right to earn income from the good, the right to transfer the good to others, the right to enforcement of property rights, and the right of ownership and management.

Simplifying, arbitrage operations can be simple or complex. By complex operations, it is understood that the operation is performed with the creation of conditions by a special agent. Classical arbitrage presents at least two contracts (agreements): a contract for purchase and a contract for sale. But in complex cases of arbitrage, there are additional participants (agents) that are creating and maintaining conditions of arbitrage and that create explicit or implicit additional contracts.

In the simple cases of arbitrage, the right of possession and use belongs to the direct participants in the transaction. For complex cases, the right of management (right to make decisions, who and under what conditions will have access to use of the good), the right to earn income (right to possess the results from use of the good), and the sovereign right (right to dispose of, lease, modify or destroy the good) may belong to a third party, which actually creates the condition for arbitrage. Also, the right to security, that is, the right to protection from expropriation of arbitral income and from damage on the part of outside environment, may belong to third parties.

There is a large set of arbitrage contracts, which may be one-off, short- and long-term, individual and collective, needing and not needing arbitrage protection, etc. Selection of the type of contract is often dictated by the desire to reduce transaction costs. If the contract turns out to be more difficult, than it is more difficult to create conditions for arbitrage and the more complex is the structure of their related transaction costs. This often does not mean an increase in the number of words on the paper of the contract; nevertheless, the period of time and the amount of informal discussion between participants can be considerably increased.

Many arbitrage transactions can be performed almost immediately by on-the-spot purchase and resale. But sometimes the transfer of ownership is delayed, representing a long-term process. Contracts in such cases turn into exchanges of promises, thereby limiting the future behaviour of the contract parties where these restrictions are taken voluntarily.

Additional participants in complex arbitrage operations are responsible for the creation of conditions to ensure arbitrage; their powers and duties are often not documented or written only very superficially. Such participants each have a long-term contract without a description of all the consequences of the bargain. It is rather an agreement on the principles of cooperation in which informal conditions prevail over formal ones. Frequently the implementation of such a contract is guaranteed mutual interest of the parties.

In this case, to adapt to unexpected changes and to ensure reliability of performance commitments, economic agents should exchange not only promises, but promises that are trustworthy. This idea is explored by Williamson (1985), who also notes that credibility can be amplified by guarantees that facilitate adaptation to unforeseen events and provide protection against opportunistic behaviour.

It should be noted that complex arbitrage contracts can never be absolutely comprehensive, as participants in the transaction are unable to foresee the mutual rights and obligations in all possible situations and record them in a written contract. Often activities are uncertain, therefore to provide a complete and accurate description of the transaction in advance is impossible. The categorisation of arbitrage operations as simple or complex bears a resemblance to ideas that have been developed by neo-institutional economists since Williamson (1985), who notes that different contract forms are subject to different regulatory structures. In classical (simple) cases, the market is a regulatory mechanism, and in this case the relationships between participants are short and impersonal and all disputes are likely to be resolved in court. In relational (complex) contracts, the hierarchical organisation carries out self-regulation. In this case, relations have a long and personalised character with disputes being resolved through consultation and informal negotiations.

A classical example of a contract with respect to arbitrage transactions is the purchase on the exchange of a batch of oil; whereas an example of a relational contract is cooperation between the firm and the official who provide conditions for arbitrage.

Complex arbitrage contracts can be implemented using a resource of authority that on one hand certainly facilitates the implementation of the contract, but on the other hand makes mutual settlements more complicated. Because the transaction structure is quite complex (primarily due to the difficulty of evaluating the creation of conditions for arbitrage), this process will require a lot of time and money. This can lead to disputes about the contribution of each participant. Therefore everyday practice of arbitrage relations, to a large extent, is caused by the subordination of all participants' numerous unwritten norms, since securing a deal can go beyond formal rights and also can be outside the law. Also, the execution of these complex contracts can never be guaranteed as participants of the transaction may be prone to opportunistic behaviour and may try to avoid fulfilling terms of the contract.

There are different mechanisms to encourage enforcement of contractual obligations in arbitrage, primarily, and most traditionally, using the court in the case of breach of contract. There is a high level of corruption in the Russian arbitrage courts, a lack of independence of judges from the executive branch and complex systems of enforcement of judgments; nevertheless judicial protection usually works well for simple contracts.

In complex contracts, the contract is often not amenable to observation or cannot be proved in court. As a result, economic agents have to create private mechanisms for settlement of contractual relations, for example, provision of collateral or concern about maintaining reputation.

Paradoxically, reputation is rather an important element because information about violations immediately becomes available for key market participants, making further complications for the offender should they wish to make future contracts. The threat of sanctions and damages caused by this deters potential offenders. Also, in controversial cases they may use an appeal to a significant third party, who may be a regional authority (e.g. the governor or chief of police), reputable businessperson or criminal leader.

One would expect that these transactions would destroy trust and mutual support. However, analysis of such practices shows the presence of honesty when signing these deals. The specific nature of the transaction means that, even in the presence of high risk, participants do not insist on a formal contract that sets out the basic structures of the transaction. In most cases transactions are based not on formal contracts but rather on oral agreements between the participants. One can say that the key element here is trust; it significantly relieves questions about the reliability of agents within transactions and allows a reduction of transaction costs.

Arbitrage operations using administrative power resources often include participants that are in administrative or hierarchical dependency, so in these cases it is possible to speak about the existence of a contract between the landlord and vassal that imposes on one side a duty to care and protect, but on the other to serve. Moreover, neither landlord nor vassal can evade compliance; the vassal trying to leave and become independent violates the implicit contract which he himself established. This leads to the appearance of sanctions such as the deprivation of opportunities to carry out arbitrage or to use special conditions for arbitrage and, potentially, the application of administrative and criminal penalties.

Arbitrage and costs of institutional transformation

Speaking about the impact of institutions, we should also mention arbitrage transaction costs, which can be defined as the costs of managing the economic system. These must be distinguished from production costs, which in the neoclassical theory constitute the essence of consumable components of economic activity. One can say that transaction costs are an economic equivalent of the energy dissipation that is the transition energy of ordered processes in the energy of disordered processes.

Transaction costs were first considered by Coase (1937). He demonstrated that transaction costs exist because for each deal it is necessary to conduct negotiations, implement relationships and resolve differences, which are all costs of using the market mechanism. Coase highlighted the following transaction costs: the cost of obtaining and processing information about prices, goods and services, existing suppliers and consumers; negotiation costs; costs of measuring the quantity and quality of purchased goods and services; costs of specification and protection of property rights; as well as the time and resources required to restore violated rights and also costs associated with misconduct that violates the terms of the transaction or directed at gaining unilateral advantages (ibid.).

Williamson (1985) identifies *ex ante* and *ex post* transaction costs. The former include the costs of preparing of a draft contract, negotiating and providing guarantees of realisation of the agreement. These actions can be carried out with the utmost care, and then compiled into a complex document which provides numerous possible future events and appropriate adaptation to participants in an agreement. *Ex post* contractual costs include adaptation costs; haggling costs which accompany bilateral efforts to eliminate *ex post* disruptions in contractual relations; setup and running costs associated with using control structures, where the parties are using to resolve conflicts; and bonding costs which are associated with the exact fulfilment of contractual obligations.

According to Eggertsson (1990), the main components of transaction costs are searching for information about products or services, searching for a partner for the deal and the collection of information; tendering, preparation and signing of the contract; enforcement of the contract; payment and registration of the contract during its implementation; and protection of contract participants from third parties such as the tax authorities.

In relation to arbitrage in Russia, this list may be supplemented by other common types of institutional cost: the costs of obtaining licences and permits necessary for arbitrage; registration of property rights; shadow costs such as bribes and kickbacks; the cost of regulation and standardisation of arbitrage processes and operations; costs of designing, implementing and changing the internal rules of the enterprise; representation allowances and costs of participation in tenders and exhibitions; the costs of monitoring the established rules and standards and identifying opportunism; monitoring costs of ongoing contracts; costs of internal approvals and permits; and finally the settlement of intra-industrial contradictions.

The size of the above costs depends nonlinearly on the degree of embeddedness of a company. At high levels of embeddedness, relative costs may be lower. For companies that are in close alliance or family relations with the regional authorities, these costs can be practically equal to zero. Conversely, for beginners without connections they are often prohibitively high. Therefore when new entrants try to repeat the success of arbitrage of established players, it frequently results in fiasco.

Polterovich (1999) proposes to distinguish between transaction costs and costs of institutional transformation. The latter are costs associated with the transition from one norm to another. In this regard, it is possible to allocate the costs associated with the formation of relevant institutional rules and regulations relating to arbitrage operations. As noted in previous chapters, companies should have conditions for arbitrage that already exist or that they can create themselves. Frequently, creation of these conditions may adjust, suspend and affect existing law and regulations that impact on the institutional environment. Moreover, the larger the scale of arbitrage, the more institutions are likely to be affected.

Using the ideas of Polterovich (1999), we can say that there are six main types of transformation costs of arbitrage: creation of a project of institutional change; promotion of a project; creation and maintenance of intermediate institutions for project implementation; implementation of arbitrage; development of arbitrage; and recapturing of attacks. We shall consider examples of some of these types in more detail.

Creating a project of institutional change

This stage is usually carried out simultaneously with the development of a general plan of arbitrage; it is the most creative type and usually relatively cheap. For example, to create the conditions for the implementation of arbitrage in the Russian Far East, the Law of the Far East was proposed (Sinjaeva 2013). This project offered exemption from payment of the federal part of the profit tax, VAT and customs duties on exports of the manufacturing industries. In addition, newly created and reconstructed enterprises would have zero tax rate on profits, property and land. Also, the idea of simplifying the creation of various types of special economic zones (SEZ) without tenders was lobbied, and also a proposal to transfer management of SEZ activity in the Far East and the Baikal region to the regional bureaucracy.

Promotion of a project

Promotion or lobbying of a project may involve establishing links with the necessary executive or legislature officials with the intention of creating the necessary legal acts or regulations for creating arbitrage conditions. Lobbying is carried out by specialists who employ very different methods, from extensive use of mass media and propaganda to criminal methods such as bribery and blackmail.

In Russia, there is strong differentiation of lobbying between regions; Moscow, St Petersburg, Yekaterinburg and Tyumen groups have the greatest influence. Regions lobby their interests through the Federation Council of Russia, which is called the 'Chamber of Lobbyists' because more than half of its members are representatives of regional business. Also, they exert their influence through the administration of the President and the government.

If a lobbyist has extensive contacts with federal executive power, he or she can bring about the realisation of federal programmes such as the construction of roads, hospitals or housing. Hence the powerful resource impact on regional authorities. Pressure groups are usually the strongest in a region where the territory is dominated by a single large corporation, or where a region is sparsely populated and industrially undeveloped. The most successful lobbyists include oil, vodka and insurance companies. Generally, this stage is relatively expensive and requires high embeddedness of managers in regional or federal authorities.

Khodakovskaya (2011) gives an example of lobbying in the tobacco industry. This industry is represented by more than 80 per cent of foreign companies in Russia and its financial flows are under strict control and verified by international auditing companies. The tobacco lobby in Russia is strong and can withstand the competing interests of pharmaceutical and insurance companies, and even the State Duma. Traditional supporters of moderate restriction of tobacco consumption in Russia are the Ministry of Agriculture, which advocates for agricultural development, and the Finance Ministry, which stands to gain revenue for the federal budget. On the other hand, an active opponent of the industry is the Health Ministry, which advocates radical anti-smoking measures.

In 2004, Philip Morris, JTI and the Baltic Tobacco Factory formed an industry group aimed at protecting its interests – the Council for the Development of Tobacco Industry, which has become one of the most influential lobbying organisations. It is interesting that one person, Nadezhda Shkolkina, is the head of the tobacco industry council and the head of the board of the Ministry of Agriculture which defines state policy on the tobacco industry (ibid.).

No less interesting are the methods of promoting interests of the tobacco business in Russia. Tobacco lobbyists regularly initiate discussion and media reports about the insignificant hazards of passive smoking, bringing the positions of the tobacco companies to legislators and society. They give grants to organisations affiliated with government officials, affecting the Ministry of Agriculture. For example, in the new technical regulations on tobacco products, the Ministry was able to maintain tobacco producers' permission to use the term 'light cigarettes', contradicting the WHO Framework Convention on Tobacco Control. Tobacco lobbyists divert attention of the community and politicians to other problems of health care, and finance secret programmes that prevent scientific research, bullying the public with forecasts that the employment rate and revenues from the sector could drop sharply (ibid.).

Creation and maintenance of intermediate institutions for project implementation

At this stage, significant negative attitudes can be formed to anything or anyone. This facilitates the subsequent decision-making of the bureaucracy because these solutions have already been agreed with the population. A good illustration is a struggle between small and large wood producers for export quotes when large companies formed the attitude in the mass media that minor wood manufacturers cannot provide logging according to high environmental standards; as a result, the business of these small companies can be captured by larger producers of pulp and paper and large trading companies. In a similar way, it can be suggested that small agricultural producers do not provide the necessary sanitary control, and so preference must be given to large companies which continually increase their market share and remove smaller competitors.

Implementation of an arbitrage project

Implementation is the main part of an arbitrage project and includes the execution of the project itself, as well as defence of the project. Project execution has been examined in various chapters of this book, so here we pay attention to protection from incessant attacks by competitors, illustrated by the great battle between the Russian beer and Russian vodka.

Despite a history of millennia of beer drinking in Russia, the consumption of beer in the USSR was negligible compared with the European average. However, the early 1990s saw a renaissance of beer in Russia, and beer consumption between 1995 (when the first Western beer companies came to Russia) and 2007 grew from 15 litres per person per year to 81 litres. This growth was driven by improvements in the quality of beer and heavy advertising by brewers. Also, new breweries were more transparent in tax payments and more consolidated in comparison with producers of spirits, which preferred to work in the shadow economy. As a result, Russia has a powerful beer lobby that can quickly coordinate guild interests and act in a consolidated manner via the Russian Brewers' Union.

Given the high popularity of vodka in Russia, beer has relative health benefits for Russians. The consumption of beer involves a general reduction in alcohol consumption, and from this point of view causes less harm to human health than vodka. For example, a bottle of vodka in Russia can be bought for about £2, and can potentially be drunk by one person. To provide a similar dose of alcohol, a beer drinker would need to drink 20 cans of more expensive beer, which is more difficult to do physically – although some beer enthusiasts may disagree with this evaluation.

As a result of the expansion of beer, sales of vodka began to decline, but vodka manufacturers were not going to give up without a struggle. They soon realised that beer is a competing product, although the vodka market is significantly different from that of beer – it is not consolidated, there is no united industrial organisation, and fewer than half of the market participants are working transparently. However, vodka manufacturers have close connections to the authorities due to the fact that a substantial part of the business is controlled directly by officials and regional elites (Tolstykh and Puzyrev 2012).

The Russian spirits market helps regional authorities, regulatory agencies and deputies to receive huge shadow cash flows. Consequently, this group has a powerful lobby in the Duma which represents the interests of vodka barons (ibid.).

Producers and distributors of vodka have great mobility: it is easier to work with cash and send it promptly for corrupting officials and parliamentarians. For example, vodka producers are among the main sponsors of the election fund of United Russia in Moscow and have a strong relationship with the Russian federal agency of alcohol regulation, which is a historically reliable supporter of vodka manufacturers (Tolstykh and Puzyrev 2012).

Such lobbying is not available for beer producers because the rigid system of control at different levels and stages (financial control, management control, control of the Board of Directors and control of the compliance office) makes the procedure for transferring significant funds for shadow lobbying virtually impossible (ibid.). As a result, spirits lobbyists were able to tighten regulation on other alcoholic products such as beer, wine and low-alcohol drinks. They have managed successfully to switch the attention of society from the problems associated with the use of spirits to competing groups of weak alcohol, presenting them as a major social evil.

They lobbied to ban beer sales at night, ban the trade in beer by individual entrepreneurs, ban the sale of beer in plastic bottles, and for the introduction of compulsory licensing of production and turnover of beer. Additionally, vodka lobbyists adopted the law 'On state regulation of production and turnover of alcoholic products' (Federal Law 2013), which virtually equated vodka to beer and set strict new sales conditions for beer, prohibiting the sale of beer on stalls. Moreover, the new law considers as alcoholic all drinks containing more than 0.5 per cent alcohol by volume, regardless of whether the alcohol is used in their manufacture.

This case shows how the vodka kings helped the Russian authorities in their struggle for sobriety to find a new enemy – beer – and managed to divert the attention of the authorities and society from vodka to relatively harmless beer, whose influence on morbidity and alcoholism is much less. They managed to implement a simple strategy: the worse and the more expensive is beer, the better it is for producers of spirits as when the price of beer increases, consumer choice leans towards vodka.

Implementation of the arbitrage project is not always done in a relaxed atmosphere; often it can be accompanied by a fierce competitive struggle. Therefore the list of the main types of transformation costs of arbitrage also includes defence from attacks and the development of arbitrage.

Arbitrage as an institutional trap

Numerous examples from previous chapters show that arbitrage has become the dominant practice in business operations and has evolved from a technical element to the dominant strategy. Moreover, arbitrage became a sustainable norm because it was unprofitable to deviate from it. The stability of arbitrage as a strategy and as a norm of a firm's behaviour is ensured by a stabilising mechanism with negative feedback (that is, the system output influences the input in a way that reduces the effect of the input signal to the system). That is, if a company does not use this strategy, the business efficiency and competitiveness of the firm often begins to fall and it is forced to adopt the arbitrage strategy or leave the market.

Also, there may be inertia in companies that commonly use arbitrage strategies which have proven effective in the past – also a mechanism of fixing norms. Inertia of an arbitrage strategy, together with the uncertainty of the magnitude of costs to move to another strategic paradigm, leads to retention of the strategy. Also, there is an additional stabilisation mechanism which is based on the effect of coordination provided by supporting externalities (Polterovich 1999). The effect of coordination lies in the fact that the more consistently all participants in arbitrage perform their roles and tasks (such as creating a price differentiation and conditions for arbitrage, as well as deflection of attacks by competitors and law enforcement agencies), the greater the damage incurred by each particular firm when it attempts to deviate from it. Here also there is a paradoxical occurrence of the mechanism of positive feedback: the more companies follow arbitrage, the less advisable it is for them not to use it; that is, the more companies adopt this strategy as dominant, the more they begin to perceive it as a norm of business.

The prevailing norm in a certain time is due to the fact that participants are trained to perform it effectively and improve the technology of its implementation. If the use of arbitrage prevails in a society with bureaucratic resources, then as a result there is improvement of the methodology of creation of conditions of arbitrage for their companies and anti-arbitrage behaviour toward competitors. Over time, this norm is linked with many other rules, that is, incorporated in other standards (a linkage effect). Therefore refusal to follow the rules may entail a chain of other changes and, as a result, high transformation costs.

Polterovich (1999) notes that under certain conditions there are inefficient but stable norms, referred to here as institutional traps. The emergence of institutional traps is a consequence of the inadequacy of formal institutions and enforcement mechanisms to fulfil their requirements and the constraints imposed by informal institutions. The term 'institutional trap' is appropriate to consider how a special economic attractor defines the domain of attraction of agents. It is characterised by significant costs during operation, but prohibitive costs associated with any exit from the current dynamic equilibrium. When the system has fallen into an institutional trap, it takes an inefficient pathway .of development, and returning later to efficient development makes no sense (ibid.).

Barter is a good example of the institutional trap which was considered earlier. In economies with a developed banking system, the share of barter is insignificant even at high rates of inflation. As noted earlier, in Russia in the early 1990s there were favourable conditions for spreading of barter. Underdevelopment of the banking system led to long-term inter-regional transactions. Sometimes it was more favourable to deliver cash by train or by plane than to transfer it from one bank account to another. Also, in the 1990s there was high inflation that sharply devalued financial assets and complicated the process of establishing a fair price for products. As a result, companies quickly discovered that the transaction costs of barter were lower than transaction costs of monetary exchange. Furthermore, relationships between companies that were preserved from the planned economy made the cost of switching to barter relatively low.

The greater the number of companies that preferred barter, the smaller the transaction costs of barter, as it became easier to find partners to build a barter chain. Polterovich (1999) calls this a coordination effect. Because of this, the growth of a barter economy facilitates connections between companies. Thus prerequisites for barter were created by changing fundamental factors – the rate of inflation and the risk of default. The effect of coordination accelerated the formation of this norm. With the passage of time, barter transaction costs continued to decline due to the effect of learning: businesses developed better ways to build a long chain of barter exchanges. In addition, an arisen norm created a large group of barter intermediaries and was a convenient tool of tax evasion (Polterovich 1999).

Despite the fact that in the late 1990s the speed of financial transfers between banks increased significantly, barter transactions were very popular because every agent who decides to withdraw from the system of barter would have to bear transformation costs in order to break the established connection with the other partners, find new companions and be ready to come under the scrutiny of the tax authorities (ibid.). Also, recall that for some participants barter exchange makes it relatively easy to increase current assets and make opaque financial transactions.

Arbitrage in the absence of control over the bureaucracy may also be an institutional trap. High levels of autonomy of the bureaucracy from citizens together with the administrative resources, blurring of moral standards and the weakness of the mechanisms of state and public control are fundamental factors contributing to the establishment of arbitrage as an institutional trap. This means that without this type of arbitrage economic systems may be less effective than with arbitrage. Due to the coordination effect, the more popular arbitrage becomes, the higher the number of firms exploiting arbitrage and the lower the arbitrage transaction costs. Moreover, people become more tolerant of this type of arbitrage as its prevalence grows.

By improving, arbitrage becomes a hierarchical structure. The massive use of this arbitrage scheme leads to the appearance of the appropriate service system: developers and consultants appear who design and implement new arbitrage schemes. The effect of training, as usual, is the complemented linkage effect: there are specific forms of business with distorted reporting; arbitrage mates tightly with corruption.

Arbitrage is embedded in the system of other rules and regulations, and a refusal to follow these rules may result in a chain of other changes. Therefore a company's exit from arbitrage strategy is associated with high costs of transformation. Domination of arbitrage generates a specific configuration of the organisational structure of the company and its functionally oriented departments. As the result, this strategy starts the process of re-functionalisation of the firm, which assumes status changes of individual production departments, working groups and staff.

This gives an impulse of transformation of rules and regulations, institutional procedures and contractual arrangements, together with changes of tradition and established stereotypes of thinking. Shifts in a firm's strategy with regard to arbitrage are difficult because the roles of participants in the process form fairly narrow business specialisations, and movement to other strategies gives rise to a high-cost re-functionalisation. All this taken together further blocks the exit from the institutional trap of arbitrage.

In Russia, for the past 25 years legislation was built with many errors which are a consequence of bounded rationality, and errors which are a consequence of opportunistic behaviour when the design of the law is to lay down a corruption trap. It simultaneously meets the interests of the corrupt bureaucracy and the different oligarch groups.

What determines the initial access of certain people to conduct arbitrage operations with state assets? The fact that they had additional possibilities that were not available to others: classified information, good relations with the government, and embeddedness.

Additionally, most market participants have prohibitively high costs of accessing information related to the conduct of arbitrage; only a minority group, which probably has close relationships with authorities and regulators, has managed to access information and consequently has low transaction costs. As a result, there is large information asymmetry between these two groups that ultimately defines arbitrage success for some and the failure of others.

Conclusion

Institutions are systems of formal and informal rules that define the relationships of people in society; the institution is a systemic social feature, acquired by a firm in a joint activity that determines the level and quality of social relations in this group. An institution is considered as a system of relatively stable traits and outwardly manifested characteristics of an organisation, which are recorded in the judgments of the organisation itself as well as judgments about it by other organisations or people.

To discuss institutions in terms of good or bad is counterproductive to understanding these processes because these institutions reflect the prevailing attitude in society and are relevant to the level of economic development of the country. After the collapse of the Soviet system, Russia actively borrowed management experience from the economies of developed countries, including the import of institutions, often without proper analysis of their suitability for the specific conditions of the Russian economy.

Institutions directly and indirectly affect the implementation of arbitrage in the context of arbitrage transactions and in the context of creating conditions for arbitrage.

Arbitrage operations may be simple or complex. In complex cases of arbitrage, there are additional participants (agents) who maintain conditions for arbitrage and also create explicit or implicit additional contracts. For complex cases, the right of management, the right to earn income and the sovereign right may belong to a third party who actually creates the conditions for arbitrage. Complex arbitrage contracts can never be absolutely comprehensive as participants in the transaction are unable to foresee the mutual rights and obligations in all possible situations and record them in a written contract.

In relation to arbitrage in Russia, there are different types of transaction and institutional costs; the size of transaction costs depends nonlinearly on the degree of embeddedness of a company. At high levels of embeddedness, relative costs may be lower. Indeed, for companies that are in close alliance or family relations with the regional authorities, these costs can be practically zero. Conversely, for beginners without connections they are often prohibitively high.

Frequently the creation of conditions for arbitrage will adjust, suspend and affect existing laws and regulations that impact on the institutional environment. Moreover, the larger the scale of arbitrage, the more institutions are likely to be affected.

There are six main types of transformation costs of arbitrage: creation of a project of institutional change; promotion of a project; creation and maintenance of intermediate institutions for project implementation; implementation of arbitrage; development of arbitrage; and recapturing of attacks.

Examples from previous chapters show that arbitrage has become the dominant practice in business operations as it evolved from a technical element to the prevailing strategy. Moreover, arbitrage became a sustainable norm because it was unprofitable to deviate from it. The stability of arbitrage as a strategy and as a norm of firms' behaviour is ensured by a stabilising mechanism with negative feedback.

Arbitrage is embedded in the system of other rules and regulations, and a refusal to follow these rules may result in a chain of other changes. As a consequence, a company's exit from arbitrage strategy is associated with high costs of transformation. The domination of arbitrage generates a specific configuration of the organisational structure of the company and its functionally oriented departments.

5 Conditions for arbitrage

Chapter 5 attempts to answer the questions: Who creates asymmetries? And how? It goes on to investigate price asymmetries and opportunities for arbitrage, as well as the causes of price asymmetries and how purposeful human activity creates opportunities for arbitrage. The chapter reveals different technologies for forming conditions for arbitrage in the Russian economy by analysing various examples in the agro, food, oil, fish and building industries. Numerous examples demonstrate convincingly that these conditions are being formed as a result of purposeful human activity of the bureaucracy which, most of the time, is a major beneficiary of arbitrage.

Creation of price asymmetries

Defining arbitrage as the action that includes buying and selling on different markets where there is asymmetry of price, with the objective of taking benefit, usually implicitly assumes independence of market prices. Also, in theory asymmetries and opportunities appear as relatively external to a firm, a result of the diversity of the objective world and business environment. However, in reality, as noted in Chapter 2, companies can form asymmetries of price and other conditions for arbitrage. The phenomenon of price asymmetries logically raises questions: Is this a product of coincidence or the result of purposeful human activity? If one accepts that it is result of human activity, it is reasonable to examine how price asymmetries and opportunities for arbitrage are created, and by whom.

To answer these questions, it is necessary to analyse the causality of price asymmetries and conditions as well as the complicated relationship between cause and effect, where results are understood as a consequence of different events. The connection between cause and effect in this way can also be referred to as a causal nexus. One can employ Aristotle's types of causation (Aristotle 1953): the first question (*causa efficiens*), 'whose influence made this reality?' and the second, (*causa finalis*) 'for what reason does the thing happen or exist?'. In other words, an event is said to cause another event if the first event precedes the second in time and the first is a necessary condition, foundation, creation, change or development in relation to the second.

However, it is important to say that often, and particularly in economic situations, there is no direct connection between a cause and a final result. The effect can be formed in a complex process where many causes interconnect.

For better understanding of the conditions for buying and selling on the Russian market, we can start from a simple example: there is a difference in the price of grain between Russia and, for example, Egypt due to different conditions of climate, different factors of supply and demand on the respective markets, and different technologies which create price disparities. There are companies that can supply Russian grain to Egypt, but there are difficulties associated with the implementation of such arbitrage, such as the capacity of the Russian port in Novorossiysk being limited, export quotas and contracts with the port to load grain and the ability to charter a grain transportation vessel at a reasonable price. Furthermore, theoretically there may be problems with buying grain, as shown in the following section, due to the export of grain from some regions being banned by the regional government, and so on. In this example, we can see that price asymmetries are determined not only by the global conditions and governments' agreements and regulations, but also by many technical nuances.

One can begin to find explanations for price asymmetries and opportunities for arbitrage from examples taken from Russian agribusiness because it is a practically perfect competitive market, with many buyers and sellers, and integrated essentially into the global agro market. Also, this market is critically important for the population so it receives attention from politicians and the federal and regional authorities, which are trying to regulate it based on their own understanding of the market and their own personal interests.

Consequently, different barriers to entry have been formed in the agro-food sector, such as various licences and quotas, restrictions on prices and trade margins, local taxes and fees, and benefits to certain business entities. In addition, there are inter-regional trade barriers which are one of the most common administrative barriers to entry on a market and thereby determine the competitiveness of the agro-food market (Csaki *et al.* 2002).

Administrative regional restrictions on the movement of agricultural and food products in Russia began to appear in the first years of reform due to the movement of livestock price-support programmes from federal to regional level. Livestock subsidies were paid for every head sold to maintain the profitability of agriculture. However, the regional authorities have begun to limit the export of subsidised products outside their territories, the explanation being that the paid subsidies should remain in their territory. This policy led to an increase in supply and consequently to relative reduction of procurement prices for agricultural products, and the effect of subsidies was eliminated (Serova 2000). Thus the subsidy paid to farmers was eventually obtained as arbitrage income by two groups of companies: firstly those that broke the regional orders and illegally exported from these regions, and secondly companies that managed to obtain authorisation from officials. Mostly these were agricultural processing companies affiliated with the regional authorities.

In the same period, various techniques of restrictions on the export of products from regions began to take shape. Many such restrictions were not fixed in the regulations of the regional administration. Frequently they could be created as oral instructions to the traffic police, who organised cordons on the borders of the region (Serova 2000). Also, authorities widely employed other methods of limitation, such as phytosanitary and veterinary controls, where restrictions were introduced under the pretext of nonproliferation of substandard or contaminated products across the country (Csaki *et al.* 2002).

The second wave of proliferation of administrative barriers to trade in the agricultural and food sector was launched in the spring of 1995, when the commercial agricultural credit scheme was introduced. Large oil corporations were asked to deliver fuel and lubricating materials to agricultural companies in the manner of repayment of their debts to the federal budget. Fuels were the main limiting resource for beneficial sowing, and agrarians undertook to repay the debt to the budget at the end of the agricultural season. Thus the agrarian sector gained free credit by deferring payments to the budget (Serova 2000).

Oil companies were allocated between different regions and could not compete with each other. Deliveries of agricultural production to the state funds were made at fixed prices. But the monopolisation of the regional markets by the oil companies allowed them to force up the price of fuel to 20–30 per cent higher than the average market price. In other words, the exchange ratio for agrarians was significantly overstated. Receiving fuel and lubricants as the state commodity credit, agricultural producers were forced to sell agricultural products at fixed prices for these loans that was significantly lower than actual market prices, which led to losses in the autumn.

Thus the government solution to lend to farmers created the conditions for arbitrage. Oil companies were made monopolists on the regional markets and they were able to establish higher oil prices, consequently there were price asymmetries between the regions. Together with the restriction on other oil suppliers, they established the conditions for arbitrage for a particular oil company. Profit from arbitrage was later shared between the oil company and the authorities that determined which oil company was allowed to work in the market.

Also, at the end of the harvest there was a second act of arbitrage. Agricultural producers sold products at fixed prices that again created price differences between the regional fixed prices of farmers and free market prices. Trading companies that were close to regional administrations were able to buy at low prices and export agro products, realising opportunities for arbitrage.

However, after these two operations the arbitrage was not over. Debts of commercial credit were not repaid on time due to large farms operating under soft budget restrictions and tolerance towards unpaid debts from regional authorities, which resulted in an increase in debt relief. Therefore, even when paying the debt, they made a profit due to the high inflation rate devaluing the debt in real terms, which enabled farmers to arbitrage their debts. Later, the debts were restructured in the debt obligations of the regions and for some time freely traded in the markets. That gave opportunities for financial mediators to make profit by the arbitrage of these debts.

Serova (2000) notes that when the federal programme was stopped, regions implemented similar schemes such as loans from their own budgets, especially in 1997–98. The schemes gave conditions for arbitrage at a regional level. Regional authorities have a strong motivation to receive agricultural products at fixed price as a payment of previous debts of agricultural producers, due to this generating solid prospects for arbitrage. Nevertheless, buying of products at the fixed price, together with farmers' inability to pay extraordinary debts, pushed agrarians to transfer their business to the shadow sphere. The decline of the regional turnover of agro products and taxation eventually destroyed the conditions for arbitrage of regional authorities' privileged firms.

Thereby, Csaki *et al.* (2002) note that the share of the shadow market of grain was about 30 per cent of its total volume. For around half of managers, a determining factor when choosing a buyer was the possibility of selling agricultural products for cash or barter. These cash and barter transactions were aimed at the reduction of tax liabilities of buyers, but on the other hand they reduced the income of agricultural enterprises because they were not able to receive a high price for their products (ibid.).

Without the ability to control the revenues of farms and thereby guarantee the repayment of regional and federal loans, regional governments began to introduce seasonal restrictions on the export of agricultural products as payment of debts by commodity and general loans. An example from Tatarstan shows how this was done in practice.

The economy of the Republic of Tatarstan has a strong agriculture segment. For example, in 2011 it harvested about 5 million tonnes of grain. However, in 2012 there was a significant decline in the gross grain harvest, by 1.5 million tonnes compared with 2011, due to severe drought. Consequently the Ministry of Agriculture and Food of Tatarstan required that producers mandatorily align with the Ministry any shipment of grain from the Republic's stockpiles to other regions of Russia. This order effectively restricts grain export from the republic.

Tatarstan was not the first region to introduce such restrictions. Article 15 of the Federal Law 'On Protection of Competition' (Federal Law 2006) establishes administrative and criminal liability for the prevention, restriction or elimination of competition, including limiting access to the market. Many regions of Russia ban the external sale of agricultural products. In this case, market restrictions negate the competitive environment; farmers are forced to sell and concentrate all the resources on the local market, leading to oversupply (Katargin *et al.* 2012). Consequently, the price of grain within Tatarstan and outside was different: for a similar quality of wheat in Tatarstan the price was 7,500 roubles per tonne whereas outside the Republic it was around 10,000 roubles and terms of payment with external buyers were more beneficial.

Katargin *et al.* (2012) note that the Russian Agriculture Ministry sent a letter to the President of Tatarstan cautioning against restrictions on competition in the sale of grain. These restrictions violate the principles of the common economic space and free movement of goods, services and financial resources, and contradict Russian law forbidding the establishment of any obstacles to the free movement of goods. According to the farmers, large agricultural holdings were the beneficiaries of this deal as small companies needed to supply grain at a dramatically reduced price (ibid.).

A similar restriction was set by the government of the Chechen Republic. Moreover, the government used the police force to prevent export of grain outside the region (Chechen Republic 2001). As a result of the existence of regional trade barriers, in 1999 almost all grain (97.6 per cent) was sold near the sites of production (Csaki *et al.* 2002).

Restrictions on the free sale of agricultural products, and the use of police cordons that prey upon countrymen on regional roads, led to the downfall of intraregional grain prices and increases in the price of grain in grain-importing regions. Thus the conditions for arbitrage were created. The beneficiaries of arbitrage are regional authorities, executives of large agro companies and large traders. In addition, many regions subsidised their poultry and livestock to support regional producers, and created extra-budgetary funds to finance these programmes. These funds, in comparison with the regional budgets, have a lack of transparency and are under the direct control of the regional administrations. Moreover, many of these transactions made use of barter that made control over regional budget spending practically impossible. Serova (2000) specifies that for the arbitrage operations of these corporations, working capital is not required; because of commercial credit, they receive the products on account.

Also, often regional governments wishing to demonstrate care of the poor supported low prices for certain agricultural products. For example, for a long time the administration of the Krasnodar region subsidised the retail price of bread by 60–70 per cent, and in 2001 loaves of bread in the Krasnodar region were made available for 2.4 roubles compared with a price in the neighbouring regions of around 6.5 roubles (Csaki *et al.* 2002). As a result of this policy, much of this bread was arbitraged in the neighbouring regions rather than being made available to the poor, and so the social effect was insignificant.

Restrictions as conditions for arbitrage

The existence of regional export barriers is not the only possible condition for arbitrage; there are other types of regional trade barriers such as import restrictions. The most common are restrictions on the import of alcoholic beverages from other regions, as this product is excisable and high-yield, and its production is a significant source of income for many Russian regions. In 2009, 22 regions of the Russian Federation, including Tatarstan, Bashkortostan and Chuvashia, restricted access of other regions to their alcohol market (Tsvetkova 2009).

Undoubtedly, vodka is a significant source of regional income; however, it is vital for regional authorities due to the regulation of the market providing beneficial conditions for arbitrage: price asymmetries between regions and arbitrage opportunities for companies operating in this lucrative market segment. In Russia, on the other hand, when the price of vodka goes up drinkers switch to substitutes such as moonshine; therefore an arbitrage game requires good performance skills, otherwise arbitrageurs do not receive anything.

In the 1990s the Moscow government restricted the import of domestic food into its territory. These restrictions allowed officials of the capital to receive impressive foreign currency loans from the federal government for the purchase of food from overseas, employing companies friendly to the Moscow government (Csaki 2002). The reason for this seemingly strange behaviour lies in arbitrage opportunities. Creating a price difference through restrictions on free entry of products to the Moscow market allowed elevated arbitrage revenues. A relatively similar strategy is employed in local agro markets of Moscow, which are controlled by different ethnic and criminal groups; authorities constrain the free trade of independent producers, consequently establishing and maintaining highly profitable arbitrage income.

Likewise, Russian regions established controls over imports to protect local producers. These measures include direct import quotas, as well as special sanitary and phytosanitary regulations, standards and certification, and labelling requirements. As a result, imported goods were disadvantaged against regional products (Csaki 2002).

Thus the Russian regions employed different instruments to create a favourable environment for agro and food companies, such as control over retail and wholesale prices, by limiting price and trade margins, rationing consumption, the creation of grain and other provisions, mandatory sale of agricultural products to regional food corporations, subsidies and other funding for agricultural programmes from regional budgets, tax incentives, licensing and food grants for poor people.

Creation of opportunities for arbitrage

In the following case studies we analyse more deeply buying and selling on different markets which depend mainly on flexible factors of human nature. Currently, in Russia, the purchase of goods for the needs of government organisations is implemented through tender systems which are conducted at federal, regional and local levels. According to the federal law (Federal Law 2011), tenders are carried out to reduce the cost of procurement and projects. However, frequently conditions of tenders decrease the number of potential participants, often reducing the number to one real participant and thus generating conditions for arbitrage. In 2013, for example, the government of the City of Moscow announced a tender for landscaping prestigious Tverskaya Street. According to the tender documentation, the winner had to plant 68 trees and 690 bushes and establish 631 stone vases for the bushes; the cost of the project was around 270 million roubles (Mitrokhin 2013). Trees and shrubs in stone tubs freeze completely and therefore they have to be replanted every six months. Agricultural specialists note that planting these plants in the special stone vessels was counterproductive. The cost of landscaping was huge due to innovative methods of gardening. Moreover, the government of Moscow provided subsidies to the winner of the tender (ibid.).

The arbitrageur (the winner of the tender) had a significantly greater ability than opponents to sell its services because of the proximity of the winner to the authorities and special conditions that dissuaded other participants. In addition, to emphasise the innovation of the arbitrageur, employing stone vessels for bushes and trees in the harsh Moscow climate created an opportunity to sell its bushes and trees every year and have regular arbitrage income.

A similar business is described by Navalny (2013), when the Russian Federal Service for State Registration, Cadastre and Cartography conducted a tender for the purchase of BMW 750 Li xDrive for $189,000. Characteristics of the car were tailored to a specific seller and the price was set dramatically higher than the market price.

Analogous approaches were realised by the National University of Mineral Resources, which in November 2012 placed the tender for the purchase of furniture for four of its dormitories. The tenders included 1,295 beds with mattresses, bedside tables and bookshelves, 1,224 desks, 643 wardrobes and 620 mirrors. Every characteristic of every piece of furniture was clearly specified by the customer: dimensions, material of goods (e.g. New Zealand pine), the colour of each item, and even the shape and colouring of knobs of wardrobes and bedside tables (antique bronze). The initial value of the contract amounted to 143.5 million roubles, around $3,500 for each student place. Information about the auction was published on 9 November and filing of applications was terminated on 28 November. Under the contract, the contractor was to supply the furniture in six weeks (Gasnikova 2013).

One can show thousands of examples of similar practices where, again and again, the strict conditions imposed by the customer in specifying the terms of the tender benefit companies favoured by the organisers of the tenders. Organisers employ approaches such as allowing a very short time for submission of documents for the tender and a very short delivery timescale of products, as in the case of the furniture delivery. Consequently, they are cutting off other participants from participation in tenders, thereby increasing the arbitrage income of friendly participants.

However, unfortunately for Russian arbitrageurs, there are geographical and infrastructure limitations which increase logistical costs and, as a result, purchases are often limited. That can be illustrated by the example of the Russian forest industry. The total forested area in Russia amounts to 1.1 billion hectares; this is more than 24 per cent of the world's forest reserves (FAO 2001). But most Russian forests are of little use to the best of commercial operations: either no transport infrastructure exists, or forests are located in the mountain regions of Siberia and the Far East, or the quality of the wood does not meet modern requirements. In these conditions it is often impossible to obtain wood, therefore companies compete fiercely for resources, typically using traditional schemes of restricting access to competitors to resources. For example, in 2006 the Russian government announced a gradual increase of export duties on round timber to reduce the export of cheap raw wood to a minimum. These duties were intended to encourage the intensive development of domestic wood processing; however, there may come a time when Russians have nowhere to put their timber, as the transition from the status of producer to processor of trees takes a long time. The process began in 2007, when the export tariffs increased from 6.5 to 20 per cent of the customs value of raw materials, and a year later the rate rose 25 per cent to €15 per cubic metre. In 2012, a month before Russian entry into the World Trade Organization, the government established new rules for tariff regulation of the industry, which provide for the growth of customs duties (Bikmuhametov 2010). However, the beneficiaries of these solutions have been the producers of pulp and paper, and large trading companies that received special export duties and, as a result, had high arbitrage profit.

The above example demonstrates how important it is for arbitrageurs to create conditions for selling of products, but for the most successful operations they should also have relatively similar conditions for buying. Examples from the oil trade during the initial accumulation of oligarch capital are interesting because they demonstrate a variety of arbitrage methods, many of which continue to exist to this day.

Balkar-Trading

In the early 1990s the Avtovaz domestic distribution network included about 300 trading companies, many of which were started by managers of Avtovaz who teamed up with friends and relations as partners. In one of these companies worked our hero, Peter Janchev, Deputy Director of the car centre in Balashikha near Moscow, on the basis of which the dealer company Balkar-Trading was established.

At that time Russia had a comparatively undeveloped car market, and strong demand for cars made them excellent material for barter; in conditions of high inflation, the car was the equivalent of hard currency. Avtovaz and its trading companies carried out thousands of barter transactions, which saved it from inflation and on the other hand provided enormous opportunities for highly profitable arbitrage which, as a rule, was realised via mediators such as Balkar-Trading (see Chapter 5).

Balkar-Trading preferred to sell in bulk. On receiving revenues, it immediately purchased some other liquid commodity such as wood or copper as it was necessary to insure against hyperinflation. However, the real success and huge money came when the company established contacts with the producers of oil from Khanty-Mansi autonomous district and began to exchange cars for oil. Balkar-Trading established a good relationship with Noyabrskneftegas (NNG), which had very large wage arrears, and the company management decided to pay salaries with cars. So in 1992 the first batch of cars from

Balkar-Trading was swapped in Noyabrsk (Ignatova 2004). To close the barter chain, Janchev was able to find profitable distribution channels for oil, partly because of his personal endeavours but also due to lobbying by his father-in-law, who was a deputy of the General Attorney of the Russian Federation.

Ignatova (2004) notes that Yanchev's scheme was stunningly profitable. Through his own channels, he bought Avtovaz automobiles for an average of about $2,000. Afterwards, cars were swapped for oil, which was sold at a fixed domestic price and then exported at prices close to world prices. Thus he was earning around $30,000 on every car. In total he sold 20,000 cars, and as a result on average each family in Noyabrsk had three cars.

Hereafter, Janchev employed a barter chain where NNG stably supplied oil, then oil was exported according to export quotas and government contracts, and the profit was shared between NNG, owners of quotas and government contracts and Balkar-Trading and its affiliated companies. For instance, the Moscow city government received a quota for export of oil for solving social problems. Janchev arranged with Moscow officials to exchange oil quotas for cash (Ignatova 2004). In 1995, with the oil company Mobil, which acted as a guarantor for the loan of the Russian government in the amount of $1 billion, Balkar-Trading succeeded in obtaining permission for preferential export of 25 million tonnes of oil over 5 years. By that time the company was one of a small number of special exporters of oil with the right to export oil abroad for specific government programmes such as the reconstruction of the Kremlin. Consequently, the company held a quarter of Russian oil intended for export (Berres and Levin 1995).

Brilliant prospects were opened for the Janchev business, such as the opportunity to buy the oil company NNG together with oil refineries and so enter into the narrow circle of Russian oligarchs; however, as always, fairy tales come to an end. Just 3 months before the mortgage auction for Sibneft, where he was going to take part, Janchev was imprisoned. He was charged with concealing income of $17.7 million and giving a bribe in the form of cars to Attorney General Alexei Ilyushenko (Berres and Levin 1995). The mortgage auction for Sibneft was won by the company of Boris Berezovsky (see Chapter 2). When privatisation of the company was finished in 1997, Janchev was released.

Janchev arbitrage was extremely effective: according to Berres and Levin (1995) he pocketed around $14 from every tonne of oil sold (at that time 1 tonne of oil cost approximately $100). This result was due to an opportunity to obtain export oil quotas; however, it was more important to buy low-priced cars and oil. One can see that, having had good relations with the boss of NNG, Victor Gorodilov and his father-in-law in the General Prosecutor's Office, Janchev had a stable source of oil.

What determines the possibility for some people to buy a scarce asset in Russia? The Janchev case shows that the arbitrageurs had private communications and information about additional possibilities that were not available to others. One can say that there was information asymmetry between the market's participants. For those who are not included in the list of front-runners there were prohibitively high costs of access to information, high costs of negotiation, and no access to the regulator, so that the costs were prohibitive.

Transneft

The opportunity to buy assets is essential for arbitrage; however, access to the market infrastructure is also crucial in many cases. Analysis of the Russian transport company Transneft, which controlled the Russian national oil pipelines, reveals new obstacles in arbitrage practice. The company owns the largest oil pipeline system in the world, with a total network length of 50,000 kilometres and transporting about 93 per cent of Russian oil (Transneft 2014).

The fundamental principle of Transneft as declared by the company management is to give all oil market participants equal access to the pipeline network in order to ensure competition and market development. Access to the pipeline network is regulated by the quarterly schedule of the Ministry of Industry and Energy of Russia and is operated by Transneft. The essence of quotas is to allocate between Russian oil exporters pipeline transportation capacity proportional to declared oil-production volumes. Oil from different fields, after injection into the pipeline system, is no longer associated with individual exporters and is instead considered as Russian export blend crude oil (REBCO) (GOST 1976). After that, exporting companies can take back the mixture from the final terminals as required for them to export according to the schedule and allocated volumes. The system of main pipelines is a gigantic common reservoir, where the oil companies continuously pump oil from the fields and then take it for export or processing. Objective monitoring of the circulation volumes in the pipe system of Transneft can be only approximate, unless the whole piping system is completely emptied.

In practice, however, the principle of enabling all market participants to have equal access to the pipeline network has been transformed by the executives into a pragmatic rule: it should be followed, but is not. In addition, part of the Russian pipeline capacity provides the CIS countries for the export of oil to Western markets. The capacity of the main oil pipelines of Transneft is not sufficient to meet the requirements of all customers, particularly in times of upsurge in the world market price of oil. Therefore there are opportunities to sell pipeline capacity to customers who are ready to pay more than the state regulated price. Also, the company artificially created this deficit by over-stating the planned capacity for the transit of oil from the CIS countries that additionally limited access to the pipelines by Russian exporters. In practice, the export of oil from the CIS countries was smaller than was announced, which led to the appearance of unaccounted capacities that could be exploited on the domestic shadow market.

In 2004, using the mechanism described, over-limit capacity was obtained to the amount of 6 million tonnes of oil, which were sold at an average price of $25 per tonne, resulting in an annual income of about $150 million. In 2005 the same mechanism was allowed to realise 3.5 million tonnes at an average price of $50 per tonne due to a high oil price that allowed the acquisition of around $175 million (Vokrug novostey 2007).

Another mechanism for the creation of above-limit transport capacity consists of the allocation to oil exporters of inconvenient terminals related to the necessity of the transfer of oil between pipelines and railway tanks. According to practice, all exporters who receive volumes for sale through the terminal Tikhoretskaya (Krasnodar Territory) try to exchange them for transportation capacity on more profitable areas. This brings additional income to managers of Transneft by way of unofficial payments for the exchange of terminals. In 2004 the terminal was planned for 5 million tonnes but actually exported 1.7 million tonnes, consequently 3.3 million tonnes was realised in the shadow market. By 2005 the volume of sales under this scheme had reached 4 million tonnes.

Two Transneft terminals in the ports of Novorossiysk and Tuapse employed a different scheme. When planning export through these ports, the limit capacities of the ports were deliberately understated and the free capacity was realised on the market. In 2004 and 2005, via Tuapse port alone, 0.22 and 0.48 million tonnes, respectively, were additionally exported at shadow market prices of $20 and $35 per tonne, respectively, obtaining income of approximately $4.4 million and $16.8 million (Vokrug novostey 2007). Furthermore, for additional revenues the company allocated small-volume quota at the Novorossiysk oil terminal. Small export quotas are typical for smaller oil companies that are doing economically impractical freight of oil by tanker, therefore it is necessary to seek additional oil for a full load. For example, for a small company with an export quota of 20,000 tonnes of oil, freight by an oil tanker with a tonnage of 60,000 tonnes is unprofitable. Increasing the export volume to use all of the tanker through the acquisition of additional oil by a small oil company is not allowed by the export schedule. The inability to implement a dedicated export quota within the schedule will lead to its loss (ibid.). In 2004, the company SUNOIL provided its oil tankers for exports of companies with small quotas in the amount of 1.79 million tonnes of oil at $10 per tonne, while receiving income of $17.9 million (Vokrug novostey 2007). The above examples clearly show the impact of the market infrastructure: Transneft creates difficulties for oil companies to sell their oil in a straightforward manner, thereby creating opportunities for arbitrage.

However, the activity of the company reveals another type of arbitrage. One can see that Transneft received from the Ministry of Industry and Energy of Russia quotas for the transportation of oil of different Russian companies. This often created some complications for the oil producers. Therefore they arbitraged profit by differences between the original price set by the government regulator and the real price for customers. In general, the major part of this income was squirrelled away by company executives.

Moreover, Transneft increased the cost of services by acquiring some part of the oil it was supposed to be transporting. We constantly note that arbitrage is buying and selling on different markets where there is asymmetry of price. However, we assume that, following the law of conservation of mass, the physical quantity of the substance does not change – but Transneft was able to surprise the scientific world by destroying the postulates of hydrodynamics when it managed to make oil disappear from the sealed pipes. The official explanation for the loss of customers' oil was oil sticking to the walls of the pipeline. In 2003, Vice-President of Transneft Sergei Grigoryev said that the main pipeline system had accumulated approximately 150,000 tonnes of crude oil and that oil accumulates in the system due to natural loss over the actual performance. This is not the first case of such a revolutionary scientific discovery. In 2001 the pipelines accumulated about 200,000 tonnes of crude oil (Pravosudov 2013). Oil attached to the wall of the pipe, regardless of how it happened, created additional costs for oil companies.

In modern times, in competitive markets, it is comparatively difficult to achieve very high profits. Therefore in these markets an arbitrageur will try to reduce the number of competitors, if possible to zero. This approach can be named as 'eliminate competitors and get arbitrage profit'. The next case shows how members of the Russian establishment virtuosi wiped competitors from the fish market and created conditions for arbitrage.

Fishing in troubled waters

In the Middle Ages, Atlantic salmon were caught off the north Russian coast. In Soviet times this fish was considered a delicacy, but after the 2000s there has been a strong market growth. For example, in 2010 and 2012 consumption amounted to 92,000 and 154,000 tonnes, respectively, and the volume of the market in value terms in 2012 amounted to 25 billion roubles (FAS 2013). The global leader in the production of salmon is Norway, which is a major exporter of salmon to the Russian market. In 2011 Russia imported 113,000 tonnes of Atlantic salmon of which 100,000 tonnes were from Norway (Marine Harvest 2012; FAS 2013).

Until 2006 the Russian salmon market was stable and more than 100 Norwegian manufacturers exported fish to Russia. But on 1 January 2006 the Federal Service for Veterinary and Phytosanitary Surveillance (Rossel-khoznadzor), under the pretext of the high content of heavy metals in Norwegian fish, completely banned exports to Russia (Kreknina 2013). Nevertheless, 2 months later the group 'Russian Sea' created the Association of Fish Processing and Trading Companies (Fish Association) in order to unite leading companies in imports, processing and sales of fish and seafood (Fish Alliance 2013). North Company and ROCK-1 joined it and in 2007 Atlant-Pacific and Defa also joined. Currently the Fish Association accounts for approximately 80 per cent of all Russian fish product imports, and through the wide commercial network of member companies the fish are sold in all parts of the country (ibid.).

In April 2007 Rosselkhoznadzor allowed eight Norwegian plants to supply fish to the companies of the group Russian Sea. Six months later, Rossel-khoznadzor opened supplies to several other Norwegian plants, which began to sell it to other members of the Fish Association. From 2006 to 2012 a close alliance between the Fish Association and Rosselkhoznadzor was established; consequently members of the Association had 90 per cent of the market share of Norwegian salmon (Kreknina 2013).

Rosselkhoznadzor offered to establish the practice of exporting without the use of intermediaries (traders, exporters). Norwegian enterprises wishing to continue to export fish to Russia had to renew their contracts in such a way as to have only a unique and direct trade with one Russian company. Among participants, this anti-competitive scheme was called 'one exporter–one importer'. Rosselkhoznadzor took the initiative for the establishment of the principles of trade policy, that is, on matters not related to the competence of the department (FAS 2013). Moreover, it actively lobbied the Fish Association and as a result, responding to requests from the Association, Rosselkhoznadzor imposed prohibitions and restrictions on the import of salmon from a number of Norwegian plants. For example, in October 2010 the Association complained about the quality of fish of 15 Norwegian companies, consequently Rosselkhoznadzor introduced strengthened laboratory monitoring of these fish suppliers and later banned some deliveries. In June 2011 the Association filed a similar complaint for 13 Norwegian suppliers, and in July Rosselkhoznadzor introduced reinforced control measures (FAS 2013). Thus the authorities imposed restrictions without laboratory confirmation of discrepancies of fish to the Russian sanitary and veterinary standards. Later, it turned out that no compelling reason for this existed: the proportion of samples that did not meet veterinary requirements decreased from 1.26 per cent in 2011 to 0.52 per cent in 2012 (Kreknina 2013).

In autumn 2011, three companies, Russian Sea, North Company and Atlant-Pacific, concluded a strategic partnership agreement with suppliers that divided among themselves the Norwegian enterprises that supplied fish to Russia. Also, participants in the agreement arranged to divide up the Norwegian plants among themselves and agreed the volume of products supplied by each participant in Russia (Kreknina 2013). Thus a cartel was created and monopolisation of the market was increased. The cartel led to an aggressive policy, for example, the Federal Antimonopoly Service (FAS) reports that in December 2011 Norwegian supplier Coast Seafood AS received threats from North Company to force them to supply only North Company (FAS 2013). In addition, FAS notes that the members of the Fish Association, in its dealings with partners and competitors, sought to emphasise the special relationship with Rosselkhoznadzor and the ability to influence its actions. FAS gives examples: in the addendum to the contract between Marine Harvest Norway and Russian Sea, Russian Sea promised to help the Norwegian company obtain a permit from Rosselkhoznadzor by the end of the first quarter 2012 (FAS 2013).

Even the giant retailer Group Auchan SA could not reach an agreement with the Norwegian producers Seaborn AS, Sekkingstad AS and Norway Royal Salmon 'because of their fear that large Russian importers may affect the closing of these plants through veterinary measures' despite the fact that they were interested in working with the retailer directly (ibid.).

According to FAS (2013), cartel participants have secured more than 50 per cent of imports of Norwegian fish. On 1 June 2013 Russian companies were able to acquire products from only 19 Norwegian fish farmers, of which eight were shipping the fish to Russian Sea and two to North Company. Interestingly, between 2010 and 2012 Norwegian companies were working with members of the cartel; prohibitions and restrictions were not applied as a result. Russian Sea and North Company managed to save their share of the salmon market, which grew by 50 per cent (ibid.).

The initiators of the cartel expected that this would lead to the elimination of competition between its members, the appearance of additional barriers to enter the market of new participants, and strengthening of the position of the cartel in relation to both other Russian buyers of fish and Norwegian producers. FAS made a decision that Russian Sea and North Company had created a cartel in the market of wholesale supplies of Norwegian salmon and also that Rosselkhoznadzor and the Fish Association had helped them by creating an anti-competitive body of state power and business organisation. FAS noted that not later than 2010 the Association entered into an anti-competitive agreement with Rosselkhoznadzor, which led to the restriction of competition and in particular the separation of the commodity market supply of Norwegian fish in Russia by volume of sales, purchase of goods, composition of sellers, limiting access into the commodity market and elimination from the market of economic agents (FAS 2013).

The history becomes more understandable if we add that Russian Sea is controlled by brothers Maxim and Andrei Vorobiev (the former leader of the major Russian political party United Russia and currently the governor of Moscow region) and oligarch Gennady Timchenko, a close friend of Vladimir Putin. It is possible to see that, thanks to their powerful lobbying capabilities, the company Russian Sea was able to restrict access for independent producers and sellers of fish and it was possible to receive arbitrage income for a long time.

GOST

Previous examples show how the leader company created barriers for other market participants using the state regulator and holding a dominant position on the market. However, Russian practice is more diverse than the theory and often provides a rather unusual scheme. Attention should be given to industrial regulators in the sphere of Russian technical standards (GOST). Adoption of state standards is stipulated by the law 'On Technical Regulation' and, according to established practice, as a rule the initiator of the GOST becomes its developer. Moreover, a new standard can be initiated by absolutely any person or company.

When GOST carries out discussion of a new standard, it is placed on the internet and reported in the media. Anyone can make comments about the text of the first edition and send them to the creator who, in principle, should take them into consideration. After such discussion, the developer produces the final edition of the standard. Often, however, for imitation of discussion, the reviews are written by friends or colleagues of GOST authors or by the authors themselves (Trushin 2009).

In our case, with the creation of the GOST on the anti-corrosion protection of concrete and reinforced concrete structures, the developer was the Research Institute of Concrete and Reinforced Concrete (Moscow). The Institute was negotiating with all major manufacturers of enamels, paints and other building mixtures. As a result of the negotiation, in the standard were included trademarks of the manufacturers of concrete protection. But it cost them around $12,000 (Trushin 2009).

Many experts who reviewed the final version of the GOST were surprised that it included no requirements for building materials, but rather concrete brands. It seemed that the experts from the Institute wrote not the standard, but rather a merchandiser's brochure. Adoption of the standard with specific names instead of describing characteristics created an almost insurmountable barrier for new entrants wishing to create competition in the market through innovation (ibid.).

In a similar way, barriers were created by various industry regulators in the sphere of technical standards and regulations. Consequently, they eliminated many participants in the market and built conditions for arbitrage for companies that managed to be included in the list of the lucky. Also, using this scheme, additional income was obtained for the management of the Institute.

Generally, the same approach is realised as in the case of Norwegian fish, but there is a difference. In the Norwegian fish case, potential participants could not buy fish from the Norwegian producers and this created additional opportunity for the key market players (in this case the company Russian Sea). In the second case, arbitrageurs could not sell construction materials because they were not included in the standard and so were not allowed to be used in the construction industry. What the two cases have in common is that the successful arbitrageur limited the involvement of other participants through active interaction with state regulators.

One can see that the capability to generate conditions for arbitrage is a significant resource of a corporation, as not all can generate such conditions for arbitrage. In Chapter 1 we described the 'valuable, rare, inimitable, nonsubstitutable' (VRIN) framework (Barney 1991) which determines key resources of sustainable competitive advantage of a company. In our cases, these abilities are valuable and rare because they create opportunities and there is a low level of their employment among competitors. Additionally, these abilities are inimitable as they have several distinctive features that do not allow competitors to do likewise and there is a lack of substitutability. Also, these resources are more important than, for example, brand names, because they lead to high incomes for a long time. The companies in these situations are protected by a resource position barrier that is, to some extent, equivalent to barriers of entry, and gives significant competitive advantage.

Brutal cut-off competitors

The logical development of the approach 'delete competitors and gain arbitrage profit' described above is a less elaborate approach where authorities create conditions for arbitrageurs by cutting off the unwanted market participants, physically preventing their activity in a region or town. Usually, cutting competitors does not occur in a frontal attack, rather it is masked and accompanied by populist rhetoric. The case of the gas capital of Russia is a vivid example of this strategy. Russians like to call provincial towns a 'capital' for their specificity; therefore in mass the media Togliatti is the 'automotive capital', Ivanovo is the 'textile capital', Surgut is the 'oil capital' and Urengoy is the 'gas capital' of Russia. There is an interesting story about the latter town.

Urengoy was founded in 1975 after the discovery the gas field. The town is exactly in the centre of the Urengoy gas field, one of the largest in the world, which produces about half of Russian gas. Urengoy has a population of 100,000 people. In 2012, the Urengoy authorities imposed restrictions on entry to the town, justifying the use of such harsh measures as necessary to protect the town from an uncontrolled flow of migrants, a sharp rise in crime and drug trafficking, as well as an influx of radical Muslims (Klevtsova 2012).

The restriction was to be limited to unauthorised entry of visitors, people arriving uninvited, without work permits or documents on a business trip. Under the new rules, those who wish to visit Urengoy should pre-apply for a special permit to enter and this procedure will take four weeks for Russian citizens.

In Russia, there are two types of cities with limited access – 'closed cities', where there are strategic military or nuclear facilities; and border towns. In Urengoy there were no military or nuclear facilities, so the authorities declared Urengoy to be a border town – a strange decision considering the city is far away from the border.

Meanwhile, crossing posts are set at the entrances to the town. Visitors who do not have permission are not granted entry to the town, and those travelling without proper documentation by rail are stopped at the station 70 kilometres from the town. Earlier, similar restrictions on admission were introduced in Norilsk, where there are nickel mines, but those measures basically concerned foreigners (Klevtsova 2012). The result of restrictions on entry to Urengoy was the creation of a more comfortable environment of arbitrage for the Gazprom entrepreneurs who were close to executives of the municipality.

The same straightforward approach to cutting competition is shown by the following case, taken from the agricultural industry of the Voronezh region. In 2012, the company AGROEKO commissioned three modern complexes in the region for about 130,000 pigs. Later, in 2013, the company announced the start of construction of two pig farms and a feed mill in the region. The total cost of these projects reached 6 billion roubles, allowing long-term production of around 100,000 tonnes of pork per year. The company was established in late 2009 in Voronezh by the sole founder of the Cypriot ECO Agribusiness Holdings Ltd and the ultimate beneficiaries are not officially disclosed. But market participants are confident that the company belong to the family of the regional governor (Stranagordeev 2013).

The company has managed to lobby a loan of the amount of 4.5 billion roubles from the state VEB (Vnesheconombank) for the construction the first three pig farms. Moreover, in December 2010 the Ministry of Agriculture included this agriculture project in the list of those receiving subsidies from the federal budget to cover the cost of paying interest on the loan (Stranagordeev 2013). But there was one problem that slowed the project: thousands of regional peasants had thousands of pigs and sold pork for a more attractive price. However, a miracle happened: by a strange coincidence, an epidemic of African swine fever occurred in 2011, in the year of launch in the Voronezh region of the first pig farm of the governor's company. It is puzzling that the former Minister of Agriculture and academic Gordeev could not contain the epidemic, which in the Soviet Union would have been done in less than a month (Stranagordeev 2013).

Markov (2013) notes that in the interest of the governor's business all of the farmers' pigs were systematically destroyed. This was done under the pretext that the region had, allegedly, a raging epidemic of African swine fever. However, a Veterinary Inspection employee stated that in the region's hunting areas there are about 3,000 wild boar, of which 250 had their heads blown off, and none of which was found to carry the disease. Moreover, in the southern region, on the border with the Rostov and Volgograd region, laboratory studies did not identify the disease at all.

In such cases, quarantine and simple monitoring by supervisory authorities would usually be enough to keep the situation under control. In terms of the epidemiological risk, of course, there was no sense in destroying the pigs on this scale (Markov 2013).

Markov (2013) notes that regional authorities selectively executed the decree of the governor in the establishment of the quarantine. They destroyed up to 4,000 pigs per week in the private farmsteads, but the population was fully preserved in large pig farms, removing competition in the region for the benefit of the business of the governor and his son. He describes the extremely cruel approach to destruction of peasant pigs. First, the 'firing squads' do not make any veterinary documents confirming the existence of swine plague. Second, the methods of destruction used were most barbaric. After the injection of sleeping pills, pigs were piled in a pit and set on fire. The pigs woke up burning alive. The top layer burned as the bottom was crawling with live pigs. Some got out, and were burned running around the field. The dead pigs lay in the sun for several days. Birds carried the meat throughout the county. If it was really a plague, it could have been a catastrophe (ibid.). Children watching this scene and then Hollywood horrors perceived them as funny cartoons.

Conclusion

This chapter reveals causes that establish price differences and specific opportunities for realisation of arbitrage. One can see that in many cases prices on different markets are a result not of the independence of market forces, but of purposeful activity of a narrow group of participants who are the main beneficiaries of purposeful arbitrage operations. However, there are opportunities for other participants to slip into the narrow hole of arbitrage – firstly for companies that are able to make an appropriate market analysis and decisions more quickly than others; and secondly for companies that are able to find legal loopholes or violate laws without sentiment.

Analysis of cases from the agro and food industries reveals that Russian companies together with regional authorities regularly create conditions for arbitrage by generating trade barriers for regional export and import operations. Authorities employ barter and non-market prices for agricultural products and limit the export of subsidised products outside their territories. This policy leads to an increase in supply and, consequently, a relative reduction in procurement prices for agricultural products, which is a foundation for price asymmetries. Additionally, the authorities employ a range of methods for creating and ensuring arbitrage conditions, such as employing police forces, and phytosanitary and veterinary controls. In addition, the subsidies paid to farmers eventually are obtained by large agricultural processing companies that are under the direct or indirect control of authorities; therefore subsidies intended for peasants are transformed to arbitrage profit of new aristocrats.

Arbitrage conditions exist across the spectrum of time; that is, they can be realised for both long and relatively short periods of time. Long-term conditions usually rely on the legislative system, whereas short-term conditions depend mainly on solutions of territorial rulers. Frequently, a relationship with a ruler is a dominant factor because the law has less influence than a ruler's decree.

Cases show that successful arbitrageurs have access to confidential information, creating possibilities that are unavailable to other market participants. One can say about this information asymmetry that, for those who are not included in the list of successful arbitrageurs, there are prohibitively high costs of access to information and subsequently high costs of negotiation and lack of access to regulators. This chapter reveals, through the different examples presented, that the arbitrageur has a significantly greater ability to sell services than its competitors due to the proximity of the winner to power and special conditions which set it apart from other participants.

Also essential for arbitrage, in many cases, is access to market infrastructure. The cases reveal the elaborate approaches taken to sidelining competitors. Authorities create conditions for arbitrageurs, cutting off unwanted market participants, sometimes physically preventing their activity in a given region.

In the Russian Sea case, thanks to its powerful lobbying capabilities the company Russian Sea was able to restrict access for independent producers and sellers of fish by using the state regulator, and it was possible to receive arbitrage income for a long time. Also, barriers can be created by various industry regulators in the sphere of technical standards and regulations. Consequently, many participants in the market are eliminated and conditions for arbitrage are built for companies that manage to build a confident interaction with state regulators.

The ability to create conditions for arbitrage is an important resource for a company. In many situations it is a critically important factor of success, as not everyone can create such conditions. In our cases, conditions for arbitrage are valuable, rare, inimitable and nonsubstitutable resources of the companies. If other firms can easily copy an arbitrage capability, it will not be a significant source of advantage.

6   Product arbitrages

Chapter 6 examines in depth goods arbitrage as a transaction of purchase and sale with settlements in the form of barter operations, and reveals how geographical disparities, poor connections and bureaucratic barriers generate conditions for price asymmetries. It shows that companies affiliated with the establishment can hedge the market risk of adverse price changes in assets trading with the federal and regional authorities. In addition, such companies can limit the access of other companies to information and participation on the market. The case of the Russian gas giant Gazprom shows that the company widely uses arbitrage of product by restricting access of independent gas producers to the Gazprom gas distribution network and also by supporting artificial quotas for gas consumers, encouraging customers to buy gas at market prices from their subsidiaries, which appear here as arbitrageurs.

Barter as arbitrage

Arbitrage is an approach of using differences between countries or regions by buying and selling, in a short period of time, in order to take advantage of different prices. Initially, arbitrage was developed as product arbitrage; for example, in medieval times, sellers merchandised goods in Kievan Rus': swapping iron for furs was an exceptionally profitable business as well as extremely risky. Historically, goods arbitrage has been the most widespread arbitrage operation.

As noted in Chapter 3, the Russian Federation includes a number of regions and there is distance between them in culture, administrative and institutional contexts and in geography. In the Soviet time, the government tried to support the development of the majority of regions through low transport tariffs, by subsidies for depressed regions and harmonious deployment of manufacturing and social facilities in the giant space of the country. Developed agriculture in the south of the country, industrial production in the centre and minerals in the north and east created the continental trade that supported the economic unity of the country.

Despite the development of transport and communication in the previous century, many Russian regions have relatively weak connections with each other. Moreover, after the Soviet planned economy was broken, the diversity of the country increased, worsening conditions for business and the sustainability of the economy. Geographical differences, weak connections and administrative barriers create conditions for price asymmetries that give opportunities for product arbitrage.

Goods arbitrage as transaction of purchase and sale can be realised with money for settlements and in the form of barter operations. Barter, that is, the direct exchange of goods and services, has existed since primitive tribes with the exchange of cows for a bride. James Fenimore Cooper describes barter between palefaces and American Indians in his novels. And, of course, constant agents of barter are collectors, car owners and other people willing to share discrete goods in order to optimise compositions of collections. In the Soviet economy, barter was the traditional method of settlement between citizens and a rather exotic operation between organisations; however, since Gorbachev's *perestroika* many non-state companies employed barter in domestic and in international trade; moreover, it was one of the principal sources of the initial accumulation of capital in Russia.

In 1992, after the liberalisation of prices, barter quickly became extremely common. Many companies did not have cash in current accounts; however, they had finished goods in warehouses, and they conducted settlements using barter and thereby managed to maintain a normal business process. Thus barter helped to accelerate the turnover of capital under the conditions of an unreliable banking system and shortage of working capital. Barter was used in all segments of the national economy, but more widely in the agrarian segment. For example, on the domestic grain market the share of products sold via barter was increased from 23.4 per cent in 1991 to 55.1 per cent in 1999. Most farmers paid for agricultural machinery, fuel, fertiliser, services of transport enterprises, and the salaries of their own employees by way of grain supplies (Csaki *et al.* 2002).

Barter transactions were actively used in linked technological cycles, for example Gazprom swapped natural gas for the electricity from power stations, and metallurgical companies swapped their products for the products of coal miners and for the transport services of railways. Makarov and Kleiner (1996) note that in the mid-1990s barter made up from 34 to 50 per cent of the total industrial turnover. Moreover, barter covered not only the relations between enterprises, but the relationships between businesses and federal and local budgets.

Barter operations used finished products of companies as surrogates for salaries. Enterprises that did not have the cash to pay salaries allowed employees to sell finished products and take the income themselves. Consequently, workers traded metal utensils, sugar, cut glass, women's underwear, toilet paper and more on primitive markets or motorways. There are some unusual cases of employing barter, for example Belchenko (2011) recounts how in the Krasnoyarsk region Hladko cold storage workers were offered to take unpaid wages and severance pay as frozen seafood and caviar. A kilogram of caviar was 1,500 roubles whereas the market price was 25,000 roubles. The workers were happy and accepted the wages; however, they did not take into account that the shops did not take caviar without sale documents, and Krasnoyarsk was not in easy reach of a city, therefore it was very difficult to sell hundreds of kilograms of the delicacy at one time.

In addition, Russian entrepreneurs found that barter transactions can create additional benefits. Participants in barter exchanged their products at prices that could be noticeably lower than the market price. As a result, companies diminished their declared turnover and consequently paid less tax. Weak fiscal agencies attempted to fight this tax evasion by forbidding trade operations at prices below prime cost, but in answer businesses created more complicated multistage barter constructions (Berezkin 2006).

Also, many companies had debts to large energy suppliers such as Gazprom or Unified Energy System of Russia, which could withdraw funds from accounts without participation of the owner. In this case, to maintain operational activity, companies needed to avoid using their bank accounts by exploiting barter.

Berezkin (2006) notes that barter is often based on the discounted price of goods. The criteria for setting the discount factors are the different views of the participants and the differences in liquidity of the products to be exchanged. More liquid goods are exchanged for discounted, less liquid products. Usually, where there are barter transactions, there is the cash price (for sale in real money); the barter price (taken on account in exchange for other goods or services); and *otkat* (kickback), which is paid to particular individuals, typically executives of the company, for assistance in signing a transaction. These three prices represent a simple variety of operating under barter, which typically involved complex chains of transactions (ibid.).

Dufy (2005) notes that the peak of using of barter came in the financial crisis of 1998, at 51 per cent of total economic activity. Makarov and Kleiner (1996) note that the economy of Russia in the 1990s may be referred to as a barter economy due to the scope of barter in industry and wholesale trade. Nevertheless, it was down to 35 per cent in 1999 and then decreased to 15 per cent in 2002. Although barter is no longer widely used in the Russian economy, it retains a certain position in the practice of business (Dufy 2005).

Under normal conditions, barter includes greater transaction costs than money transactions (Polterovich 1999). Therefore after 2000, when economic conditions improved, barter was used mainly in situations of significant deficit of working capital, to carry out transactions between business partners and as an instrument of trade intermediaries, which exploit mostly traditional arbitrage: simultaneously selling and buying goods or services.

There are two different groups of mediators, although this division is rather arbitrary. The first group of intermediaries are concentrated around a large enterprise or group of enterprises of a particular industry. Having significant industrial knowledge and good relationship with executives of a company, for example Gazprom, they build a chain of barter combination in the sale of products of the main company (Gazprom). They arbitrage difference in prices of gas and other products that participate in the barter exchange. As a result of this chain, gas can be swapped for pulp, which is exchanged for tyres, which are sold to car distributors for cash, which is distributed between participants.

Intermediaries can have working capital and use it for buying manufactured goods and then sell them either to the consumer or use these products for further processing. Additionally, there are considerable variations in the time taken to get cash, from zero to a few months. Frequently, enterprises are forced to accept proposals of the mediators for the supply of intermediate goods, which are raw materials for these businesses, and to pay their finished products due to the lack of capital for the independent purchase of the raw materials on the market. If the company has an intermediate which purchases ready products and also supplies raw materials, it can transform from an independent producer enterprise to a service provider, working exclusively with 'customer-furnished' raw materials.

This approach was used by Trans World Group (TWG) in the early 1990s when the company controlled a large share of the Russian aluminium industry by using a species of barter – tolling schemes. TWG supplied imported alumina to Russian manufacturers, which refined the alumina, producing aluminium which was exported from the country by TWG (Behar 2000). In this case, the mediator had excellent opportunities to control the prices of final products; it managed to employ the production capacity of the large aluminium enterprises and yet did not have the associated amortisation and labour expenditures.

The second group of mediators are organisations that have sufficiently broad connections and communication capabilities and these intermediaries develop multi-way barter combinations. Usually they do not have a significant initial capital, but they have to have good relationships with executives of companies that participate in barter.

Berezkin (2006) gives an example of the scheme of non-cash payments between industrial companies with the involvement of intermediary firms. Two large enterprises, which had previously worked in one production chain, had overdue receivables. So the first company, VostSibUgol (VSU), was ready to supply coal for $4 million but subject to cash settlement. The second company, Sayanskkhimprom, used the coal but, due to financial difficulties, it bought coal with a significantly delayed payment that was not satisfied with the vendor. Hence there was a gap in the normal operation of both companies.

At the same time, there were commercial firms that specialised in import and export operations and there was asymmetry of prices between the domestic and foreign markets: on imported goods, domestic prices were higher; on exported goods, external prices were higher than domestic.

This situation with the price asymmetry can be converted into a base for organising the arbitrage scheme. The main idea of the scheme is: VSU sells coal to Sayanskkhimprom and it pays using its products, not to the supplier but to certain intermediary firms. These, in turn, after a series of export–import operations carried out under commission, will pay VSU. Accordingly, a multi-lateral treaty was concluded. The essence of the agreement was: VostSibUgol supplies coal for $4 million to the arbitrageur (fund FP). FP undertakes to pay this delivery fully within two weeks. Then FP supplies this coal to Sayanskkhimprom, provided the immediate transfer of the same amount of products to company AIS.

AIS accepts the chemical products on $4 million and sells it on the foreign markets, and in one week it supplies to FP imported products by the same amount. FP sells imported products on the domestic market to the amount of $5 million. From the proceeds from the sale of imported products, FP pays to VSU $4 million. As a result, VSU sold coal with no receivables, Sayansk-khimprom got coal without using cash, AIS received interest on a commission, and fund FP had an income of $1 million.

One can see the positive results of arbitrage – but there is a fly in the ointment. We may suppose that products were sold on the Chinese market with a large discount, and when Sayanskkhimprom wanted to sell its chemical products there, it would meet customers with expectations of low price. Unquestionably, the arbitrageur could not create high profit without a favourable relationship with the executives of Sayanskkhimprom. This financial scheme was widely employed for 20 years of the Russian reform, and continues to a lesser extent.

As noted above, the peak of barter was at the end of the 1990s. More recently, barter has been used mostly for tax optimisation (see Chapter 8). However, the new financial crisis of 2008 gave a new impulse for barter and opportunities for arbitrageurs that offered new approaches. For instance, in late 2008 the Anti-Crisis Settlement and Commodity Centre (ARCT) was created by Herman Sterligov with a view to creating a barter chain between enterprises that had complications with selling of their products in the absence of effective demand. ARCT's network was based on the franchise scheme, where regional partners received software from ARCT and had to pay a monthly fee to the central office. ARCT used a simple mechanism: a client reserves an application in the computer system which indicates what items it needs and what it can offer in return, such as money, goods or debts of its customers. A program automatically builds a chain of exchange from five to ten units long, and circulates it to all participants. Subsequently, members of the chain independently realise a deal (Belchenko 2011).

The last link of the barter chain is always a company with money, and money is treated as a product in the system. For example, a barter chain could be as follows: metallurgists supply steel for a machine-building plant that makes and sells harvesters to agribusiness. But an agrarian cannot pay for the harvester and cannot borrow from the bank; consequently the whole chain is stopped. ARCT finds a company with money and that needs grain. It pays the debts of the machine-building plant to the metallurgists and consequently obtains grain from the farmers. The chain is closed (ibid.).

Entrepreneurs transfer to ARCT 2 per cent of the stated amount of the transaction. This money is a guarantee that the company has goods. When the agreement is closed, its members can pick up half the guarantee fee; the other half is ARCT's commission. In 2009 ARCT managed to collect bids for $1 billion. However, shortly afterwards the project was cancelled due to internal problems between business partners and because 'the crisis was not as deep as we thought, and our anti-crisis mechanisms were not in demand' (Business Petersburg 2010). The ARCT case demonstrates again that barter originates as a compensatory mechanism in the lack of working capital of companies and provides a good opportunity for arbitrage. However, undeveloped institutions were blocking implementation of multistage barter proposed by ARCT.

Time arbitrage

Theoretically, it is possible to arbitrage commodities employing differences between prices that arise at different times, provided the cost of money for a particular company (own or debt) is lower than the difference between prices. This strategy looks like a traditional speculation where a speculator in a commodity tries to predict the future, accepting the market risk in return for the opportunity for additional income as a result of favourable changes in market prices. Nevertheless, in the Russian case the market risk of adverse price changes in asset trading could be hedged by the federal and regional authorities due to the close relationships between business and authorities. A hedge in this context means that, in the case of unfavourable development of the situation, the losses will be covered by the state. This strategy is easily described by a simple phrase: failure divides equally but earnings distribute to yourself. Also, this strategy could be performed if the company could borrow money on the market at a relatively low interest rate. The case of the coal industry demonstrates this arbitrage strategy.

Characteristic of the business of many enterprises in 1990s was highly speculative resale of material resources such as metal, petroleum products and construction materials (Kuvalin 1995). A number of companies were able to acquire these resources at prices significantly below the average by using barter or by obtaining products subsidised by the state. The rapid growth of the price for resources, opportunities to store them and, after some time, to sell these stocks gave a significant profit. The procurement department of the mine Raspadskaya at first used an opportunity to purchase large quantities of metal, even if the mine did not need it. But after some time, when the management of the mine ordered the purchasing department to buy the necessary materials or equipment, it used their accumulated stocks of metal as currency. Metal was being sold for obtaining the necessary money or exchanged by barter. After the purchase, the price of the metal usually rose more than the price of the necessary equipment and for such transactions the mine received additional financial benefits.

Therefore such transactions allow the purchasing department to compensate rather effectively for the shortage of working capital (ibid.). It may be noted that delayed payment in times of high inflation was extremely profitable in Russia. Undeveloped institutions and poor work of bailiffs created conditions for such delay of payment. In this regard, it can be said that the delay in the payment of high inflation can be considered as a sort of arbitrage.

In many regions, companies sought to receive from the authorities the right to delay their payments to creditors. For example, in 1994 refineries and chemical plants of Bashkiria, thanks to the support of the government of the Republic, paid no more than 10–15 per cent of the cost of utilities (heat and electricity). Moreover, regional authorities actually prohibited the electricity and energy providers from stopping the power supply to the plants, threatening to dismiss the management of the company (Kuvalin 2009).

Gazprom arbitrage

Russian Gazprom is the largest extractor of natural gas and the largest company in Russia. Gazprom accounts for 15 per cent of global gas output and controls an 18 per cent share of worldwide gas reserves. The company produced around 513 billion cubic metres (cbm) of natural gas. Russia is the principal gas market for Gazprom. The company sells 262.1 billion cbm in the domestic market, more than half of its production. Unified Gas Supply System (UGS) is the world's largest gas transmission system and represents a unique technological complex, which includes 161,700 km of trunk and lateral pipelines, 215 linear compressor stations and 25 underground gas storage facilities (Gazprom 2013).

In addition, Gazprom has the fifth top position among Russian oil producers and produces the largest share of electricity in the country. In 2011 it accounted for 8 per cent of Russian GDP. The company has subsidiaries in different sectors, including finance, media and aviation, and controls a majority stake in various companies (Gazprom 2013).

Considerable size and diversification, together with its significance to state authorities and Gazprom's activity in various social projects (often with opaque objectives and budgets, such as the sponsorship of the football team Zenith or participation in the construction of the Olympic arenas in Sochi), make the company a participant in arbitrage with a variety of financial outcomes. Several cases reveal arbitrage more clearly.

Purchase of equipment

In June 2008, the small enterprise Slavimpeks signed a contract with OJSC Power Machines, which is one of the largest manufacturers of power equipment in Russia, for the supply of steam turbines and turbo-generators. The cost of the contract was about €60 million and the customer paid a prepayment around $1 million (Navalny 2009).

A month later, Gazprom finally adopted a programme of development of its power segments where it stipulated the purchase of the turbine and turbo-generator for the Cherepovets power station which belonged to OGK-6. OGK-6 is large energy producer with capitalisation of around $1 billion, and the main shareholder of the company was Gazprom, which owned around 60 per cent of its shares. Two months after the start of the Gazprom programme, Slavimpeks offered the equipment to Gazprom (ibid.). Gazprom did not consider for long, and by the end of 2008 Slavimpeks agreed to sell the contract OGK-6, ceding it for about $10 million (Navalny 2009; Mazneva and Peretolchina 2009).

Consequently, Power Machines made the turbine for Gazprom, the turbine was worth €60 million, but Gazprom paid €60 million and the additional $10 million. The simple arbitrage operation gave a profit to Slavimpeks of $10 million (Navalny 2009). Of course, one can find cases, for instance in the machine-building industry, where contracts for the supply of something are outbid. But it generally happens when the manufacture is intensely overloaded. In the case of Gazprom, nobody was in a hurry.

Purchase of gas at independent producers

Most of the major independent gas producers in Russia, such as Northgas, Novatek and Itera, were created with the active participation of Gazprom executives and were given Gazprom gas fields into operation. In 1998 six independent companies delivered 28.2 billion cbm of gas, but in 2010 23 independent companies sold 89.3 billion cbm of gas (Gazprom 2013).

Russian Gazprom, in contrast to US or EU companies, is a closed monopoly, protected from competition by the legislative restrictions. The Russian market consists of a regulated segment where the major supplier, Gazprom, is selling gas on the domestic market at prices regulated by the Federal Energy Commission (FEC); and an unregulated segment where independent gas companies have the right to sell gas at market prices. However, independent gas companies cannot sell gas on the foreign market, and their opportunity to sell gas to Russia at market prices is offset by higher transportation tariffs, which are established by Gazprom.

Russia has legislation which regulates access of organisations to the gas transmission system (GTS) and gas distribution networks; according to the legislation, owners of gas supply systems (Gazprom) are required to ensure non-discriminatory access by any organisation to the free capacity of their gas transmission and distribution networks (Presidential Decree 1992; Federal Law 1999; Government Decree 1997).

According to the government resolution, the monopolist must provide access to pipelines of independent companies if Gazprom has free capacities, if these companies have a licence to extract gas and a contract with the buyer of gas, and if their gas corresponds to technical standards. But the key concept 'free capacity' was not disclosed by the legislator, which gives Gazprom, the owner of the Unified Gas Supply System, the right to determine free capacity. The law does not provide for the possibility of regulatory bodies to monitor the technical capabilities of Gazprom. A regulatory framework for liability of the GTS for failure to provide, or untimely provision of, access to the gas transmission system in the presence of technical opportunities was not installed. All this places users of the GTS in an almost feudal dependence on Gazprom.

On the Russian domestic market, Gazprom operates via its 100 per cent subsidiary Mezhregiongaz, which is able to buy some gas from the independent gas producers (MRG 2013). In the case analysed, Mezhregiongaz bought gas from the independent gas producer Novatek via an intermediary, Trastinvestgaz (TIG), which was an insignificant wholesale trader of crude oil in 2005–06 (Mazneva and Nikolsky 2008). TIG sold gas at the same points of the pipeline systems from which it bought the gas from Novatek, and therefore it did not have gas transport expenditure. In 2005 the average contract price between Mezhregiongaz and TIG was 915 roubles per 1,000 cbm, whereas the direct contract price between Mezhregiongaz and Novatek was 540 roubles per 1,000 cbm, around 70 per cent of the TIG price. In 2006 the price ratio had fallen further, to 44 per cent. In total, Gazprom bought 4.5 billion cbm from TIG and the arbitrage difference (i.e. Gazprom losses) was 1.49 billion roubles (Mazneva and Nikolsky 2008).

It is interesting that executives of Gazprom have considered that Gazprom did not suffer damage from contracts with TIG because resale of the gas from TIG brought Mezhregiongaz more than $20 million in 2005–06 and the company did not have enough gas from Novatek. Moreover, TIG was the owner of the additional gas and bought gas on the free market (ibid.). However, Gazprom profit could be higher if there was a direct contract without intermediaries. Concerning this, Navalny (2008) notes that TIG was credited by Gazprom and all money earned by TIG was channelled through consulting services that reduced taxation to zero. A criminal case about theft of money from Mezhregiongaz was opened but it did not reach any result because, as supposed by Shleinov (2008), TIG was controlled by people close to friends of the Prime Minister.

Anti-arbitrage strategy

The Russian gas legislation, together with exceptionally powerful Gazprom lobbyists (such as Prime Ministers Viktor Chernomyrdin and Dmitry Medvedev), made it possible to destroy arbitrage of insignificant competitors: realisation of an anti-arbitrage strategy.

Derbilova and Reznik (2004) give examples of practical implementation of this strategy when, in 2004, Gazprom completely stopped gas extraction from the independent producers Rospan and reduced gas intake in the pipelines by 50 and 30 per cent from Northgas and Novatek, respectively. Gazprom justified this decision by demonstrating that the gas produced by these companies was not picked up entirely by their customers. After that, Gazprom tried to put pressure on gas producers, forcing them to sell the gas to it at about a third of the price. Consequently, Rospan sold to Gazprom all gas produced directly at the well (about 10 million cbm per day) at a mutually beneficial price (Grivach 2004). Also, Gazprom accepted applications for pumping gas for an exceptionally long time (Derbilova and Reznik 2004) which hampered opportunities for short-term gas arbitrage.

For 15 years the Federal Antimonopoly Service (FAS) quietly considered limiting access by Gazprom to the gas transport networks, and in early 2009, for the first time, the FAS fined Gazprom 157.7 million roubles for refusing independent gas producer TransNafta access to the main pipeline. According to the FAS, Gazprom was hindering the realisation of long-term contracts of independent producers. Moreover, FAS found that Gazprom had free capacity to satisfy the request of TransNafta (Rybalchenko 2009).

A comparable approach was realised by Gazprom with oil companies in the utilisation of associated petroleum gas (APG). In 2009 alone, the top seven oil companies burned 19.96 billion cbm of APG, 64.3 per cent of total APG (Kostenko and Malkova 2010). As a result, the losses of the oil industry could exceed $1.3 billion in damages based on the domestic price of natural gas (1,920 roubles per 1,000 cbm). If damages were calculated using the average Gazprom price in Europe ($285), losses would have increased to $5.7 billion. For example, in October 2009 the Russian largest oil company, Rosneft, said that the gas monopoly refused to accept its associated gas via the transportation system. As a result, Rosneft needed to burn gas to the value of 151.8 million roubles and additionally was fined 14.7 million roubles for violation of environmental laws (Oreanda 2009).

Despite the state regulation of prices, the Russian gas market has always been attractive for Gazprom. Even at undervalued prices, unsatisfied demand allowed the company to sell to consumers additional volumes of gas at a price significantly higher than the regulated price. Additionally, declining capacity in the traditional Gazprom gas fields forced the company to buy gas at the wells of independent companies to cover the deficit of its own gas. For this purpose, Gazprom sought legal and technological loopholes and as a result, complicated access to the gas pipeline system; this forced independent producers to sell their gas at the wells thereby diminishing the arbitrage income of independent gas producers.

Such anti-arbitrage strategy of Gazprom, and its monopoly as a supplier of gas transportation services, does not allow independent producers to develop dynamically. Gas field development projects require considerable investment; the payback period exceeds 5–7 years, therefore it is very difficult to attract investment. Frequently, transportation in the domestic market at market rates is unprofitable. Transit fares and transportation routes are established by Gazprom on its own terms and do not take into account the interests of other market operators which cannot access profitable foreign markets. The declared goal of the company to become a global energy leader was unachievable because the company used a narrow range of strategic tools. As a result, Gazprom could not foresee the technological revolution in the gas industry that has resulted in a large-scale expansion of liquefied natural gas and the shale revolution.

Currently, in the global market there are dissimilar approaches providing flexibility in the supply of gas. For instance, the US gas-supply system actively uses storage to balance high and low gas pressure as well as to cover peak fields. Other various technological and financial instruments help to maintain the balance of supply and demand. There are contracts with customers such as take or pay, and special system rates that are charged for exceeding the selection and not fully taking gas from the system (Natural Gas 2014). Gazprom does not use these tools widely. The Russian system of gas supply does not have the necessary flexibility for further effective development; there are no economic incentives for the development of a fair market for natural gas.

Gazprom realises simultaneously two generic strategies: arbitrage and anti-arbitrage. In this approach there is no contradiction, however, rather they complement each other. The anti-arbitrage strategy helps to reduce competition in the gas market and reduce supply on the market, whereas the arbitrage strategy forms high price asymmetry, making high company returns. In the analysis of these two strategies, we are faced with the dialectical relationship between them: the unity and struggle of opposites (the concept of Hegel and Engels). On one hand, both strategies complement each other by increasing the margin from operations and will eventually profit the company. On the other hand, these strategies have different orientations: the arbitrage strategy aims to increase the difference between prices in different markets, whereas the anti-arbitrage strategy aims to reduce the impact of competitors. Also, it should be noted that full implementation of the anti-arbitrage strategy – elimination of all rivals – can lead to the degradation of the company's resource base, thus Gazprom needs to offset its arbitrage and anti-arbitrage strategies.

Selling of gas

Russia is the primary gas market for Gazprom. The company sells 262.1 billion cbm in the domestic market, which is more than half of its production. Currently the Russian market consists of two segments: regulated, where Gazprom is the major supplier; and deregulated. According to Russian legislation, gas produced by Gazprom is marketed to domestic consumers, mainly at state-regulated prices. The Federal Tariff Service (FTS) of Russia approves particular regulated wholesale prices for different price zones with regard to consumer types and distance from gas production regions (Gazprom 2013).

There is a difference in price formation for gas between domestic and external markets. On the external markets, Gazprom operates mainly under long-term contracts linked with oil prices that are generally derived from intergovernmental agreements. In the long-term contracts, price formulae take into account oil prices for the preceding 6–9 months. Also, many contracts employ take-or-pay commitments that the purchasers should pay for the volumes that have not been accepted by them for the period of a year, and these may be received afterwards after distribution of the minimum annual volumes contracted for the specified year and with the applicable additional payment (ibid.).

Gazprom's export market, and arbitrage operations acting upon it, are of interest for analysis. Consider the long-term gas conflict between Russia and Ukraine, where intermediaries play an important role carrying out arbitrage between the external and internal gas prices. This extraordinary story goes beyond the scope of this book. On the Russian internal market, prices are regulated by federal and regional authorities. However, since 2006 the government has been taking steps toward developing the Russian gas market in accordance with market principles. Consequently the company was allowed to distribute gas to a certain consumer group at contract prices, while the FTS regulates the upper price threshold which was equal to 10 per cent of the regulated price in 2011.

In 2010, the government specified a transitional period when wholesale gas prices would be regulated for all industrial consumers on the basis of a price formula stipulating staged transition to homogeneous gas sales on both external and internal markets, taking into account the cost of alternative fuels. From 2006 to 2008 natural gas was experimentally traded at free market prices via the electronic trading platform (ETP) of Gazprom Mezhregiongaz, the company's trading subdivision, and in 2008 the total sales volume at the ETP made up 3.1 billion. The bulk of gas was purchased by power-generating companies (Gazprom 2013).

As a result of state regulation in the gas industry, Gazprom's subsidiaries establish quotas for gas consumers, namely a set limit of gas which a particular user can obtain from the main gas pipeline. This scheme is related to the fact that the gas pipeline capacity is limited and the volume of transported gas is distributed in advance, in accordance with the submitted quotas for gas. Of course, any company can buy gas from independent suppliers at free market prices, which are much higher.

Usually the quotas were set at the time of the connection of a company to the gas pipe and at this stage correspond with real demands. But after some time, when an enterprise's need for gas may increase, it will find it difficult to increase the quotas. As a result, a company needs to buy gas on the free market, which is controlled by Gazprom. This forms a situation for arbitrage where there is both a consumer capable of paying a higher price and an arbitrageur capable of buying gas at a discounted price. However, there is one unclear question: Who will be the beneficiary of arbitrage? The next case shows how it was done in Gazprom.

Quotas for gas

TGC-1 was created in 2005 and is the principal manufacturer of electricity in the North-West region of Russia. It operates 55 electricity-generating stations in four regions of Russia which use natural gas from the Gazprom pipes (TGC-1 2013). In 2006, demand from TGC-1 for servicing St Petersburg and the surrounding region in natural gas amounted to 4.86 billion cbm. However, the quota allocated by Gazprom was only 4.34 billion cbm a year. Thus there was a deficit of gas and TGC-1 needed to find an additional 10 per cent of gas over the quota (Kozyrev 2011).

The energy company sent dozens of letters to various divisions of Gazprom trying to increase the quota of gas, but to no avail. Fortunately, the company found a mediator which offered to find contractors and sign agreements with them for supplying additional volumes of gas of around 400 million cbm. In turn, TGC-1 had to pay for gas with a premium of 50 per cent. Through the mediation of PoiskKoma, TGC-1 received from Mezhregiongaz, and its affiliated Peterburgregiongaz, about 400 million cbm. Thus the hole in the fuel balance of the company was almost completely covered (ibid.).

Kozyrev (2011) noted that there were many similar cases. For example, in 2006 Eurocement, the largest cement producer in Russia, needed to pay an intermediary for the supply of an additional 200 million cbm of gas worth about $1 million; TGK-2, located adjacent to the TGC-1, paid about $18 million to an intermediary for additional gas (ibid.).

Krasavin & Makeev (2006) note that in 2006 there was misbalance between data from Gazprom and Mezhregiongaz. According to the group itself, it amounted to 307 billion cbm, but according to Mezhregiongaz data the figure was lower, at 290 billion cbm. Companies did not talk about the fate of the rest of the gas, which at current prices was worth in excess of $600 million, and it is possible that this gas was sold at above quota conditions.

In the three cases of Gazprom: purchase of equipment, purchase of gas from independent producers, and selling of gas on the domestic market, Gazprom bosses used arbitrage of product. They themselves created conditions for arbitrage, such as price asymmetries between the purchase price for Gazprom and the sale price of the real supplier, and by restricting the access of independent companies to information about, and participation in, tenders. This allows accumulation of profits in the accounts of arbitraging firms.

In the case of the purchase of gas by independent producers, one can see that Gazprom managers restrict access to the Gazprom gas distribution network. This reduces the price of the gas from these independent producers, allowing further resale of this gas, accumulating profits in the accounts of the arbitrage firms. In the third case (selling of gas on the domestic market), Gazprom creates conditions for arbitrage by supporting artificial quotas for gas consumers and by closing the access of independent producers to pipelines, thereby creating price differences and enabling arbitrage.

The ability to create conditions for arbitrage is an important resource of a company; in many situations it is a critically important factor of success of the business, as not everyone can create such conditions for arbitrage. Moreover, in some situations the ability of a company to create conditions for arbitrage is a more important resource than brand names, technology, skilled personnel, trade contacts and equipment, because it can lead to high incomes for a long time. As Wernerfelt (1984) notes, in some circumstances a holder of a resource is able to maintain a relative position with regard to other companies, on condition that they act rationally. In these situations the holder is protected by a resource position barrier that is, to some extent, equivalent to entry barriers, and gives competitive advantage. Wernerfelt remarks that resources are stable factors and could not be varied in the short run, but the concept of time in economics is rather relative, and in our case an ability to create conditions for arbitrage depends on the embeddedness of a company, which is also variable with time.

Arbitrage in state companies

In previous chapters arbitrage has been determined as the purchase of goods and their subsequent sale at a higher price. However, by analogy with the opening of short positions in securities trading, one can create an arbitrage strategy that will initially sell the goods and then will buy them on the market. Simplifying, the arbitrageur always has two contracts: one for purchase and the second for sale, therefore the sequence in which buying and selling are implemented is flexible. The example below reveals some nuances of this strategy.

The Eastern Siberia–Pacific Ocean (ESPO) oil pipeline is a 4,857 km pipeline for exporting crude oil to the Asia–Pacific markets, built and operated by Transneft (the organisation of Transneft is described in Chapter 4). The first stage of the pipeline is 2,757 km long and runs from Taishet (Irkutsk region) to Skovorodino (Amur region). It was built in 2009 and cost around $14 billion (including the export terminal) (CUPVSTO 2013).

In 2006–07 Cyprus and Panama companies, with unknown owners, received contracts from Transneft. These companies did not have the technical, human and financial resources for effectively completing the design, installation and construction of oil pipelines (Rupor 2009). Consequently, the whole business of these companies was limited to a search for subcontractors who performed the work at a much lower cost than those that appeared in the contracts of Transneft with contractors, and for which the government funded the construction of the ESPO (Accounts Chamber 2008).

Then subsidiaries of Transneft concluded subcontracts with these companies according to directive letters of Transneft at recommended prices. The share of these subcontracts for subsidiaries and affiliates of Transneft was about one-third of all work on the ESPO. The difference between the value of the work for the general contract and subcontract ranged from 5 to 60 per cent (ibid.).

The most famous contractor of the project was a Cypriot company, Krasnodarstroytransgaz (the name appears as though the company was registered in the Krasnodar region of the Russian Federation). This off-the-shelf company was bought just before the start of the project and had only a title. However, the company received materials and equipment for approximately $1 billion plus more than $0.25 billion prepayment from Transneft (Rupor 2009).

A similar story occurred with design and survey works (R&D). The full volume of R&D was performed by a reputable design organisation, Giprotruboprovod, with its traditional subcontractors, but Transneft signed the agreement with VNIIST, which bought the main contract and sold it on to Giprotruboprovod and other subcontractors, a classic example of arbitrage. Net profit from this operation was around 20 per cent of the full cost of R&D, more than 2.1 billion roubles (Accounts Chamber 2008).

In 2009 the Accounts Chamber of the Russian Federation once more checked the expenditure of funds for the construction of the oil pipeline. Following the inspection, a criminal case was opened against the managers of the company for fraud amounting to 3.54 billion roubles (Accounts Chamber 2009). However, the results of the investigation of the Accounts Chamber were rapidly retracted, and Vladimir Putin stated that the results of audit of the Accounts Chamber of the activities of Transneft for the construction of ESPO found no criminal aspect to this case (RIA Novosti 2010).

A reader can say that some examples of arbitrage, such as the building of ESPO, are brilliant examples of corruption in Russia, where a manager of a state company uses their position to make a contract with affiliated offshore firms, consequently putting huge money into their own pocket. From an ethical point of view, it is straightforward. However, from an operational point of view it is arbitrage, therefore it enters the sphere of our analysis. Moreover, the modern understanding of the corrupt behaviour is not always relevant to the Russian economic system due to the Russian quasi-capitalism, where a position in the state company is often bought for money or is awarded to an associate under a condition of lifetime loyalty. Given such a position, managers often become eligible for feeding (*kormleniye*). Feeding is a relatively new phenomenon; however it has centuries-old historical roots. The Laws of Yaroslav the Wise, written in the first half of the eleventh century, had requirements that the population had to pay maintenance to princely officials (feed them), due to them having no salary entitlement from the Prince, hence the term 'feeding'. Such a system existed in Russia for nearly 700 years. Nevertheless, the philosophy of feeding as a form of relations between the authorities and society indubitably remained. In the system of feeding, official remuneration is not important, whereas opportunities for feeding (that is opportunities for self-enrichment) are extremely important. In accordance with this concept, the official salary of an officer or manager is not important because the appointment to the post of Minister is accompanied by a stake in state-owned companies and enjoys the profits from them. Every Russian administrator or official in any city or village receives a similar demonstration unequivocally: if it is possible for them, why not us? The following examples reveal the relationship of feeding and arbitrage in more detail; they also show the new technique of using arbitrage.

In Russia there are problems with the quality of assessment of state assets such as land, properties and businesses. This creates good opportunities for arbitrage of these assets. Russian privatisations of the 1990s gave numerous examples of near-simultaneous buying and selling of assets with high profit. The latest examples show that these practices never disappeared despite all the political rhetoric.

In the Moscow suburbs, land is cheaper than in the centre of London or New York, but it is of interest for investment. When the results of auctions that took place on 18 December 2007 and 14 March 2008 were published on the site of Mosleskhoz (Ukolov 2008), many citizens were extremely surprised. The auctions were notable not only for the sale of green belt land reserved for forestry, but also for the fact that the Moscow region land went under the hammer at a very low price – from 10 to 15 pence per square metre. In general, there were one or two bidders per lot and a maximum of three bids, not greatly increasing the final cost of the land. The largest lot (397 hectares) in the Bakovsky forest district, which is around 25 km from the Kremlin, was sold to Eco West for 24.39 million roubles, around 12 pence per square metre. Eco West belonged to Roman Abramovich (Ukolov 2008).

One year later, the government decided to promote innovation and so began to seek land for a dedicated innovation area. Among many offers of land, many of which were practically free, officials chose the most expensive plot of land, which belonged to Abramovich. According to the Russian legislation, withdrawal of lands can be made only by a special federal law. The land owner is compensated according to an independent evaluation of the market price. Thus the Abramovich land was bought back at a market value, which for the Skolkovo area is around $1 million for 1 hectare of land according to various estimates (£100 per square metre) (Sichkar and Granik 2010). Previously it was assumed that the innovation centre could be accommodated in Tomsk, Novosibirsk, St Petersburg or Obninsk (ibid.), which are traditional Russian scientific centres with cheaper land, infrastructure and staff than on the outskirts of Moscow. However, that would significantly reduce arbitrage opportunities for the project participants.

Also, near the Skolkovo Innovation Centre is a farm, Matveevskoe (about 2,000 hectares), of which a substantial part belongs to the company Millhouse, owned by Abramovich (Sichkar and Granik 2010). These lands were not initially included in the project, but they are near the Skolkovo Innovation Centre and development projects related to the Centre are likely to affect the land. Therefore the Abramovich company was able to sell the land profitably to investors.

Schemes of arbitrage with Abramovich land are not unique. In the past 10 years, with the state conducting nationalisation in some segments of the economy, arbitrage with land became very popular among companies affiliated with the authorities. For instance, when Transneft started to build the ESPO pipeline (see above and Chapter 5), it was planned that the oil terminal in Skovorodino, with a capacity of 15 million tonnes of oil, would be joined to the ESPO pipeline (Gavshina and Reznik 2010). However, it turned out that by that time the land for the terminal in Skovorodino was owned by the company ESN which belonged to Gregory Berezkin, who in the past was a close associate of Roman Abramovich and an executive of the large oil company Komi TEK (Novaya Gazeta 2004).

Transneft was given the task of carrying out the construction of ESPO in the shortest possible time. Therefore Transneft was forced to settle for the proposal of the owner of the land, Berezkin, in joint implementation of the project. Later, in August 2008, control of the terminal was passed from ESN to Transneft (Gavshina and Reznik 2010). Initially a private company, using inside information about the location and timing of the construction of the pipeline, bought the plot of land which then was sold to Transneft, effectively to the state. One can see that the state itself created the conditions for arbitrage: it knew about the construction and nevertheless sold the land.

Relatively similar cases can be seen in other segments of the property market. For instance, at the peak of the financial crisis in 2008, when all property rapidly lost value, the Russian Ministry of Regional Development bought the building of the Hungarian trade mission of 17,612 square metres based on two government contracts with Diamond Air for a total amount of 3.5 billion roubles (Luxembourg) (Dmitrienko 2012).

The company Diamond Air operated under an agency agreement with Innovative Technology Renova, which belongs to Russian oligarch Viktor Vekselberg, number four in the Russian listing of Forbes for 2013 with a net worth of $15.1 billion (Forbes 2013). In this case the Hungarian participant sold the building to Diamond Air for $21.3 million (about 575 million roubles). After the arbitrage operation, Diamond Air was liquidated (Dmitrienko 2012). One can see that with a flick of the wrist, signing two contracts, the arbitrageur profited by around 500 per cent. As a result Russian–Hungarian trade relations will be weaker; the budgets of both Hungary and Russia lost money because the first country sold the building at a lower price and the second bought it at inflated cost.

The successful bid of the Ministry of Regional Development for the Hungarian building sparked debate in the Russian mass media. Later a criminal case was opened, which established that the price of the building was set on the basis of the evaluation reports carried out and paid for by representatives of Renova. However, the enthusiasm of the detectives quickly dried up and they could not find evidence that Renova transactions were not made in full compliance with the Russian legislation (Dmitrienko 2012).

Schemes of arbitrage with land and property such as those analysed above are not unique, and have been used by many. The deputy of the head of the Legal Department of the Federal Property Agency, Konstantin Fradkin, describes some schemes that were implemented in the privatisation of state property (Pasmi 2013). The property can be transferred from federal to regional ownership under the pretext of performance of public social functions. Then the local parliament changes the intended purpose and the property is sold at reduced prices to close people. This is described as the 'primitive scheme' (ibid.).

Until recently, by the law, any deals with the assets of federal enterprises were considered null and void if they were carried out without the knowledge and consent of the owner (the Russian Property Management Agency). But

recently the Supreme Arbitration Court made a clarification that such transactions, even if they are held in direct violation of the law, are not negligible,
but disputed. By law the statute of limitations begins at inception rather than
from the time when the owner found out about the deal. As a result, the deal
makes out an afterthought after the registration of the property when the
owner finds out the statute of limitations had expired. Consequently the
transaction is fully legalised. This is called the 'new scheme' (ibid.).

Soon after the acquisition of property at a reduced price from a federal
enterprise, the buyer enters into a transaction with the offshore company. The
Russian register registers the transaction marvellously quickly, so the Federal
Property Management Agency does not even have time to make a claim. To
prove the bad faith of companies registered overseas is difficult. This is called
the 'widespread scheme' (ibid.).

Fradkin describes these schemes as within the law, but the attentive reader
can certainly find flaws and could suggest that the above-described schemes
are beyond the law. Without attempting to resolve the legal collision in this
chapter, we can note that the purchase of the first-class land at the price of 15 pence
per square metre by bureaucrats raises the question of social justice for the
millions of Russian citizens (Pasmi 2013).

Conclusion

Geographical differences, weak connections and administrative barriers create
conditions for price asymmetries that give opportunities for product arbitrage.
Goods arbitrage as transactions of purchase and sale can be realised with
money or in the form of barter operations. Barter was widely carried out
during the initial accumulation of capital in Russia in the 1990s and was well
incorporated into the shadow system of the Russian economy. Barter maintained
normal business processes and helped accelerate the turnover of capital under
conditions of an unreliable banking system and a shortage of working capital.
Barter gave good opportunities for arbitrage; moreover, the opacity of barter
gave additional income to arbitrageurs.

The Russian economy gives opportunities for arbitrage of commodities,
employing differences between prices which arise at different times, provided
the cost of money for a particular company is lower than the difference between
prices. For companies affiliated with authorities, the market risk of adverse
price changes in assets' trading could be hedged by the federal and regional
authorities due to a close relationship between business and authorities. Specific
post-Soviet Russian institutions and poor work of bailiffs created the conditions for delay of payment. In this regard, the delay in the payment of high
inflation can be considered as a sort of arbitrage.

Analysis of Gazprom activity shows that Gazprom bosses widely used
product arbitrage. They restricted the access of independent gas producers to
the Gazprom distribution network. Accordingly, the drop in the price of this
gas allows further resale of the gas by Gazprom, and consequently the

accumulation of profits in the accounts of arbitrage firms. Also they restrict the access of independent companies to information and participation in tenders which allows the establishment of large gaps between market price and tenders' price. In the third case (selling of gas on the domestic market), Gazprom creates conditions for arbitrage by supporting artificial quotas for gas consumers, encouraging them to buy gas at market prices from their subsidiaries, which appear here as arbitrageurs.

In Russia there is no adequate valuation of state assets such as land, properties and business. Moreover, private companies using inside information bought undervalued assets with subsequent resale to a state company. 'Feeding' in Russia became an element of social life and an element of management where executives of state companies use arbitrage technology for self-enrichment.

7 Labour arbitrage

This chapter reveals how Russian companies are arbitraging labour costs, transferring operations into low-labour-cost regions to take the benefit of interregional differences in working hours and wages per hour. The chapter investigates the transfer of production processes to deprived regions where there are low salaries; the transfer of the workforce from deprived regions to developed parts of Russia; and the use of special closed zones where it is possible to establish special conditions for working and with reduced labour expenditure.

Global labour arbitrage

Throughout human history there has been a difference between countries' levels of economic development, which creates substantial disparities in social settlements. These disparities create conditions where, as Haslam *et al.* (2012) note, multinational companies are arbitraging labour costs, transferring domestic operations into low-labour-cost economies to take the benefits of international differences in working hours and wages per hour. Moreover, labour arbitrage suggests the possibility to transfer the balance of value-added distribution away from labour cost to cash.

Roach (2003) offers a definition of global labour arbitrage, noting that its main factor is the unstoppable pressure to decrease costs, which encourages US corporations to replace high-wage workers in the USA with low-wage workers abroad. Consequently global labour arbitrage has become an increasingly crucial approach for firms' existence in the developed countries. Milberg and Winkler (2008) note that between 1998 and 2006, 35 US manufacturing and service industries employing offshoring managed to get a higher share of corporate profit in total value-added.

Numerous US corporations increased their share of industrial capacity and employment in low-labour-cost economies. As a result, between 1992 and 2001, each year around 100,000 manufacturing jobs in every major industrial sector, from high-tech businesses to low-wage businesses in food and textiles, moved from the USA to Mexico and China; in 2004 this figure increased to more than 400,000 jobs (Bronfenbrenner and Luce 2004). For example, a factory in southern China paid a wage of just $2 per day (2003), labourers worked long days under deprived workshop conditions, which gave Wal-Mart the opportunity to spend $15 billion on Chinese-made products, constituting more than 80 per cent of Wal-Mart's production in the 6,000 factories in its worldwide network of suppliers (Gereffi 2005).

However, labour arbitrage is not just exploitation of blue-collar workers, but also transferring modern technologies between countries. Couto *et al.* (2007) note that offshoring is not only about reducing costs by moving manufacturing and back-office operations to low-labour-cost destinations. Currently, off-shoring is also the discovery of talent needed to support innovation. Providers of offshoring services perform work such as new product development, research and development, and engineering.

Despite some positive aspects of labour arbitrage for developed countries, there are disadvantages. For example, Roberts (2004) notes that US managers are replacing low-cost foreign labour with US labour in the goods and services that they supply to internal and external markets. Consequently American employees are being redeployed to untransferable services and job growth is concentrated in internal services that cannot be outsourced.

Transfer of production to regions

Labour arbitrage in Russia is a socio-economic phenomenon where business moves to regions, where labour expenditure is lower than in the initial place of business, and a poor workforce moves to regions with wages higher than in their initial location. In the context of Russia, there are two main paths in which higher-wage labour can be substituted for low-wage labour: the transfer of production processes to deprived regions where there are low salaries, and the transfer of the workforce from deprived regions.

The key factors of labour arbitrage in Russia are the movement of both business and workforce, for which businessmen and labour force need to have both the desire and opportunity to move to a new region. Despite a large differentiation in labour cost between regions, not many can get barriers to interregional operations due to various factors, which will be analysed in this chapter. Theoretically the result of both movements is a rise in the supply of labour compared with the demand for labour, resulting in cuts in labour expenditure. Moreover, the poor regions integrate better into the Russian economy and workers' incomes and standards of living rise. However, the reality sometimes differs greatly from the theory.

The second path, the transfer of the workforce from deprived regions, can be supplemented by transfer of the workforce from poor Central Asian countries that have exclusive cultural and political relationships and a special immigration regime with Russia. Also, there is a third path which is not typical for EU and North American countries: using the existence of special closed zones, where it is possible to establish special conditions for working and have lower labour expenditures. Of course, in real life businesses may use relatively complicated schemes which do not lay in the Procrustean bed of theoretical constructions, but which are more interesting to analyse.

The first main path in which higher-wage labour can be substituted for low-wage labour is the transfer of production processes to deprived regions where there are low salaries. During the economic boom in Moscow in the 2000s, there were two interconnected tendencies: the growth of remuneration in almost all segments of the regional economy, and sharp growth of immigration which offered a low-cost labour force. As a result, in many sectors where management could not use the cheaper labour of migrants, wages became two or three times higher than wages outside Moscow for similar jobs. This creates the opportunity for labour arbitrage by transferring production between the Russian regions. Also, there are other drivers for transferring activity, such as the high cost of property in the capital, high cost of living, and high transaction costs (bribes) of business. Consequently many corporations are opening offices in the regions and transferring their production, call centres, accounting and analytics.

In general, Russian companies are moving along with a global trend – a similar strategy has been implemented in developed countries a decade earlier. For example, Gordon *et al.* (2005) show that there are three central groups of servicing functions that are subject to transfer. First, call centres of different types for marketing, standard business investigations and advanced technical support. Second, IT operations such as data processing, programme checking, software development and adjustment. Third, operations support, publishing and statistical analyses, accounting procedures, paralegal work and record maintenance.

The largest Russian bank, the Savings Bank of the Russian Federation, is a good example of this strategy. Between 2010 and 2012 about 75 per cent of the large banks moved from Moscow into the Russian cities. The Savings Bank had only a call centre in Moscow, but within two years it opened call centres in several regional centres including Novosibirsk, Rostov-on-Don and Yekaterinburg (Danilova 2012). In 2012, the Savings Bank of Russia opened a new Unified Contact Centre in the subsidiary office of the Omsk branch, which has around 2,500 workspaces (Call Center Guru 2012).

An analogous strategy is employed by mobile operators which are moving to cheaper regions of Russia. Operators have expensive call centres in the Moscow region and have to pay high salaries to staff. Movement towards the East decreases labour costs as well as decreasing payment premiums for night work (Call Center Guru 2012). For example, in 2010 VimpelCom, the second-largest telecoms operator in Russia (operating under the brand name 'Beeline'), opened the largest in Russia call centre in Perm. Perm is one of the fastest-growing Russian regions, with highly developed industrial complexes as well as transport links. This project will provide jobs for 1,130 city residents, and total investment in the construction of the call centre will be about 1 billion roubles. The city was selected due to the geographical position of the region, relatively cheap labour force, and the region's offer of a regime of tax exemptions (Properm 2010).

In addition, large Russian companies follow the same logic of transferring labour force from expensive to cheaper regions. For example, in 2011 the largest Russian oil business group Lukoil, with sales of over $133 billion, which has 0.8 per cent of global oil reserves and 2.2 per cent of global oil production (Lukoil 2013), organised an accounting centre in Perm. This city was chosen due to the good conditions and high quality of the regional labour force. Branches participating in the project to move accounting from Moscow to Perm will reduce the cost of accounting by around 60 per cent (Kashina 2011). In addition, the creation of an accounting centre provides a united global accounting service for Lukoil. In 2011 the centre had more than 700 employees who served 12 large branches of the company. Transitions to a new and more advanced model of accounting have reduced the time of preparation and significantly reduced the cost of accounting (Perm neft 2012).

The company uses a management model that looks like accounting out-sourcing, but there is a difference: Lukoil has created a subsidiary accounting firm, which serves the oil giant. This company does not use third-party accountants due to a desire to contain confidential information. Accounting outsourcing is undeveloped in Russia in comparison with the EU countries.

In both cases, Lukoil and VimpelCom, it is important to recognise the contingent factors impacting upon the success of transfer of business to the region: staff qualification and loyalty (available in many large Russian cities), political influence of the company (good relationship with authorities) and, for VimpelCom in particular, a good time zone which offers the possibility to serve clients 24 hours a day.

Another example of transferring labour force from expensive to cheaper regions is the case of the car plant ZIL, which was founded in 1916 and was the first Russian car manufacturing plant. Over the years it produced about 8 million vehicles, including the ZIS-5, ZIL-130 and ZIL-131 as well as top-class Soviet cars (Gorshkova 2012). Serial production of the light truck family ZIL-5301 ("Young Bull" trucks) was launched in 1994, and it was the most popular car among consumers. The company aimed to produce 250,000 trucks a year, but production declined dramatically in the 1990s. In the past 10 years the company has transferred production to branches located in different regions of the country due to their lower labour costs. The transfer of production from the capital to the regions is the first stage of a company recovery programme. As a result of this programme, production of ZIL-5301 was transferred to the Petrovsky auto-parts factory in the Saratov region (Gorshkova 2012).

In this example, one can see how the industrial company reduces expenditure by transferring production to the region with a cheaper labour force. Of course, there are other reasons to move from Moscow, for instance the desire of the Moscow government (the owner of the company) to use the company's industrial land for other projects. However, as Gorshkova (2012) notes, the car plant ZIL does not have a modern truck model and many of its traditional supply lines were halted during the crisis at the plant. Therefore the relocation of manufacturing in the Saratov region will do nothing but postpone the death of the company.

Confectionery companies expanding their businesses have the same scenario. For example, Holding United Confectioners, which is the largest confectionery company in Eastern Europe, brings together 19 Russian plants including Moscow's largest enterprises, Red October, Babaev and Rot-Front. It has 17,000 employees (Uniconf 2013). The major assets of the holding are in Moscow, where the cost of labour is dramatically higher than in other Russian regions. For that reason, in the past decade the holding increased its share of production outside Moscow. At this time, most of the factories belonging to the holding did not have a clear specialisation. One company could produce different products, such as chocolate, candy, waffles and cookies. This tradition was developed in the USSR, when a factory had to supply a whole range of products to its region. However, both Moscow and the regional enterprises of the company managed to produce the popular federal brands. As a result, the holding changed its strategy: the leading company brands have replaced less popular local brands and each of the company's factories has its own speciality. Expensive products should be made at the Moscow enterprises. However, other plants have limited product specialisation which increases efficiency and facilitates logistics and the management of the group; for example, modern equipment for a particular type of product being installed in only one factory gives higher efficiency than when it is installed in fifteen different factories (Shokoladka 2013).

Rustabak (2013) shows a similar approach in the tobacco industry. British American Tobacco (BAT) is one of the world leaders in the manufacture of tobacco products. The company has operated in Russia since 1994 through 'BAT Russia'. It manufactures and sells cigarettes in Russia under the brand names Dunhill, Kent, Vogue, Rothmans and Lucky Strike. In October 2011, BAT Russia transferred part of the production capacity of the Moscow factory to Saratov. In autumn 2012 it was decided that to continue production in Moscow was impractical and the production lines should be transferred to the plant in St Petersburg. Later, BAT closed the factory BAT-Java in the centre of Moscow.

Generally, it is incorrect to attribute low regional remuneration to low productivity. Wages are low due to the additional supply of labour that over-hangs in many Russian regions' labour market. However, low remuneration does not automatically mean low production costs in many Russian regions. Many areas of Russia, including single-industry towns, small towns and villages, have a low-cost labour force, but often they have poor infrastructure and an unfriendly business climate, and the cheaper labour force does not provide sufficient incentive to warrant investment. That there is no possibility of labour arbitrage in these areas halts their development, completing a vicious circle of regional unattractiveness.

Transfer of labour to large cities

The second main path by which higher-wage labour can be substituted for low-wage labour is the transfer of the workforce from deprived Russian regions. Migration of low-wage labour in Russia is directed to the largest cities, which have large population growth. Moreover, as noted by Zubarevich (2011), the agglomeration of the two federal cities attracts workers from across the Russian Federation, concentrating a large share of the total net migration, and other major cities mostly absorb migrants from their region. This second path also applies to transfer of the workforce from former Soviet Union Republics as well as post-communism countries such as China and Vietnam. These countries have a surplus of poor labour force, which moves in the direction of more wealthy nations. This increases the supply of labour relative to production capacity in the wealthier countries and, as a result, decreases salaries in those segments of the poorer nations' economies most sensitive to migration.

Between 1999 and 2008, the demand for labour in Russia increased considerably due to the economy's rapid economic growth, and the level of employment grew by more than 10 million workers. The major source of labour force was migration from the eleven members of the Commonwealth of Independent States (CIS) (Shelburne and Palacin 2007).

There are different data about migration in Russia: according to the World Bank (2008), Russia has around 12 million migrant workers; Kallioma (2009) notes that Russia ranked first in Europe and second in the world after the United States in the number of *gastarbeiter* (migrant workers). In Moscow alone, 2 million *gastarbeiter* come each year but only 300,000 are officially employed.

After geopolitical reorganisation of the post-Soviet space in 1990s and the collapse of large industrial enterprises in the post-Soviet countries, the Russian Federation has become a leading centre of immigration in the world. Between 1992 and 2005, the country absorbed around 610,000 people annually (Astakhova 2005). In addition, Russia has a stronger economic position and a higher standard of living compared with other CIS countries. For example, in 2005 the average monthly salary based on exchange rates in Azerbaijan was $64.80; in Armenia $46.10; Belarus $106.20; Georgia $46.30; Kyrgyzstan $34.50; Moldova $50.20; Tajikistan $12.40; Ukraine $70.50; and in Russia $141.20 (CIS 2005). Eight years later, the disparity between Russia and the CIS in general remained. For instance, the difference in wages between Russia and Kyrgyzstan was 3.6 times (Global Wage Report 2013).

According to official data, the influx of immigrants to Russia from CIS countries during the reform years was dominated mostly by residents of Kazakhstan, Ukraine, Uzbekistan, Kyrgyzstan, Georgia, Moldova and Turkmenistan, and from non-CIS countries by China, Turkey, North Korea and the republics of the former Yugoslavia. A third of the foreign labour force is concentrated in the central region, in the Khanty-Mansi and Yamal-Nenets autonomous districts – and about one fifth in the Belgorod region – more than 5 per cent; Seaside (about 5 per cent); and Krasnodar regions (3.5 per cent). Officially, the sectorial structure of foreign workers in Russia in 2005 was as follows: industry 22.5 per cent (in 1995 25.8 per cent); agriculture 12.6 (14.7); construction 7.6 (9.3); transport 6.5 (6.6); trade and public catering 14.9 (10.1).

This migration moderately balances the negative natural growth of the population in Russia due to a high level of emigration and mortality.

The high level of migration could be explained by huge differentiation of living standards and wages between Russia and CIS countries. For example, in 2005 per capita income in Armenia, Kyrgyzstan and Tajikistan was 46.2, 17.7 and 11.8 per cent, respectively, of Russian income. For all eleven CIS countries (excluding Russia) the ratio is 48.4 per cent (author's calculations).

Despite the fact that many migrant workers were working illegally and consequently not reporting their earned income to their host country, migrant remittances from Russia to the CIS-11 increased more than nine times between 2000 and 2008 and reached about $10 billion (Shelburne and Palacin 2007). Migrant remittances to CIS were around 4 per cent of GDP, and for some economies such as Armenia, Tajikistan and the Republic of Moldova the share of remittances in GDP was 34, 52 and 42 per cent, respectively, which was increasingly important for their economies (ibid.).

In Chapter 3 we analysed Option 2, strong price asymmetries and a robust opportunity for arbitrage. An example of this option is the building industry in Moscow and other big Russian cities where there is large dissimilarity between native higher-wage labour and low-wage immigrant labour. Opportunities to employ this dissimilarity were created by the special resolution of federal and regional governments and weak social institutions. Also, the contractor companies, having had potential for labour arbitrage, put a lot of effort into organising special conditions, lobbying for special state resolutions to allow the employment of migrants.

In the Russian capital, the driver of this was Mayor Luzhkov who, together with his wife, the richest businesswoman in Russia, Elena Baturina, realised grandiose building projects. Moscow, as well as other Russian cities, had an extraordinary explosion of construction and as a result it has created millions of new workplaces largely filled by migrants from countries of the former Soviet Union.

As noted by Human Rights Watch (2009), approximately 40 per cent of migrant workers are employed in the highly unregulated construction sector. Generally, migrant construction workers are young men who leave their family in their home country and enter Russia for six to nine months of seasonal employment, often for many years in a row. These workers enjoy higher wages in Russia and often send money to their families. Building workers usually live in deprived conditions, and often employers commit violations of Russian law such as requisition of identification documents, withholding salaries and forcing *gastarbeiter* to work long hours. Some managers practise violence or threats of violence against employees. Numerous cases have been documented that establish forced labour of migrant workers.

Employers routinely fail to provide migrant workers with written contracts as required by Russian law; 77 per cent of *gastarbeiter* do not have contracts that prevent the proper migration registration. The absence of a written employment contract also leaves *gastarbeiter* vulnerable in situations of workplace accidents due to their not being able to access accident insurance: because of their illegal status, employers avoid paying for their insurance. Moreover, often managers do not make any assistance available to injured employees (ibid.).

According to our estimation of *gastarbeiters'* salaries in the Moscow region, they are about 35 per cent of the wages of Russian workers who have a permanent labour contract. This example shows the well known type of economic arbitrage which exploits low-cost labour as a reaction to growing competition in markets and the huge demand for labour force.

However, the Russian model of offshoring arbitrage is dissimilar to that observed elsewhere. Russian business transfers labour from developing countries to the relatively more developed Russia; more generally, offshoring arbitrage transfers capital and technology from advanced economies to developing economies with lower labour costs.

In addition, this case reveals two complementary advantages for companies moving to emerging markets: undeveloped health and safety regulations, and labour law. Health and safety compliance is very expensive in manufacturing but is often ignored in developing countries. As a result, relocation into countries with more lenient health and safety regulations can create reduced operational expenditure.

Labour law in developing and transitive countries in comparison with developed countries does not provide adequate terms of employment, anti-discrimination, unfair dismissal and child labour protection. In addition, usually trade unions are dependent upon executives and this reduces union effectiveness. Consequently companies conducting business in developing countries can often reduce effective labour costs.

Vozhdaeva (2012) gives an example of a medium-sized business in a village south-east of Moscow. The company used around 100 Vietnamese, who were being forced to work up to 18 hours a day without weekends and holidays. The workers were poorly fed, frequently beaten up and forbidden to leave the workshop buildings. Seventy-five Vietnamese lived in four small rooms without facilities, including electricity, which blocks the use of any communications. They could not take a shower for more than two months. The Vietnamese could not leave their rooms to walk and had to stay indoors all day.

Gastarbeiter were picked up from different Vietnamese provinces lured by promises of high salaries. Many workers were forced to pay intermediaries up to $2,000 in order to obtain the job. According to a preliminary labour agreement, the average salary had to be about $220 per month. However, this was never paid in full: more than 50 per cent of the money was withdrawn as payment for food and accommodation.

In 2012 the *gastarbeiter* went on strike; the company management invited Vietnamese diplomats, who reminded workers that they had a legally binding labour agreement and must follow its terms and conditions. Executives of the company reminded the staff that they could work elsewhere, but the new employers of the workers would have to pay the workers' debts, moreover, the workers could leave for Vietnam but they would also have to pay their debts first. After the strike, some workers were beaten up. However, the Vietnamese embassy stated it could not find people who were beaten up, denied accusations of any abuse and forced labour, and stressed that workers come to Russia in order to work, not to go on strike.

Later, the Russian migration service made a raid on the factory and found 75 people locked up in small rooms. No migrants had any documents on them; 24 workers were identified as illegal migrants and were deported to Vietnam (Vozhdaeva 2012). This is not a unique case – this factory was just one of hundreds of similar factories run in Russia and of migrant workers employed in Russia facing similar conditions.

Nguyen (2010) notes that often Vietnamese workers' companies officially do not exist for the Russian authorities, which of course know about their existence. However, factory owners pay bribes to police, tax officials and migration authorities to ignore the Vietnamese businesses and Vietnamese citizens. Consequently, employees can easily be exploited. In addition, working in these invisible factories is very risky because it is illegal and many *gastarbeiter* overstay their visa and live in constant fear of being deported. Russian law gives permission for work for five years and then a person has to leave the country. Nevertheless, people have found ways around the system. Some workers have bought new passports with new names and come back to Russia.

In Zelenograd (the administrative district of Moscow), police officers stopped the work of three underground shops making counterfeit clothing of world-famous brands including Gucci and Armani, and 400 illegal workers from Vietnam were arrested. The cost of their illegal activities is estimated at 800 million roubles. Migrants lived and worked in the same place – directly in the premises of the former military plant. Police officers found 500 workstations equipped with sewing machines and devices for cutting and making patterns, and seized more than 15,000 ready-made products with illegal trademarks of Chanel, Dolce & Gabbana, Gucci, Armani, Hugo Boss and Roberto Cavalli (Dni 2010b).

A similar story was seen in 2008, when the Moscow police found about 150 illegal Vietnamese immigrants sewing fake Dolce & Gabbana. The illegal manufacture was established in the resort complex 'Sunny' in the Moscow region. Entrepreneurs rented three large rooms: two were equipped with a sewing shop and the third was used as a large bedroom for *gastarbeiter* who had no registration or work permit. These repetitive stories show the large scale of production of counterfeit clothes of well known companies (ibid.).

In Yegoryevsk (Moscow region), police officers rescued 30 Vietnamese from slavery. *Gastarbeiter* were trafficked from their home countries into forced labour in an illegal garment factory. Managers employed violence and threats of violence against employees. These included managers' refusal to provide contracts, extremely long working hours, unpaid salaries and unsafe working conditions (Dni 2010a). There was an interesting multinational character of this business: the management were migrants from Armenia, the guards were

Russian and the labour force was Vietnamese. Vietnamese *gastarbeiter* did not have documents and could not leave the factory. There were attempts to escape, however they were not successful; for example, two girls were trying to escape through a window using a rope ladder and fell to the ground, one breaking a leg and the second breaking her spine. Representatives of the Vietnamese Embassy were informed of the situation and took part in the operation to free their citizens (ibid.).

Generally, employers do not meet fire safety requirements. For example, in 2012 near Moscow police established that the *gastarbeiter* from Vietnam who died in a fire at Yegoryevsk were locked in a garment workshop. Vietnamese were kept under lock and key due to fear of audits from the migration service. The door to the workshop, where the foreigners lived, was opened only once a day for delivery of food, sewing materials and accessories for the job. The fire killed 14 Vietnamese. After the tragedy, the Moscow Federal Migration Service organised an inspection of the factory and identified 60 illegal migrants. Earlier the factory had appeared in four criminal cases of illegal migration and entrepreneurship (Krylov and Rogoza 2012).

Quong (2012) notes that there are a number of Vietnamese firms which include compatriots in their list of employees, thereby legalising their position in Russia. As a result of this transaction, the authority gives permission to live in Russia. Also, many Vietnamese issue their documents as members of the international exchange students programme, then by paying bribes annually to the university they manage to maintain their position. Thus officially these people are students and have the right to reside in the territory of Russia.

In the latter examples the labour force were immigrants from Vietnam. However, this model of business can use workers of any nationality and any age. For instance, in Moscow police freed from slavery 15 children aged 11–17 years from the Kyrgyz Republic, who were forced to work in a clothing factory. On the territory of one of the industrial enterprises of the Noginsk (Moscow region), an illegal textile producer used minors as its workforce (Dni 2009). The children's documents were taken away from them, they were lodged in barracks unsuitable for living and guarded around the clock. They were forced to work night shifts; and were cruelly punished if they failed to meet production standards. Wages were not paid to the children and they had no days off. The juvenile slaves were fed twice a day, usually on a diet of bread and mayonnaise. Medical care for the children was not provided; in cases of disobedience or refusal to work, children were punished. Children were taken from low-income families and parents were promised that their children would work in the garment industry with a monthly salary of 5,000 roubles, and provided with three meals a day, excellent accommodation and two days off (ibid.).

Again and again, it is possible to see how local authorities knew about the existence of the illegal migrants with their exceptionally long working hours, hazardous working conditions and forced labour, but they did not interfere with these businesses despite their being prohibited by to Russian law. Dozens of witnesses saw this exploitation of children and nobody called the police;

however, if calls to police or other authorities were made, they may have been ignored.

As a rule, violation of immigration laws exists together with violation of criminal laws. For example, an underground plant for the production of plastic doors and windows was identified in the Khabarovsk region. The illegal production under the disguise of an agricultural firm received official authorisation by the Federal Migration Service for the use of 20 foreign guest workers on the farm. The company produced low-quality products, which were in high demand by construction companies. Production was carried out using equipment imported from China, apparently smuggled. A similar illegal production of plastic windows operating from China recently closed down in the Primorsky territory and Yakutsk (Regnum 2004).

In 2010 in the town Ussuriysk (Primorsky territory), police officers identified an underground factory where around 700 Chinese produced thousands of pairs of shoes hazardous to health. The footwear manufacture was established three years ago and was controlled by a Russian executive. His Chinese partner supplied components of footwear from China: tops for different models of shoes, laces, insoles, heels and all sorts of accessories and components. Import of raw materials from China was very profitable due to zero tax duties. The workshop had terrible working conditions due to the use of toxic glue and soles: the sharp, acrid smell irritated the nose and throat. However, workers did not use even a basic respirator. Workers lived on the site of the company in the extremely cramped dormitories and every day produced more than 21,000 potentially dangerous pairs of shoes. The products of this factory were mainly distributed in the Russian Far East, in Moscow and St Petersburg (Regnum 2010).

According to a laboratory study by the regional Centre for Hygiene and Epidemiology, the shoes contain four substances in concentrations much higher than the norms permitted by Russian legislation. For example, the figure for vinyl chloride exceeds the occupational exposure threshold by more than 10 times, which provokes cancers of the liver, brain, lungs and blood. The investigation established that quality certificates for factory shoes were issued illegally (Regnum 2010).

There is an opinion that Russia needs massive foreign labour, which has a considerable impact on the economy of Russia. However, the argument about the need for large-scale use of migrant labour contradicts the fact that, in Russia, the level of productivity is greatly inferior to that in developed countries. Generally, labour costs of *gastarbeiter* are cheaper than labour costs of Russian workers, because the price of labour is only the migrants' salaries, whereas the price of Russian workers includes, in addition to wages, income tax (13 per cent of salary) and social contributions (34 per cent of salary). In addition, a standard company has to pay VAT whereas most companies that employ illegal as well as legal migrants minimise VAT to zero. Moreover, the large supply of cheap labour force from Asia often exceeds demand for labour, therefore it reduces the price of migrant labour. As a result, the price of Russian labour becomes uncompetitive compared with the price of migrants performing the same job.

Rodionov (2013) similarly notes that the average hourly output per worker in Russia amounts to a third of that in the USA; therefore the increase of productivity can be the main driver for the growth of the Russian economy. The massive migration from neighbouring countries discourages institutional and technological modernisation of the Russian economy, removing any incentive to invest in the technological development of production and retraining of staff. This leads to the preservation of Russia's backwardness compared with the developed countries, and the substitution of Russian employees by foreign slaves is making Russia a country with low social capital and limited opportunities for modernisation.

Employers prefer to employ migrants due to the absence of contracts or formal agreements. Consequently, a *gastarbeiter* is not registered in Russian tax accounting and the employer does not pay tax. In addition, citizens of Central Asia agree to live in inhuman conditions, be fed twice a day, and do any hard and dirty work for meagre money. This creates the conditions for the creation of large ghettos in the Russian megalopolises that are becoming a source of unsanitary and delinquent behaviour.

There is a high cost to be paid for Russian society's large-scale influx of migrants, including the large burden placed on the domestic health care system due to widespread severe infections of hepatitis C and tuberculosis among migrants (Ivakhnenko 2013; Nafeev *et al.* 2013). In addition, the educational system is not ready to accept migrant children because of their lack of knowledge of the Russian language and simply because of the deficit of student places in schools.

In all main Russian cities there are consolidated national diaspora groups, which often provide cultural, economic and legal support to migrants (Human Rights Watch 2009). However, this consolidation of ethnic migrant communities helps to monopolise the supply of labour on the Russian markets and as a result they can dictate terms to employers.

Migration gives a new impetus to Russian corruption and disruption of the law. According to Garnachuk (deputy district council), the official wage for a janitor at a site in Moscow is 52,000 roubles, but workers from Central Asia receive 10–12,000 roubles. The difference goes into the pocket of the heads of management companies.

The struggle with illegal migration appears as a military operation. For example, the Moscow Department of the Russian Ministry of the Interior stated that on 29 May 2013 the Migration Service, Russian Emergencies Ministry and Federal Drug Control Service officers, supported by riot police force and the Second Operative Police Regiment, held an event in the industrial zone, located at Khoroshevskaya Street where thousands of foreigners were living in workers' sheds. Consequently 952 foreign citizens were detained in order to establish their identity and allow investigation into any previous involvement in crime. According to the report, 117 migrants of the Republic of Tajikistan, Uzbekistan, Kyrgyzstan and Turkey were illegal migrants (Moscow Police 2013). It is likely that many of these migrants will soon return after extradition.

Tactically, police operations are necessary, but they cannot be a state strategy. The Deputy Prime Minister (Izvestia 2013) says that in Russia there are now 86 million people of working age, of whom only 48 million are working legally, the other 38 million working in the black market. In addition, she notes that the government does not know in what spheres these people are working and what they do. Due to the large size of the illegal sector, the budget does not receive a significant portion of taxes. She notes that the labour market in Russia is now almost illegitimate, and only a small part of it is functioning according to the normal rules (Izvestia 2013). Her position once more confirms that Russian economy has a huge shadow/informal sector, a large share of the population work illegally or semi-legally, the state cannot monitor the situation of the labour market, and the poor quality of statistics cannot present any real information about the labour market. When there is no fundamental governmental idea for its own citizens, no-one expects a good strategy towards migrants.

As noted earlier, labour arbitrage in Russia is a phenomenon where business moves to areas where labour expenditure is lower than in the initial place of business, or a deprived workforce moves to areas with higher living costs than in their home area. However, there is a third path in which higher-wage labour can be substituted for low-wage labour. This path is not representative of modern EU and North American countries, but has a long historical tradition. It is the use of special closed zones, where it is possible to establish a special environment for jobs, to use mainly forced labour, and to pay symbolic salary – or not pay one at all. Examples of these closed zones include corrective colonies, colony settlements and settlements of slaves in the mountains or steppe areas.

Russian zones

The Federal Service of Punishment Fulfilment (FSIN) is responsible for the security and maintenance of prisons in Russia. In May 2013 its correctional institutions, including 736 corrective colonies, contained around 693,000 people (FSIN 2013). It is interesting that 693,000 prisoners are guarded by 337,800 full-time staff of FSIN. Russia has second place in the world (after the USA) in the relative number of prisoners, now standing at 655 prisoners per 100,000 people (MCPR 2013). The Russian penal system is not Stalin's GULAG (concentration camps for political prisoners); nevertheless it has a few important problems that impede its performance. Firstly, it is common knowledge that the living conditions of prisoners in most institutions are equal to torture because of overcrowded cells. The most famous case is the 'Novokuznetsk tragedy' when, in July of 1995, in the Novokuznetsk Investigation Isolator, 11 people died due to lack of oxygen and dozens of prisoners were placed in intensive care units. However, this tragedy was not an exception, according to the head of GUIN (now FSIN), Yuri Kalinin, 'Cases of deaths from asphyxiation took place practically at all big isolators of Russia' (ibid.). The general type corrective colonies are overfilled to 110 per cent of their capacity. Secondly, insufficient funding, which was only 46 per cent of the required financing, causes shortages of food, medication and fuel. Thirdly, the problems of the accommodation and maintenance of the different categories of convicts keep increasing (ibid.).

Nadezhda Tolokonnikova (leader of Pussy Riot) noted that in the Mordovia penal colony in June 2013, her salary was 29 roubles ($1) per month, which means the actual legalisation of slave labour and termination of the Labour Code (Tolokonnikova 2013). She writes that:

> All my team is working in the sewing workshop on 16–17 hours a day from 7.30 am to 0.30 am. Sleep – in the best case, four hours a day. Day off happens once a month. Almost all Sundays are working days. Convicted persons write statements for access to work on weekends with the wording 'at his own request'. In reality, of course, nobody wants to work on Sunday. These statements are written at the request of superiors and prison leaders transferring the superiors' will.
>
> (Ibid.)

According to the law, prisoners must work, but only around 60 per cent of able-bodied prisoners have jobs. In 2008 their average salary was 2,545 roubles, roughly one tenth of the country's average. In practice, work in the colonies is voluntary in most cases. Moreover, often colonies cannot provide work to all those who are willing (Petrov 2009).

The employment of prisoners depends strongly on the management and the geographical location of the colony. In practice, the majority of prisoners are employed in the forest and metalwork industries; for example, in the Arkhangelsk region a large amount of timber is harvested through the labour of convicts. The former President of Russia, Dmitry Medvedev, noted that the industrial base of the Russian colonies and prisons needs to be optimised. It is very out of date, and the goods that prisoners produce often are not wanted (Petrov 2009).

In general, every Russian colony has a good infrastructure (electricity, heat, water, sewage) and they are near railway stations or federal highways. Many have workshops. Therefore, despite many disadvantages, correctional institutions are an interesting object for investment, mainly for medium-sized and small companies.

In 2012 in the Novomoskovsk colony number 6 (Tula region), a new manufacturing plant opened for the production of secondary polymer pellets. In the production area of the colony new technological equipment was established, worth about 7 million roubles. The plant produces 200 tons of pure recycled polymer granules per month from plastic waste material. The new production initially employed 45 convicts. They receive wages, but part of the wages of those convicts who are under the sentence of court proceedings covered the expenses of the investment (News Tula 2012).

However, the selection of industrial sites, the structures of industrial buildings and fire-explosion protection equipment were not selected correctly; therefore fire and explosion protection of the technological process as a whole was not good enough. The production of secondary polymer pellets has many different harmful elements, such as temperature, humidity, air mobility, the presence of gases and organic dust in the air, thermal radiation, noise and vibration exposing the human body at work to physical stress. All these factors fall outside the current health standards.

Moreover, when polyethylene is heated above 140°C it can begin oxidative degradation, and volatile products containing organic acids and carboxylic compounds including formaldehyde, acetaldehyde and carbon monoxide, which are mutagens and carcinogens and can cause respiratory diseases as well as diseases of the musculoskeletal system and gastro-intestinal tract. Also, when the concentration of these substances in the work area exceeds permissible amounts, acute chemical poisoning can occur (Samykina et al 2013).

The production does not provide personnel with protective equipment: special clothing, shoes, gloves, goggles, masks and hand cream required to protect workers from exposure to harmful substances. The explosion and fire safety of the process are not controlled correctly and the ventilation systems to remove gaseous side products from the upper areas of the work area do not satisfy health and safety standards.

Wage bills are half of those for workers at liberty, and the management company can decrease taxation dramatically due to the colony being hidden from tax inspectors. The cost of auxiliary equipment (ventilation, cooling and air purification, fire and explosion protection, anti-noise equipment, etc.) is more than 50 per cent of the cost of tangible assets. Payments for protection, co-payment for the harm to the worker and for early retirement are also relatively large in this business. Also, all risks are taken by the corrective colony and mostly prisoners, which means that in a case of an injury the company will not pay any compensation. Consequently, return on capital employed in operations in the colony will be about 40 per cent higher in comparison with a similar operation outside. However, it is impossible to evaluate the personal benefits of the colony staff and how loyal the prisoners will be; therefore no-one can make a conclusion about the project in a long-term perspective.

The President's Representative in the Siberian Federal District Anatoly Kvashnin (he was a Chief of the Russian General Staff) suggests using convicts serving sentences in correctional colonies for processing and sorting of household waste. According to him, in Siberian correctional colonies there is high unemployment, and without much effort colonies can organise recycling and sorting of rubbish. He supposes that using innovative approaches, prisoners can solve the problems of persistent organic pollutants, of utilisation of household and industrial waste, and even toxic substances (Actual Comment

2010). However, he does not take into account that advantages of slave labour exist only in organisations closed for society, and arbitrage opportunities decrease dramatically when civil institutions start to work properly.

A similar approach is realised in some territories of the Russian Federation, relatively closed to state and civil control, where businesses can use low-priced labour. Yuzhnyy (2013) gives examples of this approach.

One resident of Smolensk was given alcohol with clonidine by strangers, and the man woke up in a brick factory in Dagestan – he was taken there in the luggage compartment of a bus along with seven more prisoners. Others go to the North Caucasus voluntarily trying to find a job and fall into slavery. One example of a typical story:

> In my home town Saratov, I was looking for a well-paid job. I saw an announcement that the South needed workers with salary of 40,000 roubles a month. Calling a specified number, I learned that I have to go to Dagestan, but on the phone it was said that the construction firm is from Moscow. I put trust in it and went there. But on the first day, my passport and money were confiscated. When I started asking questions about the job, I was badly beaten up and was told that I would be working here until death.
>
> (Rybin 2009)

In general, there is a whole network of paid agents throughout Russia, who select from a number of potential victims in the ranks of the homeless, the mentally retarded, or persons simply caught in a difficult financial situation. They are taken to North Caucasus republics, where slaves are sold to brick factories or agriculture farms. Their documents and passports are confiscated and they are forced to work 12–14 hours a day, fearing that if they try to escape then the bandits will kill them.

According to one estimation (Yuzhnyy 2013), about 10,000 people are currently in slavery in that region, and the cost of a slave in Dagestan is only 15,000 roubles (about $500). In the modern history of the new Russia there have been two criminal cases for slavery, because the fact of slavery is very difficult to prove – factory owners say their captives work hard day and night completely voluntarily, for good money (ibid.).

Newspark (2011) gives the example of a person, Sergey Oborin, who was in slavery for 16 years. He was a commercial traveller and was robbed on a train. Than he was sold to a brick factory at Nogai Steppe, which lies between Chechnya, Dagestan and Stavropol regions and is practically unsettled. Sergey Oborin worked for 16 years at four brick plants. In 2007, when he was 53 years old, after the 16 years of slavery, his health had almost gone. The owner of the plant pitied the unhappy Russian and gave freedom to him.

Like Odysseus of Ithaca, Sergey Oborin returned to his hometown, where he had stopped being expected by everyone a long time ago. In 2001 he was officially declared dead by the decision of the court. His wife had long considered herself a widow and over the years managed a few times to get a divorce and marry again. His son Anton erected a monument to his father at the local cemetery Chusovsky, under which there was no body, but the tablet with the date of birth and death, and a photograph (ibid.).

This story of human tragedy, which could have been the scenario for a film, once more demonstrates the situation with slavery in Russia, as well as revealing the problem of a vast number of people who have disappeared without a trace in recent years. They disappear suddenly, without a rational reason, and many disappear forever. The number of missing has almost doubled and in 2007 it exceeded 120,000 people (59,000 men, 38,000 women and 23,000 children). Thus, in a single year, the population of an average town vanishes. Fortunately most are found alive, sometimes after a month of searching, sometimes after a few years (Kozlova 2008).

Moscow and Dagestan slaves have a lot in common, but there is one small difference: Vietnamese or Uzbek slaves go to Moscow for money and crime, whereas the Russians in Dagestan are driven in by force and fraud. But in general there is no difference between labour arbitrage schemes in Dagestan's brick plants, which use Russians, and Moscow's regional plants making counterfeit clothing and using Vietnamese illegal migrants – both use slaves. Slave labour is slave labour, regardless of the specifics of the business.

Conclusion

The period of reforms was characterised by a large differentiation in living standards and wages between Russia and the CIS countries as well as between Russian regions. These factors formed and maintained price asymmetries and opportunities for different types of arbitrage in the Russian economy. Labour arbitrage in Russia is a socio-economic phenomenon and there are two main paths in which higher-wage labour can be substituted for low-wage labour: the transfer of production processes to deprived regions where there are low salaries, and the transfer of the workforce from deprived Russian regions as well as from the former Soviet Union Republics. In addition, there is a third path: the use of special closed zones, where it is possible to establish special conditions for work and have lower labour expenditure.

In general, Russian companies are moving with the global trend; similar strategies have been implemented in developed countries a decade earlier. Many parts of Russia have a low-cost labour force but they often have poor infrastructure and an unfriendly business climate, so the cheaper labour force does not provide sufficient incentive to warrant investment.

There are complementary advantages for companies moving to regions with low wages: emerging markets and exploiting asymmetries between high and low levels of labour safety cost, labour law cost, environmental pollution cost and knowledge cost to boost earning capacity.

The central idea of labour arbitrage in Russia is an increase in surplus value by considerably cutting wages and reducing qualification requirements of the workforce by the replacement of the national labour force by a foreign labour force. In contrast with current trends, where entrepreneurs increase income by substituting the labour force with new equipment and technologies, Russian entrepreneurs substitute expensive labour with cheap labour.

The actual economic impacts of an influx of cheap labour are an increase in the revenues of companies that employ migrant workers and a consequent increase in unemployment among Russians, a significant reduction of wages in the Russian economy, deficits in the pension and medical insurance funds, cash outflow from the Russian economy, and the braking of Russian modernisation.

Russia shows a 'traditional' approach to labour arbitrage which has neither improved the quality of the labour force nor increased labour productivity. However, there is another scenario for development, as in the USA, for example, where in the past 15 years immigrants have started a quarter of American start-ups, where market capitalisation of these venture-backed companies surpasses half a trillion dollars, and 40 per cent of publicly traded venture-funded firms operating in high-tech segments today were started by immigrants. Intel, Solectron, Sun Microsystems, eBay, Yahoo and Google were founded by immigrants (Anderson and Platzer 2012). They note that immigrants have huge innovative capacity, mainly in technical areas. Software, semiconductors and biotechnology are the top industry sectors for immigrants. The share of immigrant entrepreneurs among publicly traded venture-funded companies is remarkable in comparison with the relatively modest number of immigrants in the total American population.

8 Outsourcing arbitrage

This chapter explores contracting with another party to perform a specific function which can provide cost savings. The chapter investigates outsourcing from a historical perspective, and in areas where it is most widely used. The chapter analyses the three types of outsourcing of personnel that prevailed in Russia. Additionally, the chapter examines tolling in sugar, ferrous metallurgy and light industries

Outsourcing – a historical perspective

Outsourcing is contracting with another subject (private company, public company or individual) to perform a specific function or a repetitive long-term task. Characteristically, the function and the task being outsourced are not considered vital to the business. Theoretically, outsourcing is able to provide cost savings and improved services through specialisation and economies of scale. Moreover, by using the services of professional firms, companies can employ their own resources in their most profitable segments. Outsourcing is an alternative way to reduce transaction costs because many operations are relocated to independent firms, that is, outsourcing is the shifting of their own transaction costs to other companies.

Companies have numerous motives for engaging in outsourcing, including reduction of the volume of investments in non-core assets; focusing on core activities; the use of highly qualified professionals with extensive experience, the hiring of whom would be too expensive or irrational; lack of company expertise in a particular field; use of the vendor's innovation and best practices; and transfer of risks to the vendor. It is a flexible response to changes in the market and within the company, as with the introduction of advanced technologies through a specialised outsourcing company and reduction of costs (Deloitte 2005). The latter point, the cost-saving strategy, is a major factor in outsourcing because companies believe that it is cheaper to pay the provider of outsourcing, which has more significant activities in a particular area, than to keep a small unit itself. According to a Deloitte (2005) survey, for 70 per cent of companies the key cause for the use of outsourcing is the desire to save money. However, outsourcing is a very complicated process and the anticipated advantages frequently fail to materialise. Outsourcing needs a compound sequence of trade-offs: cost savings against growth, speed against quality of service delivery, and maintaining organisational cohesion against knowledge and innovation. Vendors and companies have fundamentally contradictory objectives, putting at risk the latter's objective of innovation, cost savings and quality. Furthermore, the structural benefits of vendors do not permanently translate into low-cost and faster services (ibid.).

It is important to note that, despite strong growth of outsourcing in the past 30 years, it is not a new phenomenon in business. Previously outsourcing was known under another name, subcontracting, and was extensively employed in Japan, USA and USSR in the 1950s. Kimura Fukunari (2001) notes that subcontracting (*shitauke*) is a contractual relationship where sizeable companies offer commissioned works to minor companies to manage under a dominant long-term arrangement. Subcontracting suggests reusable transactions, and these relationships are included in risk-sharing arrangements, technology diffusion mechanisms and distinctive subcontractor control, such as the '*kanban* system'. Also, the relationship is not essentially exclusive: a subcontractor may have multiple clients.

The car industry has shown that the stratified subcontracting system improved both static and dynamic efficiency. Since then, subcontracting has been considered a significant mechanism of the Japanese industrial system, with supposed benefits in saving costs of searching and selection of new suppliers, achieving positive quality development and cost reduction in cooperation with subcontractors, effectively providing motivation for subcontractors' investment in relation-specific assets, having efficient risk-sharing mechanisms and periodically owning a certain number of shares in a subcontractor to maintain beneficial relationships (Fukunari 2001).

Subcontracting arrangements vary widely across industries. For example the food, petroleum and coal industries do not make great use of the subcontracting system. In contrast, industries that employ subcontractors significantly include such spheres as labour-intensive production processes (textiles and clothing) and multi-layered vertical production of machinery. The nature of production technology affects the efficiency of subcontracting systems, and the share of subcontracting in each industry is mostly stable over time (ibid.).

In the Soviet Union, subcontracting was used largely in huge military programmes such as the development of the orbital spaceship 'Buran' by the Ministry of the Aviation Industry (MAI). MAPSSSR (2013) notes that in December 1973, the Presidential Committee of the Council of Ministers of USSR made a resolution to develop reusable launch vehicles (RVL) (Energia-Buran project, 11F35) as a response to the US Space Shuttle programme. The MAI was determined as the chief company for building the orbital plane Buran, an airplane for the transport of the orbital plane to the launch–landing complex, and the landing complex with the necessary equipment. Creating Energia-Buran was one of the largest R&D projects carried out in the USSR.

To perform this task, the MAI organised a governance structure, which established intra-cooperation of subcontractors, realised the planning and financing of the project, and controlled the timing and spending of budget funds. The need to create this structure, which was untypical for MAI, was determined by a huge amount of work in the project, which surveyed 124 research institutes and design bureaus and 52 production plants of the MAI. For these subcontractor organisations this project was not the main one, and their share of the project did not exceed one to a few per cent of their capacity. It is important that it was only the primary cooperation which determined control by MAI, whereas the secondary cooperation, established by the agreement of company-performers, was much broader. For example, the Tushino Machine-Building Plant (TMP) supplied materials, semi-finished products, components and manufacturing tooling required for manufacture, assembly and testing of the orbital plane and its systems of more than 450 enterprises of various ministries and departments.

The Chief Designer of the organisation was named Gleb Lozino-Lozinski and the head manufacturer of Buran was determined as the TMP and the NPO Molniya, which had sufficient experience and an adequate production base for manufacturing rockets and the construction of supersonic aircraft. These two companies had a large share of the work to design, build and test Buran. The 'Soviet Shuttle' was launched on 15 November 1988, but that was its first and last voyage (MAPSSSR 2013).

Comparison of Japanese and Russian subcontracting experiences and modern outsourcing practices shows that they have a relatively similar nature: subcontracting has all the features of outsourcing. But subcontracting has a narrower usefulness; it covers mostly industrial, scientific and manufacturing areas. Therefore subcontracting is a narrower concept than outsourcing, and can be seen as part of outsourcing. However, for simplicity, in this book we use outsourcing and subcontracting as synonyms.

Outsourcing of personnel

Modern Russian outsourcing is in the early stages of development due to a late start; however, there are already companies that provide outsourcing services. The most outsourced functions are information technology, accounting, payroll, administration, corporate property services, catering, office cleaning and security. Industrial outsourcing in Russia, when the company shuts its workshops and transfers the manufacture of products or components partially or wholly, is not as developed as in Japan due to Russia's undeveloped small and medium-sized enterprises and undeveloped market infrastructure. The specific feature of Russia's industrial structure is large Russian companies developing against the background of weakly developed small and medium-sized businesses.

The leader of the Russian outsourcing market is information technologies, which has surpassed the threshold of $1 billion (Melnik 2009). The locomotive of IT outsourcing is IT infrastructure services. The key customers of IT outsourcing are the telecom sector (MegaFon, MTS, Beeline and Svyazinvest), together with large Russian oil and gas and retail companies. But in the latter there is also strong growth in the public sector. Apart from this segment, there is growth in the creation of electronic information resources, which includes the processes of preparing an array of paper documents (jointing, grading, restoration), scans, retrospective conversion, combining the knowledge base and scanned images into a single resource, and service support, primarily of telecommunications equipment (Melnik 2009). Despite the generally positive trend, experts note the following distinctive characteristics of the Russian IT outsourcing market: the low level of maturity and lack of transparency and common industry standards, a low level of knowledge in the field of outsourcing, and the leadership of enterprises. According to experts, the key factors contributing to the development of IT outsourcing in Russia today are optimisation of company costs, changes in the technology of management, and the growth of competition (Melnik 2009).

Accounting outsourcing is another relatively large area. This trend has developed intensively due to support from government organisations. For example, the government of Moscow has launched a joint programme, Standard accounting services using ASP (Application Service Provider) technology, which supports creating accounting centres to provide outsourcing for small business in the region (Stabus 2013).

However, there is a distinction between IT outsourcing in Russia and in the EU. EU banks are the main consumers of IT outsourcing, whereas Russian banks suppose that all business processes have to belong to the banks themselves. Outsourcing entails fundamental risks, many of which are structural, thus it is impossible to completely eradicate them (Deloitte 2005). Frequently, global companies are unable to find the global vendors to use standardised services in different regions; therefore they need to cooperate directly with many outsourcers, which can reduce the efficiency of outsourcing. The main concern is the potential loss of intellectual property and corporate knowledge, and breach of confidentiality (ibid.). The transfer of the administration of IT systems to providers gives them opportunities to access all the company's data, and it is difficult to reduce this risk. Correspondingly, the risk of loss of key knowledge increases when outsourcing functions that provide leadership in the market. Therefore many companies do not outsource key areas of their business.

There is also a demand for outsourcing of HR processes. In recent years, call centres were established in the major Russian companies and banks. One of Russia's leading suppliers of solutions for call centres is the company Golden Telecom (Golden Telecom 2013). However, there is another area of outsourcing – human resource management – where Russian companies establish other targets and employ other HR approaches for outsourcing. Outsourcing arbitrages internal settlements against external suppliers, where a gradient of difference can be identified and captured. In Russia, outsourcing of personnel emerged after the 1998 financial crisis. Outsourcing HR, where the company transfers some function to another company, looks like offshoring labour arbitrage because the vendors generally use a cheaper labour force by placing the business, for example a call centre, in regions with cheaper labour, or inviting a cheaper labour force from poor regions (countries) to more developed regions (countries) (see Chapter 7).

Outsourcing of personnel is hiring skilled workers without legal registration through specialised agencies. This business model helps to achieve tangible competitive advantage. Presently, in Russia three types of outsourcing of personnel prevail: staff leasing, temporary outsourcing and outstaffing.

Staff leasing is a sort of outsourcing in which an employer transfers personnel management tasks (payroll and workers' compensation) to another company. In the first type (staff leasing), a recruitment agency enters into an employment contract with an employee on behalf of the agency, after which it sends an employee to work at the company for more than 3 months. Its essence is as follows. In company A, the employer creates a workforce of a particular category, calculates their pay, pays social and personal income tax, deductions to social funds, benefits, etc. Company A provides the personnel to company B for participation in the manufacturing process or in other functions of company B (Ermoshina 2005).

Agreement on the provision of personnel is to be distinguished from agreements to provide services or recruitment. Under the agreements on the provision of personnel, one organisation provides other organisations with workers with the essential qualifications to carry out certain functions in the interests of the other organisation. In this case, an organisation that provides staff has only the obligation to provide qualified personnel and accepts no obligation to provide any services. Payment for the provision of personnel is set to a predetermined amount, regardless of the fact that the staff made the scope of services (Ermoshina 2005). The document confirming the actual fulfilment of the obligations under the agreement for the provision of personnel is for the provision of personnel, not for the provision of services (ibid.).

Temporary outsourcing is where staff are selected for short-term projects, from one day to three months. Typically, temporary staff are recruited for a period of illness or vacation of regular staff members, or to be service personnel at trade shows, fairs and conferences. This type of outsourcing of personnel is more applicable to traditional temporary employees such as interim, contractual and seasonal jobs.

Outstaffing (often called payroll outsourcing) is the relocation of HR management functions to external entities. The core of outstaffing is in taking the personnel out of the staff of the customer-company and its registration as the staff of the provider-company (often a recruitment agency), with further provision of these staff to the customer on behalf of the provider-company. In this case the employees continue to fulfil their duties at the same workplace, but the provider-company is their employer.

However, it is necessary to note why this form of employment is popular among different companies: the Russian system of simplified taxation permits companies to avoid taxes on salaries by freeing them from the duty of paying the 26 per cent Unified Social Tax. By outstaffing, companies that employ standard taxation relocate some of their employees to a company that uses simplified taxation, or a company that somehow evades taxation. This reduces the number of personnel in the host company and subsequently its payroll and tax burden. Also, between the provider and customer-company there is a need for a contract identifying services rendered. The cost of this service can be written off under various expenses, reducing the customer-company's taxable profit (Sitnikova 2006).

In general, an outsourcing provider who realises staff leasing and temporary outsourcing employs similar taxation schemes to staffing. Labour arbitrage employing migrants (see Chapter 7) often uses outsourcing schemes.

Also, as noted by Sitnikova (2006), outsourcing is an activity that is not precisely regulated by Russian legislation, therefore tax inspectors are likely to pay attention to the opportunities apparent in outstaffing contracts.

A company uses the services of staffing at the stage of activity when it is clear that not all business processes are effective, and are suffering from the activities of the business itself. And the weak point in this case is in the staffing structure.

Outsourcing of personnel provides Russian companies with a number of opportunities in the optimisation of business, such as more efficient distribution of resources; reducing legally binding responsibilities for personnel; reducing expenditures connected with employment of personnel and maintaining their records in accounting and human resource departments and the calculation and payment of salary; reducing costs for sacking employees; evaluating new employees without entering into labour contracts; diminishing the volume of HR paperwork and related expenditure; diminishing the volume of administrative work connected with formalities of business trips and provision of social privileges; and optimising costs for training and remuneration packages (LinkedIn 2013).

Andreyeva (2006) notes that generally firms favour outstaffing of white-collar roles: managers, finance, engineering and IT; and leasing of blue-collar roles: workers in retail, warehouse packers and loaders. The key reason for the popularity of HR outstaffing is the shortage of personnel on the market. But the core problem with outstaffing is that there is no particular juridical framework that regulates the rights and duties of the client company, outstaffing provider and outsourced personnel. The latter have limited rights, which cause complaints from trade unions (ibid.).

Companies practise outstaffing for simplification and adjustment of business processes and to allow more flexibility of employment. As a rule, employees may not mind such a style of work and do not see any significant difference between being a staff member of the company or a contractor.

On the other hand, outsourcing of personnel can create serious problems. Firstly, there could be a lack of involvement in the organisation's business by external workers and inattention of external staff to the reputation of their temporary employer. Not everyone from the supernumerary body perceives the company as actually their workplace, and this can violate corporate spirit. Moreover, outstaffing, that is, the transfer of personnel out from the company to the provider-company, increases the alienation of workers from the product of their labour, and from other workers. Additionally, agency workers do not qualify for holiday pay and sick leave, are not eligible for compensation in the event of redundancy and can be dismissed much more easily than regular staff members.

In the case of occupational disease or injury, they do not receive compensation. Employers save on pension contributions and reduce the number of staff positions in the workplace because expenditure is higher when employing people for a permanent job. Also, contracted staff have dramatically lower salaries compared with full-time employees. There are examples where the salaries of workers hired directly and hired through an agency are different by a factor of two or three, despite their doing equivalent jobs (HR-Portal 2011).

Outsourcing companies have many conflicts with various government organisations (tax, legal, labour, health, etc.); however, outsourcing companies reduce the risk of strikes and poor quality of staff. Additionally, providers take responsibility for employees working in hazardous industries and being injured in production (Auto-sourcing 2013).

However, Vahonicheva (2007) has an alternative opinion: outsourcing of personnel is a semi-legal form of work, for which Russian legislation is not comprehensive, but is nonetheless widespread. Recruitment agencies invite people, through the regional employment service, to major cities, promising them favourable conditions of work and residence, but the reality turns out to be different from the initial offer.

Vahonicheva gives the example of Maria Ryzhkova. A recruitment agency in a small town of the Tambov region invited women to work in Moscow's JSC Confectionery Concern Babaevsky for a few months. The agency promised free accommodation in a hostel with meals, free transportation and wages of 80 roubles per hour. When the job was started, the agreement changed: wages were reduced to 23.32 roubles per hour. Living conditions in the hostel were disgusting, with one stove for 40 women in one room (ibid.).

The company did not offer transport for the night shifts and workers were not given money for transport costs. Complaints were sent by the women to the recruitment agency, which proposed if the conditions were not to their liking, they could go home.

Maria Ryzhkova and other leasing workers were dealt with in brutal violation of Russian labour legislation. However, it is practically impossible to demonstrate these violations due to the fact that, from a legal point of view, they were hired by, and were working for, the outsourcing company. They have no legal relationship with the famous factory and therefore the factory is not responsible for these women. Usually the outsourcing company rapidly disappears in such cases.

The State Labour Inspectorate and prosecutors now usually carry out documentary checks of labour rights. This means that they are looking for documents and they usually ask for proof that the person was really working in the company. It usually turns out that people have no evidence to suggest that they attended the workplace, except for testimonies. In this case the woman could not present any evidence of her work because it is a totally informal sector of labour relations, in which nothing is formalised. There are many more people like her in a similarly hopeless situation, where they can prove nothing (ibid.).

Outsourcing schemes are increasingly being implemented in various companies, mostly in industrial enterprises and catering organisations. The essence of this approach is highlighted in the Russian HR advertising of one outsourcing company: 'we will replace two of your regular loafers with one of our freelance, hard-working and humble Tajik. He will do the same job for less money. He will not skive off or protest about rights' (Vahonicheva 2007).

Many outsourced employees have contracts of service with companies, or have no contracts at all. It is important that, according to Russian legislation, contracts of service, in contrast with labour contracts, do not require any benefits or pension plans. Outsourced workers are not union members and lack opportunities to defend their labour rights. Current flaws in labour law allow employers to escape responsibilities for temporary workers. If some-body was employed by a workshop as a short-term worker and he was hit by a brick, it is unclear who would be responsible. The person can go to court, but he will not win the case (Bratersky 2013).

Analysis of outsourcing in Russia shows that outsourcing HR, where the company transfers some function to another company, is relatively similar to offshoring labour arbitrage that employs migrants or workers in cheaper Russian regions. Companies exploit a cheaper labour force by transferring some functions and operations to other companies with the cheaper labour force. Also, outsourcing as well as offshoring labour are activities that are not adequately regulated by the law. However, outsourcing of HR is not the only way of outsourcing in Russia. There are other approaches, which are analysed below.

Tolling in Russia

Tolling is a relationship between two companies in which the ownership of the raw materials passes to the enterprise that manufactures from them and returns the finished products to the first company which, in turn, pays the man-ufacturing cost of processing and an agreed income. An important condition for classifying operations as tolling is that the raw materials, whether imported or purchased in the country of processing, are placed under the customs regime of processing. Thus tolling represents the processing of raw materials imported into the country using duty-free treatments and can be subdivided into tolling with or without the provision of tax incentives (Belova 2000).

With the implementation of tolling, contractual relations are formalised by an agreement where the ownership of the raw materials and the finished product remains with the holder of the raw materials, and all costs incurred in processing are included in the price of tolling. In Russia there are two sorts of tolling: external tolling, where raw materials are imported from abroad by a foreign firm; and internal tolling, where a foreign company purchases raw materials in the territory of the Russian Federation.

In current business literature the concept of tolling exists independently from the concept of outsourcing. Nevertheless, we suggest that tolling is specific case of outsourcing. The common definition of outsourcing is contracting with another subject (private company, public company or individual) to perform a specific function or a repetitive long-term task, where characteristically the function and the task being outsourced are not considered vital to the business. In tolling there are two active subjects: a customer and a processor of raw materials. For the first participant, tolling is just outsourcing of peripheral manufacturing operations, such as IT operations. The second participant in tolling becomes a workshop without traditional business functions such as marketing, procurement and logistics.

Belova (2000) notes the motives of a customer for the implementation of tolling: the desire of companies to reduce production costs through the implementation of all or part of the production process in countries with lower salary costs; and the lack, in the country of the customer, of the technology or capacity to produce the required product. The motives of a processor-company are the desire to reduce idle production capacity; and a lack of working capital for buying raw materials coupled with the unavailability of loans.

According to Burkov (2001), the practice of tolling in Russia uses four major forms of payment: first, payment in cash; second, payment of raw materials where the contract is made in such a way that a certain percentage of raw materials is supplied by the supplier as payment for the processing; third, payment in finished products where a certain percentage of production is taken as payment for services; and fourth, payment may be absent. In this case, the standard output of finished products is understated by an amount that compensates for the processing expenses. This method does not allow an accounts department to legitimately form a cost of processing for the finished product, so enterprises with legal accounting do not use it. The method is included due to its popularity in agribusiness.

After the start of the Russian reforms in 1991, many companies had a shortage of raw materials and underutilisation of their capacities due to the destruction of the vertically integrated production chains of the Soviet economy. However, at the same time the newly formed private companies could purchase raw materials in various ways, including complicated barter schemes. Consequently these companies, having had financial resources, used tolling to produce profit from the sale of the final product. In other words, these companies were doing arbitrage. This system of economic relations was very common and tolling was widespread in Russia in all sectors of the economy. According to the State Statistics Committee of Russia (Avdasheva 2001), in 1998 76 per cent of polyethylene and polypropylene, 43 per cent of synthetic rubber, 81 per cent of motor petrol, 94 per cent of cast iron, 94 per cent of steel, 45 per cent of flour, 75 per cent of vegetable oil and 89 per cent of sugar were produced using tolling. We will now consider the practice of tolling schemes in different industries.

Light industry

Since the beginning of the 1990s, tolling schemes have been used extensively between textile mills. For example, a spinning–weaving factory gives the finishing factory the fabric for bleaching and printing and then sells the finished fabric. Payment is made in raw materials. In 1995–96 there were large independent firms importing cotton from Uzbekistan and processing it by way of tolling. Light industry was included in the global production chain based on tolling schemes when a foreign company or joint venture gave factories raw materials for processing and then took the finished products and paid for services. Such schemes have proliferated for spinning, weaving, garment and knitwear factories. Tolling in this case allows manufacturing of products under the brand name of a Western company (Burkov 2001).

Prior to 1992, the garment industry had a high degree of concentration and almost completely satisfied the domestic consumer market. After the collapse of the Soviet Union, links between raw material suppliers and processors were lost. But on the other hand, restrictions were removed and large volumes of clothes began to arrive from all over the world for the Russian market. In a very short time, foreign imports virtually wiped out domestic producers. Huge enterprises of the garment industry were not ready for such a radical change and many businesses went bankrupt. Nevertheless, there were companies that found a way to work with foreign companies through a tolling scheme. They managed to survive and maintain their production capacity, and did not lose their qualified staff of seamstresses, designers and engineers.

After the default in August 1998, when the rouble was depreciated, the costs of domestic products and imported products were indistinguishable. Therefore Russian manufacturers had opportunities for growth, and many small-scale producers with insignificant manufacturing facilities and little available capital entered the market.

The following case is taken from Bibliofond (2013) and reveals the use of tolling and outsourcing in the outerwear company Sirius, which was organised after the 1998 default and operates in a moderate price range of outerwear for children of all ages. It was related by the owners to small businesses due to small businesses have a number of advantages in taxation. The model of Sirius' business was to buy fabric in South Korea due to the low cost and timeliness of delivery, make clothes by employing contractors, and sell its products to Moscow and regional wholesalers as well as major chain stores. The company did not have production capacity, so chose outsourcing as a key strategy. The company placed orders for sewing (employer tolling) in factories with large capacities of more than half million units per year. Most of these factories did not have competitive brands or strong marketing and had inadequate working capital.

Additionally, Sirius applied a system of outsourcing in other areas of its activity. The company had an outsourcing agreement for providing services for accounting, tax and record-keeping. Development and maintenance of corporate identity, brand names and trademarks were performed by an outsourcing company. Certification of products was held by an independent company, untypical in the sewing industry. Information and computer support were similarly outsourced.

Manufacturing outsourcing allows companies to focus on developing new products, which is important with rapidly changing fashions and levels of demand, as well as to increase the flexibility of production that enables successful competition, in this case in the marketing of a jacket range. However, the company saved for itself the key business functions such as detailed planning of marketing and operations, developing sketches of models by its own artists, fashion designing and sewing samples, together with testing new samples on the market.

Sirius preferred to work with a company from the Republic of Belarus. The main criterion of a partnership with Belarusian companies was the cost of providing services for processing. The apparel industry of Belarus had significant production capacity and provided high-quality products. Belarusian enterprises operated in a competitive environment. The vast majority of factories fulfilled orders for the tolling scheme. It is also important to note that there were no tariffs on the export of goods produced in the Republic of Belarus and into the territory of Russia, and there was a uniform rate of VAT in the two countries.

The main criteria for choosing of vendors of outsourcing were the experience of vendors in working as outsourcers; their production capacity, technical equipment, size and number of processing lines; availability of special equipment necessary for the production of special features, such as embroidery equipment, wet heat treatment and tie-off machines; qualification of staff and their experience in the manufacture of the jacket range; and distance from Moscow and transport links with vendors. The designer and technologist of Sirius participated in the testing of raw materials, cutting and running products into production, and they monitored both the technology of tailoring and the quality of products.

The most important item in determining the cost of outsourcing is the interests and goals of participants in the outsourcing contract. As a rule, each factory calculated the cost of its standard hours, then considered the complexity of the product, and on the basis of these two parameters determined the cost of outsourcing and the required amount of services. Knowing approximately the complexity of their products and the cost of standard hours of vendors, Sirius was able to predict the cost of the service. Usually the company bartered, using fabric from South Korea and China, for payments of service.

The company paid serious attention to the outsourcing contract. The contracts provided for the right of refusal of manufactured products if they did not conform to the details of the contract (technical level, quality and compliance with delivery schedules) or did not comply with copyright law. Additionally, after two months of the contract, the buyer could terminate the contract by paying the amount specified in the agreement without any penalty.

A simplified comparison of the use of outsourcing and in-house labour in situations where the production programme consists of one model in one month and includes 1,000 products shows that the outsourcing cost is 316,600 roubles, and the transportation cost for delivery of raw materials and finished products is 9,000 roubles. Overhead costs for the implementation of the outsourcing process (communication with the factory, travel expenses and incidental expenses) account for 10,000 roubles, whilst wages of the technologist controlling the production process plus social taxes account for 11,000 roubles. The total cost of production in terms of outsourcing is 346,600 roubles (without the cost of raw materials). An alternative solution would be the creation of the company's own production facilities. Consider the appropriateness of this approach with the same production programme. Rental costs are 36,400 roubles, utilities are 12,000 roubles, depreciation of equipment is 20,000 roubles, wages including social taxes amount to 478,800 roubles, with incidental expenses of 3,000 roubles. The total cost is 550,200 roubles.

From the data it is clear that the maintenance of its own production would cost the company considerably more than outsourcing. Aside from the financial benefits, outsourcing gives a firm additional mobility. At high levels of consumer activity, the organisation can produce the required number of items in the shortest time. Having its own production, the organisation will be limited in capacity. Certainly these are theoretical calculations and they involve a number of simplifications. However, this case demonstrates the potential of using arbitrage in Russia and Belorussia.

Sugar industry

The Russian sugar industry is highly dependent on the supply of imported raw sugar. Until 1993 these supplies were provided by state-owned foreign trade companies. In 1993 companies started to produce these supplies themselves. However, many did not have sufficient resources to fund the large-scale supply of raw materials (Pakhomov and Burlakov 2012). Therefore large mediators affiliated with the Russian banks, such as Menatep-Impex and Alfa-Eco, offered raw sugar from Cuba on a tolling scheme. This tolling scheme, along with large corporations, sourced great quantities of supplies of imported raw sugar from the rural producers such as collective farms and farmers interested in the processing of customer-owned minor amounts of sugar beet to produce a finished sugar which is more convenient to use for barter (Burkov 2001).

Avdasheva *et al.* (1997) note that in the sugar industry tolling contracts are most common in areas where there is a complete process chain from the production of sugar beet to manufacture the final product – sugar. Additionally, they note that using tolling contracts is largely displaced for sugar mill executives, who do not satisfy the conditions for tolling.

Often tolling in the sugar industry is used to optimise tax (transfer pricing), for example, the Russian sugar plant Ertilsahar contracted for refining raw sugar and beets with a Moscow company, Prodex-Import, with loss-making for the company and super profitable conditions for the customer. According to one of the contracts from 15 September 1999, Ertilsahar committed to processed sugar beets at the rate of 150 roubles per tonne. However, according to the costing of tolling of beets for the company, drawn up at the same time, the processing cost was 284 roubles per tonne. Thus, even at the time of the contract, the potential losses from implementation were 26.8 million roubles (about 200,000 tonnes of beet), which subsequently caused enormous damage to the sugar firm (Kalyuzhny and Anohin 2000).

In reality, the sale of sugar was carried out through trading houses, which accumulated a significant part of the revenue and profit, and the sugar factory carried false losses. As a result, a significant amount of taxes were not contributed to the development of the district and created a significant imbalance in the relationship between the sugar factory, the community and the authorities (Pakhomov and Burlakov 2012).

Tolling was extensively employed in the sugar industry; moreover, there was high monopolisation of this service. Avdasheva and Dementev (2000) note that in the 1990s in the Tambov region all five sugar companies completely worked via tolling and had only one intermediary company; in the Belgorod region 10 sugar mills used tolling and 45 per cent of raw materials was supplied by the one mediator.

Statistical data and polls show that the proportions of the distribution of finished production are such that the incomes from the sale of finished products of processing enterprises can practically only cover running costs. Tolling contracts provide savings on transaction costs that are associated with the execution of the most basic obligations of enterprises, in particular searching for suppliers and the obligation to pay for the supply of raw materials (Avdasheva and Dementev 2000).

Ferrous metallurgy

In Russia, due to a shortage of capacity of processing hot-rolled steel to cold-rolled sheets, an external tolling scheme existed for processing in other countries. For example, according to the order of the government (Government Decree 1992), the tolling scheme for the Cherepovets Steel Mill was granted exemption from customs duties. In 1992, in accordance with the scheme, the company sent 600–680 tonnes of hot-rolled steel sheet in coils to Germany, Italy and Romania, with the payment of the cost of services for the processing completed by Russian raw materials (Burkov 2001).

Aluminium industry

Tolling was widely used in the 1990s in the Russian aluminium industry in the processing of foreign and domestic bauxite, with further export of processed products abroad. The industry was an undisputed leader in tolling, in both the variety and the degree of use; the share of primary aluminium on a tolling scheme reached 90 per cent of total production. The peculiarity of tolling in the aluminium industry was significant benefits in tax and customs duties. These features deserve special attention, and are analysed in Chapter 9.

In tolling model, where it is assumed that both mediator and processors sell their products at the same price – that prevailing in the market – the profit of processing enterprises is significantly lower when there is a traditional market interaction between them. In turn, the profit of the mediator is increased. Tolling, compared with market transactions, increases the risk for the supplier of raw materials: if market demand for the final product decreases in the period of the contract, its profit will be reduced. In this context, additional income is the risk premium of an intermediary (Avdasheva and Dementev 2000). Another factor in the reduction of transaction costs for the raw material supplier is moving its marketing operations to market products with a high degree of processing. All products made from raw materials have greater liquidity than the raw material. A company that produces a product with a higher degree of processing will face a lower risk of revenue loss due to fluctuations in commodity prices than other firms producing simpler products (Avdasheva and Dementev 2000).

Conclusion

Outsourcing is contracting with another subject to execute a particular function or a repetitive long-term task that is not significant to the business and is able to provide cost savings and improved services through specialisation and economies of scale. Outsourcing was known under another name – subcontracting – which suggests reusable transactions, and these relationships are included in risk-sharing arrangements, technology diffusion mechanisms and distinctive subcontractor control.

Currently, the frontrunner in the Russian outsourcing market is information technologies, where IT infrastructure services dominate. The main customers of IT outsourcing are the telecoms sector, and large Russian oil, gas and retail companies. The important factors contributing to the development of IT outsourcing are optimisation of company costs, changes in the technology of management, and the growth of competition. The other large areas of outsourcing are accounting and human resource management, where staff leasing, temporary outsourcing and outstaffing prevail.

Outsourcing of personnel provides Russian companies with a number of opportunities in the optimisation of business. However, using outsourcing generates a lack of involvement in the firm's business by external workers and inattention of external staff to the reputation of their temporary employer. Moreover, outstaffing increases the alienation of workers from the product of their labour and from other workers.

Outsourcing companies have many conflicts with various government organisations (tax, legal, labour, health, etc.); however, outsourcing companies can reduce the risk of strikes and similar disruption. Additionally, providers take responsibility for employees working in hazardous industries being injured in production.

Outsourcing of personnel is a prevalent semi-legal form of work, for which Russian legislation is not comprehensive. Outsourcing HR is relatively similar to offshoring labour arbitrage which employs migrants or workers in cheaper Russian regions.

Tolling is a particular case of outsourcing and often represents the processing of raw materials imported into the country using tax-free treatments. There are two sorts of cross-border tolling: external tolling, where raw materials are imported from abroad by a foreign firm; and internal tolling, where a foreign company purchases raw materials in Russia.

For a customer-company, the main reasons for tolling are the desire to decrease production costs through implementation of the production process in countries with lower salary costs, and the lack of the technology or capacity needed to produce the required product in the country of the customer. The motives of a processor-company are the desire to reduce idle production capacity, and a shortage of working capital for buying raw materials coupled with the inaccessibility of credit.

9 Transfer pricing arbitrage

This chapter examines transfer price, which operates as an instrument for the distribution of costs and profits between different units and does not represent real market prices. The chapter shows how Russian companies transfer a firm's profit to the Russian region with extraordinary conditions for business. The chapter investigates how national transfer pricing generates profit centres in regions, and how the distribution of revenue among diverse regions influences the sustainable development of territories.

Definition of transfer price

Modern multinational companies are the drivers of the growth of international integration. They present relatively complicated structures consisting of holding companies, subsidiary companies, associate companies, shell corporations, affiliated units and joint ventures, as well as legal entities under either partial or complete control. These entities have extensive interactions which often cross national and regional borders. Different economic conditions and the economic distance between them create the conditions for transfer pricing. That is a type of arbitrage.

Horngren *et al.* (2002) define transfer pricing as the price a company charges for a product, service, loan and the use of intangibles to related companies (subunits). The transfer price creates revenues for the selling subunit and purchase costs for the buying subunit, affecting each subunit's operating profit. Transfer pricing operates as a tool for the allocation of costs, income and profits between different units. Transfer prices can be in relation to tangible goods and services, as well as intangibles such as intellectual property, royalties, leasing, interest payments, expenses and management charges.

Simplifying, a transfer price is a cost at which goods are relocated from one unit to another. A large share of transactions takes place between related units within international corporations without transitions through the independent market, allowing the corporations to manipulate internal prices of their goods to their own benefit. These internal prices, or transfer prices, between the related businesses do not represent real market prices. Often transfer pricing indicates sham operations between related enterprises in order to adjust business income or profit.

Sikka and Willmott (2010) note that transfer pricing is of increasing importance to corporations as in a globalised economy their operations extend to countries with diverse taxation regimes and regulatory capacities. Boosting profits, attaining marketing goals and competitive advantage across different forms of affiliation demands evaluation of costs to measure corporate performance. Under these conditions, companies should improve methods for allocating costs and create strategies for employing transfer prices. Cost-allocation methods are highly subjective, therefore companies use great discretion in allocating costs to particular products and geographical jurisdictions. Such discretion can permit companies to reduce taxes and thus amplify profits by ensuring that, wherever possible, a substantial share of the profits will be placed in low-tax or low-risk areas. Transfer pricing becomes exceptionally significant for corporations in a globalised economy, therefore their activities extend to countries with different tax regimes and regulatory capacity (ibid.). Practically every international company transfers profits at will around the world using transfer pricing (Baker 2005).

The Russian company Norilsk Nickel offers a beneficial illustration of transfer pricing phenomenon. After the 1990s, the company quickly became one of the main suppliers for the European non-ferrous metals market, and it supplied approximately half of the world's platinoid and 20 per cent of its nickel (Norilsk Nickel 2003). As an element of the company's transcontinental market-oriented distribution policy, Norilsk Nickel USA, Norilsk Nickel Europe Ltd and Norilsk Nickel Asia were created, and these companies distributed products to the global markets. The compound configuration of marketing branches abroad assisted in regulating the earnings capacity of the company by establishing transfer pricing between geographical subsidiaries, and exploited fiscal differences between Russia and other countries, decreasing the company's customs and tax payments.

In 2006 the average Norilsk Nickel contract price of nickel was $21,689 per tonne, whereas the price at the London Metal Exchange (LME) was $24,254 per tonne, which is 10.57 per cent higher. The company exported 99,000 tonnes of nickel in 2006, and as a result the reduction in export income was $254 million. Between 2001 and 2006, the reduction in nickel export income fluctuated between $35 million and $254 million (Katsik *et al.* 2008), consequently the reduction of export income in cash from operations was around 30 per cent. The company had a similar reduction of export income for other metals.

When taxation of international companies is discussed, transfer pricing is a central element. By transfer pricing, a company is able to adjust its profit which is attributed to its subsidiaries (or business associates). Overpricing by a company results in high profit for it and low profit for its subsidiaries, whereas underpricing by the main company has the opposite effect. One can illustrate transfer pricing by an example. A company has two divisions: one operates in a Russian low-tax region with a 5 per cent corporate tax rate, and sells products to the second division in a high-tax region with a 25 per cent corporate tax rate. As a result the company experiences the following financial results in, for example, millions of roubles:

- sales revenue in the high-tax region   1,000
- cost of sales in the low-tax region   600
- gross profit   400
- operating expenses in the low-tax region   200
- operating expenses in the high-tax region   100
- profit before tax in the high-tax region   100
- tax in the high-tax region (25 per cent corporate tax rate)   25
- net profit   75

If the transfer price costs 800 = 600 + 200, then the tax payable is 25. However, tax could be reduced by setting the transfer price at 900, which means that the net profit of 100 is shifted to the low-tax region where it would experience tax at 5 per cent, which is 5. Thus the company's after-tax profit would be changed from 75 to 95, that is, an increase of 26 per cent.

Russian companies use many such schemes for tax reduction by transfer pricing.

Russian offshore zones

A firm's profit can be transferred to a region that offers special conditions for business, such as internal offshore zones and special economic zones (SEZ), which permits the firm to use a reduced corporate tax rate. Often these zones, which are analysed below, can permit supplementary acceptable expenses against income as higher depreciation rates and carrying forward of business losses of the company. Second, the profit may be shifted to a region where tax avoidance is easier because of tax administration being fragile and having less strict enforcement of fiscal laws. And third, taxation may be shifted to a region with high corruption, where tax can be reduced to zero or where the state will refund the tax.

World Bank officials state that numerous huge Russian companies profit from transfer pricing by using mediators to avoid taxation. They sell their products to subsidiaries at below-market prices; these trading affiliates subsequently sell the product to the final purchaser at market prices and take the margin. Usually these shell companies are registered in distant districts and quickly evaporate soon after a few financial transactions (Ruehl and Schaffer 2004).

When discussing transfer pricing and tax optimisation, it is important to note that Russia widely uses nonmonetary taxation where federal, regional or local authorities invite a company to participate or invest in some sort of project where it is implicitly understood that the company will not show a profit. For example, a governor of the Russian region asks the owner of a regional brick plant to help build a nursing home by giving 1 million bricks without payment, motivated by the absence of regional funds and the importance of the project for the region. For the company boss, this is not a request but an order. There are many reasons why he agrees to it; however, it is important that for the regional producer a free-of-charge delivery of bricks is a sort of taxation, and he will seek to be compensated for this expenditure. Using nonmonetary taxation gives authorities additional opportunities for realisation of important projects without dipping into the official budget, as well as developing opportunities for the personal enrichment of members of the authorities. On the other hand, it gives an indulgence for transfer pricing and tax optimisation.

As noted above, corporations utilise differences between countries, but in a country as large as Russia it is often relatively easily to use distinctions between regions, primarily the various internal offshore and economic zones of the Russian Federation. Special economic zones have long been established in Russia. Their creation and existence reflect the transition in the direction of market economy and the development of a new legal base.

According to the International Convention on the Simplification and Harmonization of Customs Procedures (Kyoto Convention 1973), a free zone is a part of a country with a specific regime where the goods are considered as objects that are outside the national customs territory and therefore are not subject to the usual customs controls and taxation.

This regime is governed by special legislation, which covers the following topics: customs regulation, taxation, licensing, visa clearance, mortgage and property relations, banking and relation to land ownership, concessions and management of the free zone. Also, labour and social legislation can have certain specificity in the SEZ. Special economic zones are considered worldwide as the active agents of public policy that can revive depressed areas and give further impetus to regional development (Prihodko *et al.* 2007).

There are a large variety of free economic zones operating in the world; however, it is possible to identify some criteria that are common to all of them. The first is the locality of the territory in which an SEZ is created. Secondly, within this special area, more preferential legal and economic regimes operate in comparison with the economic and legislative conditions prevailing in the country as a whole. Thirdly, zones experience specialisation in business and investment activities (Prihodko *et al.* 2007).

In developing countries, the main function of an SEZ is to achieve a higher level of industrialisation and to improve the country's role in international trade. The main, or even the only, source of capital employed in this case is foreign investment (Prihodko *et al.* 2007). A good example is China, which effectively employs six SEZs, 14 open maritime cities, 15 duty-free trade zones and 53 high-technology zones for the development of the national economy (Carter and Harding 2013).

In developed countries, the establishment of an SEZ is used primarily as a tool of regional policy: SEZs are created in those areas where it is necessary to increase the level of economic and social development. The level of unemployment and the income of the population act as the criteria for choosing a site for the establishment of an SEZ. The number of regions that enjoy special economic conditions is always limited because the characteristic feature of an SEZ in industrialised countries is an attempt to give an impetus to economic development of certain territories, and the main driving force is national private capital, government grants and loans (Prihodko *et al.* 2007). For example, Japan has established free economic zones in order to increase foreign trade and regional development. Japan carries out a national development planning system, and in the framework of this plan the country established free economic zones which generally are concentrated in the development of techno parks (Japan Special Economic Zones 2009).

Organizational structures of SEZs are moderately diverse, and from time to time it is difficult to determine the characteristics of a free economic zone because each has a variety of features. Nevertheless, they can be reduced to few major types: export processing zones (EPZ); free trade zones (FTZ); export processing free zones (EPFZ); free export zones (FEZ); industrial free zones (IFZ); and special economic zones (SEZ) (ILO 2006).

In 1990 and during the following ten years, the process of creation and operation of these zones occurred chaotically due to a lack of suitable legislation, an unstable political situation, and constant tension between regions and the federal government for the governance of free zones.

The law 'On Investment Activity in the RSFSR' of 26 June 1991 contained a chapter on free economic zones and, in particular, regulated their creation. In compliance with the law, free economic zones were to be established to attract foreign capital, advanced foreign equipment, technology and management experience, and to develop local export capacity. Free economic zones implied a beneficial regime of economic operations for foreign investment and enterprises with foreign participation, such as simplified procedures of registration of enterprises with foreign participation (Federal Law 1991).

Specifically – enterprises in which foreigners had invested up to 75 million roubles were to be registered directly in the SEZ; benefits included beneficial tax rates with up to 50 per cent of tax rates set for foreign investors in the territory of RF; lower fees for the use of land and other natural resources; provision of the right for a long-term lease (up to 70 years) with the right for sublease (beyond SEZs the term was just 50 years); lower export and import customs duties; a simplified border-crossing procedure and entrance and departure procedures for foreign citizens, including no visa procedures; the right for unlicensed export and import granted to enterprises fully owned by foreign investors, as well as for joint ventures with the proportion of foreign investment over 30 per cent. Such enterprises could also keep their forex denominated gains from export of their output at their own disposal (Federal Law 1991).

In Russian practice, the first form of special economic regimes became SEZs, which were spontaneous, irregular and poorly regulated. The first SEZs were perceived as an area of market relation and the capitalist economy. There was a lobbying struggle between the regional elites for taking SEZ status as it allowed those regional elites to order their financial resources freely (Turovsky 2006).

In the first years of the exploitation of SEZs, there was a lack of clear criteria for their selection and of clear rules of their operation. Many SEZs did not have prerequisites for development, they were a result of lobbying by regional leaders and many had a dubious reputation because they did not bring any benefits to federal or regional budgets (Turovsky 2006). Also, in 1992–95 the government made decisions on specific zones, for example Sheremetyevo free trade zone (1992), Moscow Franco port free customs zone (1993), and Ingushetia favourable economic zone (1994). However, the collapse of the Russian economy and political unpredictability did not permit efficient realisation of SEZs in Russia (Prihodko *et al.* 2007).

There are different types of free economic zones in Russia: first, federal-level SEZs, free trade zones such as Sherizone by Sheremetyevo international airport; R&D zones such as Zelenograd SEZ with a focus on micro-electronics; and informatics and tourist resort zones such as Kavkazskiye Mineralnye Vody. Tax rates were lower and customs procedures were simplified in all these zones.

The second type of SEZ was established to implement specific economic programmes such as the production zone ElAZ in Tatarstan. Thirdly, closed administrative territorial entities (also known as ZATO or the so-called research towns) were territorial objects where high-tech weapons and their components were designed and manufactured. And fourthly, SEZs of the offshore type were territories with special tax regimes such as Kalmykia, Ingushetia, Altay, Buryatia, towns of Uglich and others. Additionally, some SEZs were formed on the basis of special federal acts such as the SEZs in Kaliningrad region and in Magadan region. Their creation can be attributed to their peculiar geographical location (Prihodko *et al.* 2007).

Prihodko *et al.* (2007) also note that the process of appearance of SEZs in Russia in the early 1990s was characterised by the absence of a clear understanding of their actual purpose and mission; the many advantages and privileges granted to SEZs; and the regional authorities' aspiration to sovereignty through the formation of SEZs.

In Russia the SEZ did not became a well organised instrument that creates new jobs, increases export and business activity, promotes regional economic development and improves the quality of regional life. Despite Russian zones having a variety of aims, conditions of formation, governance and other features, most of them could not create beneficial conditions of making business and acceptable social and engineering infrastructure. They managed to create only tax benefits and, as a result, most of them were shut down.

Also, for many years around 40 Russian cities had a special economic regime: closed administrative territorial entities (ZATO). Mostly these relate to the nuclear industry or the Ministry of Defence. They were founded according to the Federal Law 'On closed administrative-territorial unit' of July 1992. ZATOs had a closed position determined by several aspects: they depended on the federal budget because they all received annual subsidies; they had autonomic positions in their regions and did not transfer tax to regional budgets. For many years ZATOs had features of offshore zones and consequently some companies actively used them as internal offshore zones. However, at the end of the 1990s the federal legislation of ZATOs was tightened and they began to lose their special economic status (Turovsky 2006).

The practice of internal offshore zones virtually collapsed in 2004 due to the introduction of federal legislation that prohibited businesses from being exempt from the regional tax rate, which was the most attractive incentive for those who used these domestic offshore services. The regions were able to save some opportunities for preservation of the offshore practices: they can reduce regional income tax rate by 4 per cent and can subsidise enterprise from the regional budget in the amount of paid tax (ibid.).

Also, there is another type of city with a special economic regime – Naukograd (science cities). A Naukograd of the Russian Federation is a municipality with the status of city district, which has high-level scientific and technical facilities (Kodeks 2012). The relevant law passed in 1999 which determines the status of these settlements, and for several years around 70 have been organised with the help of presidential decrees (Ivanov and Matirko 2001).

Generally, foundations for Naukograd were closed nuclear cities in the USSR, which have concentrations of scientific research and production. Many of them belong to the Ministry of Medium Machine Building of the USSR (Minsredmash), which was responsible for the complex of development of nuclear energy (military and civil), and had the whole cycle of works from full-scale basic research and production of raw materials, to manufacturing industrial products, their use and disposal of waste. Many of the Minsredmash cities, Obninsk, Protvino, Arzamas-16, Chelyabinsk-65, Chelyabinsk-70, Krasnoyarsk-26, Sverdlovsk-44, Tomsk-7 and Penza-19, were included in the list of closed administrative-territorial formations and later received Naukograd status. Also, science cities were created in other industries: aerospace (Zhukovsky), electronic technologies (Zelenograd) and biological research (Puschino).

Assigning a municipality the status of science city is the basis for federal transfers to the budgets of the science city. Science cities gave to taxpayers, implementing innovative projects, different tax benefits in VAT, profits tax, tax on land and property, tax for the maintenance of housing stock and socio-cultural sphere, payment for the maintenance of police and health, and tax on advertising (Ivanov and Matirko 2001)

During the Medvedev presidency the idea of Naukograd was partly trans-ferred in the project Skolkovo. In April 2010 it was proposed that a particular legal regime (Skolkovo) be established by a separate law (Kremlin 2010). The Federal Law (2010) was established with the following features: tax and customs privileges, simplified procedures of urban development and simplified rules of technical regulation, special sanitary regulations and fire safety regulations, sheltered interaction with the authorities, and the introduction of a 10-year tax holiday on income and other tax privileges.

Beyond all doubt, SEZs and their derivatives in Russia were an important element of transfer pricing and tax optimisation, but there was always a risk of rejection by the state of eligibility for the application of such schemes. Below, the case of the oil giant Yukos reveals transfer pricing between subsidiaries, which utilised fiscal differences between one region and another, reducing the company's effective tax rate; and shows how the Russian authority evaluated the Yukos approach.

The case of Yukos Oil Company

Yukos Oil Company (Yukos) was created on 15 April 1993 and, according to the Resolution of the Government (Resolution 1993), the company included the oil extraction enterprise Yuganskneftegaz, three oil refineries in the Samara region, oil distribution networks in a few Russian regions and a number of construction and service companies. On 1 September 1995, under Decree of the Government, the oil extraction company Samaraneftegaz and several research and industrial organisations were added to the assets of Yukos (Government Resolution 1995).

By the end of 1995, the Russian government decided to sell state-owned shares. The sale was carried out in several stages: 45 per cent of the shares, formally enshrined in the public domain, were put up for auction escrow; 33 per cent of the shares at an investment tender and 7.96 per cent at cash auctions. Another 7.04 per cent of the shares were distributed among the workforce of Yukos and 7 per cent of the balance transferred to the company for resale in the secondary market.

The winner of the auction and the investment competition was the firm Laguna, which was owned by the bank Menatep. Shares traded on cash auctions were mostly acquired by structures close to Menatep. In December 1996, Menatep bought the government stake in Yukos, which was in pledge, and became the owner of 85 per cent shares of the company (NGFR 2008b).

After privatisation, Yukos began to recover very quickly and over the course of several years became one of Russia's largest oil companies and a leader in corporate governance reform. In 2003 Yukos assets in Russia comprised more than 600 subsidiaries, a team of approximately 100,000 professionals, total production of oil 80.8 million tonnes, 19.2 per cent of Russian oil production, proven oil reserves of 14,709 billion barrels, market capitalisation around $46 billion and dividends of $2 billion. In April 2003, Yukos and Sibneft reached an agreement in principle to merge the companies (Yukos 2006).

In the summer of 2003, the relationship between the company and the country's authority deteriorated, and in October 2003 Yukos Board Chairman Mikhail Khodorkovsky was arrested in Novosibirsk airport and delivered to Moscow, where the Russian Prosecutor General's Office charged him under six Articles of the Criminal Code. Khodorkovsky was charged with acting illegally in the privatisation process of the former state-owned fertiliser company Apatit. In addition, he was charged with large-scale tax evasion.

In November 2004, Yukos received a tax claims audit report for 2003 to the amount of 169.9 billion roubles. The total amount of Yukos' tax debt for the period 2000–03 exceeded 582 billion roubles; including claims made by the subsidiary and the executive collection it was 703.1 billion roubles. This high value of claims was due to an unprecedented level of fines. Yukos' fine was 80 per cent of the principal amount of the debt, whereas in conventional practice the fine does not exceed 20 per cent of the debt. The motivation of the tax authority was deliberate nonpayment of taxes, so fines increased from 20 to 40 per cent, but due to the fact that the company was prosecuted twice for the same offence, the penalty was doubled up to 80 per cent (NGFR 2008b). In July 2004 a consortium of banks, including Societe Generale, Citigroup, Commerzbank, Credit Lyonnais, Deutsche Bank, HSBC and ING, presented Yukos with notice of default. The banks began writing off funds from the Yukos affair from the obligations owed to them.

Analysing the path of Yukos from triumph to financial disaster, leaving aside the relationship between Putin and Khodorkovsky, is a very interesting psychological exercise, as is trying to analyse the major elements of the oil company's financial strategy. According to Russian tax legislation, oil companies have to pay a significant share of their profits to the state treasury. Prior to 2001, oil production was subject to differential excise duty and tax on the reproduction of the mineral raw materials (10 per cent) and royalties (6–16 per cent). The latter two taxes were calculated as a percentage of the commercial oil sales revenue of oil companies. According to the developed scheme, an oil extraction enterprise sold wellbore fluid subsidiary companies, which were registered in ZATO territories with preferential tax treatment. Tax rates in such territories were dramatically lower than in other parts of Russia. All the companies were created in December 1997 and fully controlled by the management of Yukos.

Wellbore fluid is a mixture of oil, water, salts and impurities (such as sand). It is not a commercial product and its production is not liable for tax because the object of taxation under the tax code is dehydrated, desalted and stabilised oil (Pronin 2007). The wellbore fluid was delivered by the Sverdlovsk's company to the plant located near the well, where commercial oil was extracted.

Golubovic (2005) notes that oil was sold to the companies (Business-Oil, Mitra, Wald-Oil and Forest Oil) registered in ZATO Lesnoy of the Sverdlovsk region (also it used other ZATO areas, for example in Mordovia) at a low price, based on the fact that this oil and raw materials were not used for production. Then the wellbore fluid was delivered by the ZATO's company to the plant located near the well, where it was extracted for the preparation of commercial oil. The ZATO's company paid taxes at the regional special rate and paid income in the form of dividends to its offshore shareholder. Dividends were included, if needed, in the consolidated balance sheet of Yukos (Golubovic 2005). Fuel producers had to pay excise. For optimising this tax, the factory capacity of refineries was rented to companies registered in ZATO. Oil and oil products were bought at the lowest prices by these companies, representing the centres of the companies' profits, and were sold at market prices on the domestic market or abroad. Export products were bought out by foreign offshore operations associated with Yukos, and then sold at world prices (Pronin 2007).

Allegedly, these schemes enabled Yukos and its affiliates to reduce its revenue for the year 2000 by 210 billion roubles, and the government sued the company for $28 billion for back taxes and penalties. These schemes were legally justified, they were assured by the large international auditors and were admired by minority shareholders, for which Yukos was positioned as the most profitable and efficient oil company in Russia (Golubovic 2005). It must be noted that similar schemes were used by all Russian oil companies, but only Yukos used the version with wellbore fluid (Pronin 2007).

On 16 May 2005 the judgment of the Meshchansky District Court (Moscow) found Khodorkovsky guilty of the crimes stipulated under different Articles of the Criminal Code and imposed a final sentence in the form of imprisonment for a term of nine years in a correctional colony. As a result, the main oil-producing assets of Yukos became the property of the state oil company Rosneft, and the company Yukos became bankrupt (Judgement 2005).

The key element of the company strategy, as noted by Golubovic (2005), was the shift from production of oil to production of well fluid, and it is not easy to find a lawyer able to establish any violation of the law within this operation. He summarises that vertical integration and transfer pricing were used by most mining companies. Other companies received a higher tax bill due to the inferior talents of their lawyers and accountants in comparison with those of Yukos, who used tax optimisation techniques and efforts to protect the legality of these activities on an extremely large scale. For a long time, the Yukos government relations department successfully blocked any resistance of regional authorities to tax optimisation, including the arbitration courts, but this led Yukos management to a loss of vigilance and they were not forced to think about urgent changes in company strategy.

Yukos is not an exceptional case; the Russian government has initiated other similar investigations against large oil companies that employed transfer pricing and demanded back-taxes and penalties. The oil giant Lukoil established a $200 million back-tax claim for 2000 and 2001 for use of transfer pricing (Komisar 2005). The TNK oil company was hit with a tax claim for nearly $1 billion for 2000 (ibid.).

However, in general their penalties were not as harsh as Yukos' punishment. Moreover, despite similar approaches using arbitrage, the Russian oligarchs experienced different results. For example, in 2003 Alfa-Bank was allowed to sell some of its oil assets to BP. The signing ceremony was attended by President Putin, showing that the Russian authorities are in many ways related to their major business: if Yukos, and by extension Mikhail Khodorkovsky, was destroyed and dismantled piece by piece, the Alfa-Bank, Mikhail Fridman and partners were allowed to sell some oil business to BP, and so in 2003 created, the third largest Russian oil producer, TNK-BP.

TNK-BP also widely applied a scheme for tax evasion through transfer pricing by employing short-lived companies in SEZ Kalmykia (Nekrasov 2009). According to the auditor of the Russian Accounts Chamber, Vladimir Panskov, TNK-BP in the Tyumen region created two companies that bought oil from production companies at low prices and sold it at normal prices to oil refineries. Their profit in 2004 amounted to 84 billion roubles. However, thanks to 4 per cent of the exemption from income tax, which was given by the Tyumen region, the company was able to save 4.2 billion roubles on taxes (Egorova 2005).

Khlebnikov (2003) noted that when a business buys state assets in the course of a backroom deal and at such a low price, it takes the large risk that its rights to the new property will never be safe. Citizens will consider this business as a fraud, and the state will take it as a custodian rather than the asset's real owner.

According to IFS (2002), in 2000 Yukos was the second Russian company in terms of tax payments among the largest Russian oil companies, and in 2001 Yukos became the leader of the largest Russian oil companies in terms of tax payments to the budget in absolute terms and in terms of extracted tonnes of oil. For example, in 2000 Yukos gave $39.7 per tonne of crude taxes and in 2001 $45.7 per tonne, whereas Sibneft gave only $28.3 and $38.9 per tonne, respectively. The average in the Russian oil industry was $36.8 and $37.6 per tonne, respectively. Furthermore, there was large discrepancy between Yukos and Sibneft in the share of taxation. For example, in 2000 and 2001 Yukos had 20.5 and 26.5 per cent whereas Sibneft had just 17.3 and 19.1 per cent, respectively. In general, one can say that all Russian oil giants employed transfer pricing. Egorova and Grozovskiy (2005) note that in February 2003 LUKOIL needed to pay to the budget $103 million due to incorrect taxation in Baikonur offshore in 2001. Baikonur is a town in the Kazakhstan desert steppe, rented and administered by the Russian Federation, where Baikonur Cosmodrome is located. Baikonur SEZ is an enclave almost independent of Kazakhstan in economic terms, because the large share of taxes collected from the registered companies in the city went to the Russian budget.

LUKOIL's production subsidiary sold crude oil at below-market prices to shell companies with practically no assets and employees, apparently affiliated with LUKOIL, and established in a Baikonur SEZ with a low tax regime. The shell companies were 'renting' the assets from refineries such as LUKOIL-Perm Refinery, LUKOIL Ufa Oil Refinery, Moscow Oil Refinery and Ufaneftekhim, which were the actual beneficiaries. Then the shell companies sold petroleum products to domestic and foreign buyers at market prices. Consequently, the total loss to the Russian budget in just 10 months of 2001 was more than 13 billion roubles (Kuznetsov 2002). Thanks to LUKOIL, Baikonur has become not only a window into the cosmos, but also a window to tax avoidance.

Comparison of net income and revenue of petroleum companies shows that top Russian oil companies had relatively similar patterns of net income and revenue. There is no dissimilarity between unit costs per tonne of oil, which is determined by as residual between revenue and net income and includes costs

Table 9.1 Net income/(loss) of petroleum companies per one crude oil tonne ($ per tonne)

	1998	1999	2000	2001	2002	2003
YUKOS	(18.77)	25.89	75.23	54.23	44.00	58.17
Rosneft	(7.92)	14.27	33.96	32.15	20.12	19.69
Sibneft	12.08	19.33	39.24	63.38	44.08	72.43
Lukoil	0.44	14.05	42.63	26.93	23.10	45.41

Source: Khodorkovsky (2010).

Table 9.2 Comparison of revenue of petroleum companies per one crude oil tonne ($ per tonne)

	1998	1999	2000	2001	2002	2003
YUKOS	70.40	93.87	182.46	162.56	163.64	204.48
Rosneft	115.36	126.61	184.10	155.84	183.91	185.77
Sibneft	102.95	107.12	139.42	173.68	181.36	213.58

Source: Khodorkovsky (2010). Data taken from the companies' consolidated financial statements and reports of independent auditors.

of transport, mining, processing and taxes paid. Indicators of Yukos from official reporting generally correspond with the industry average indicators and are relatively similar to the data of Rosneft. Additionally, operating income (revenue minus expenses) for the period between 1998 and 2003 was the same as the industry average. Tables 9.1 and 9.2 confirm the opinion that transfer pricing was the dominant strategy in almost all large Russian oil companies in the 2000s.

In all cases, large oil companies' production subsidiaries sold crude oil at dramatically below-market prices to shell companies which were established in SEZs and were affiliated with the central companies. Shell companies sold oil and/or petroleum products to domestic and foreign buyers at market prices, they also managed to resell oil or oil products a few times between different affiliated companies which could be in different jurisdictions and had different tax benefits.

Companies strictly controlled the full processes of the shell companies through placement of directors, force support and contracts with the shell company. Under contracts, oil giants organised the purchase, transport, processing and sale of oil and petroleum products. The shell companies received the main part of the profit resulting from the sale of oil. The transfer pricing policies allowed oil giants to avoid taxes as the shell companies had large tax privileges in different sorts of taxation.

Resurrection of economic zones

On 22 July 2005, President Putin signed the Federal Law 'On special economic zones in the Russian Federation' (Federal Law 2005), which aims to create favourable conditions for the development of the country's economic and scientific potential through the creation of SEZs. An SEZ is a part of the state and customs territory of Russia set by the government decision, where a special regime of conduct of entrepreneurial activity in the part of taxation, customs regulation and activities by controlling bodies is set. The Federal Law (2005) sets two types of SEZ: industrial, and research and development, with a total area of no more than 10 and 2 square kilometres, respectively, and for a term of no more than 20 years (Federal Law 1991). An essential condition for obtaining resident status of industrial SEZ is the responsibility of companies to make capital investments of not less than €10 million.

According to this law, the central purposes of an SEZ are the additional attraction of domestic and foreign investment in the manufacturing sector, promoting the equalisation of the level of economic development of the regions, the development of high-tech industries and the service sector, and the creation of new, highly skilled jobs. In order to stimulate investment activity in SEZ, in an SEZ a free customs zone can be established and residents will have tax breaks such as diminished rates of unified social tax (rates ranging from 14 to 2 per cent), using accelerated depreciation, including R&D expenses in expenditure, and cancellation of property and land tax (Federal Law 2005).

On 28 November 2005 the Russian Ministry of Economic Development held a contest. According to the results, it was decided to create four technology-innovative SEZ – in Zelenograd (microelectronics), Dubna (nuclear and physical technologies), St Petersburg (information technologies) and Tomsk (new materials); and two industrial production SEZ – in the Lipetsk region (household electrical appliances and furniture) and Tatarstan (automotive and high-tech petrochemical products) (Vasiliev 2006). The SEZ of technical innovation type was created in order to increase the share of Russia's presence in the global markets for high-tech products, concentrating intellectual and other resources to address priorities in science and technology.

The SEZ in New Anapa (Krasnodar region) located on the Black Sea shore was created in 2007 (Government Resolution 2007). The SEZ's area was 780 hectares, and the resort had to take about 360,000 people a year; it was planned to build 43 five-, four- and three-star hotels, 300 villas, a golf club and six trade-entertainment centres. Originally a plan of public investment in the development of the site was 30 billion roubles (Serbina and Perova 2010). In reality, since 2006 the project has received 170 million roubles of budget funds. The income tax for residents was reduced from 24 to 13.5 per cent (Government Resolution 2007).

However, during the three years of existence of the SEZ in Anapa nobody made an investment agreement and not a single investor wanted to invest in this tourism. As a result, in 2010 the government eliminated the zone (Government Resolution 2010). Apparently the authorities gave up on the idea of creating such zones as a mechanism to attract investors' funds (Serbina and Perova 2010).

On the other hand, the state does not provide an attractive SEZ for business, and it was clear that those benefits that were offered to residents of the zone were significantly different from similar projects in Turkey. The costs of tickets for working in the zone and transaction expenditures were higher than the economies from tax, consequently it was impossible to make arbitrage. In recent times new SEZs have often been maintained by enormous investment from the federal budget, which offers good possibilities for profitable business, but in the Anapa case money was given instead to the Olympic Games in nearby Sochi.

In recent years the government has paid more attention to transfer pricing controls in the country. For example, in July 2011 President Medvedev signed a Federal Law based on OECD Guidelines, taking both taxpayers and tax administration to a new legal environment, and consequently increased transfer pricing controls in the country (Federal Law 2011). This Federal Law defines associated organisations, controls transactions and details the information sources required to perform transfer pricing analysis. The new law is founded on the arm's-length principle, a new concept in Russian tax law. It introduces different transfer pricing methods to use the arm's-length principle following OECD rules, and thus connects the Russian legislation with international practice.

The use of domestic offshore zones for tax optimisation has been quite popular for many companies, including state-owned companies. However, there are exceptional companies to which the government gave exceptional opportunities for tax optimisation and arbitrage. Of course, such uniqueness could only be given by an exclusive relationship with the supreme authority, and the undisputed leader was, and is, Gazprom. It has economic advantages (huge export capacity, monopoly position in the Russian market, very significant impact on the markets of the CIS and many European countries). The company's executives widely used arbitrage, participating in the creation of mediators which accumulated profit, for example the second largest Russian gas producer, Itera. However, Gazprom employed the more interesting arbitrage approaches.

In order to facilitate the solution of its own financial and economic problems, Gazprom, using its huge economic and political weight, in the autumn of 1992 obtained from government the right to create a stabilisation and development fund (Presidential Decree 1992). This fund was formed by payment which directly increased the cost of natural gas and also by transfer to the fund of about 48 per cent of profit from gas exports for federal purposes. No tax was levied on the money that entered this fund. In 1993 and 1994, federal exports accounted for 83 per cent of total gas exports (86 billion cbm) and 53 per cent (58.3 billion cbm), respectively. About $35 for 1,000 cbm exported gas was allocated to the fund, which allowed transfer to the fund from this source of approximately $3 billion and $2 billion, respectively. The value of exemptions for income tax associated with export revenues amounted to at least $500 million in 1993 and $150–250 million in 1994 (Kuvalin 2009).

These amounts were only a fraction of the additional funds remaining in the possession of Gazprom, because the above estimates did not take into account any other tax exemptions, such as additional revenue from the share of the production cost, which essentially constituted the same as nontaxable income (ibid.). However, Gazprom stated that the total value of the stabilisation fund was only $1 billion in 1993 and $1.3 billion in 1994, which still makes the size of tax exemptions very significant – for income tax alone it was around $200 million in 1993 (ibid.).

By the beginning of 1994, the total volume of all extra-budgetary funds was comparable with the federal budget. Every industry and each ministry and agency tried to create their own extra-budgetary fund. Thanks to these funds, many enterprises have access to extra money that helped them solve the financial problems of the transformation and privatisation of state property. Extra-budgetary funds were formally liquidated in early 1996; however, Gazprom received compensation for some time, the company did not pay export duties for the export of gas (Shulga 1996).

Tolling

In Chapter 8 we defined tolling as interactions between two companies in which the possessor of the raw materials delivers them to the second company, which uses these materials for manufacture and returns finished products to the first company, which pays the production cost of processing and an agreed income. In this chapter we will discuss the use of tolling for affiliate structures.

The main effect that tolling gives the affiliates is free redistribution from the supplier to the processor obtained during the processing profit. This is obtained by varying the norms of output and the cost of processing (Burkov, 2001). Tolling allowed transferring of part of the taxation in the Russian offshore areas such as Altai Republic and the Republic of Kalmykia. Thus for export-oriented industries that depend on imported raw materials, the use of tolling is stimulated by two important factors: the reduction of customs duties, and transfer of corporate profits to low-tax internal or external offshore zones.

Also, when using tolling, tax administration is more difficult for a tax inspector due to the tracing of the chains in the schemes that are involved in tolling. These are more complicated than the chains based on purchase and sale agreements, as the trade flows do not coincide with the financial flows (Burkov 2001). The extraordinary history of Trans World Group (TWG), which was unconditionally a leader in the use of tolling in Russia, discloses nuances of Russian tolling in the 1990s.

TWG was launched by David and Simon Reuben in the early 1990s. Together with two Russians, Lev and Michael Chernoy, they built a considerable vertical empire in the former Soviet republics in the 1990s. In 1996 TWG was the world's third-largest producer of aluminium; also the company had considerable holdings in steel, coal and many other raw materials (Behar 2000).

Tolling schemes have been used in Russia for 90 years in the aluminium industry in the processing of foreign and domestic bauxite. Russian companies then export processed products abroad. The peculiarity of tolling in the aluminium industry was significant benefits in terms of tax and customs duties.

In such a scheme, neither imported alumina nor its products were subject to customs duties (5 per cent) or VAT (20 per cent). As a result, the share of primary aluminium on a tolling scheme reached 90 per cent of total production.

TWG imported tax-free bauxite, produced primary aluminium and further shipped the metal abroad tax-free. The plants such as Bratsk, Krasnoyarsk and Sayan aluminium smelters received a fee that just covered operational expenditure. According to Behar (2000), TWG made a profit of $500 per tonne of aluminium, which was sold on the world market for about $1,500 per tonne.

At the time of privatisation they captured the stakes of the Bratsk, Krasnoyarsk, Sayan and Nadvoitsky aluminium smelters, Novosibirsk Electrode Plant and Achinsk Alumina Refinery. Only stakes controlled by Vekselberg's Ural aluminium smelters were too tough for them, as they had their own raw material base.

The TWG shareholder activity was only portfolio investment. Trans World bought no more than 10–20 per cent of the share capital, insufficient to have a lever of pressure on company executives or the ability to hold its people in boards of directors. TWG's efforts were not focused on the capture of the property, but on the management and control financial flows (Borisov 2003).

To get around the legislative restriction of participation of a foreign partner in the charter capital of a Russian enterprise, an offshore company which was a part of TWG created a Russian company with 100 per cent foreign ownership, and this in turn established a purely Russian company, which bought up the shares of the plant in its name (Borisov 2003). Around 200 companies were created in the West and about 100 in Russia. The companies were like Russian dolls, with one nestled inside another, many with similar names created in offshore zones such as the Bahamas, the Cayman Islands and the Isle of Man. All these companies were served by TWG's private banks in Western Samoa, Moscow, Bermuda and the Bahamas. Companies conducted the flow of documents poorly, with documentation not being stored; moreover, most of the Russian documentation was destroyed because of potential tax audits (Behar 2000).

The crisis in Russia in the early 1990s and breaking links between companies created problems for aluminium plants (notably a shortage of working capital and raw material supply). TWG arrived at the right time and executives were willing to use any methods, including some beyond the edge of the law. They managed to set up close relationships with the Russian authorities, including the First Deputy of Prime Minister of the Russian Federation, Oleg Soskovets (Moscow News, 2009). Consequently, directors of the smelting plants were forced to agree to tolling, especially due to the fact that the offer of tolling was supported by the participation of aggressive men with guns. According to Behar (2000), Makarkin (1999) and Borisov (2003), during 1995 a few company executives, officials and investors were killed due to their participation in the Russian aluminium business. That allowed speculation of the mass media that the alteration of the Russian aluminium market took place to the accompaniment of gunfire.

However, there is another point of view as to why executives accepted tolling. In that time, executives wanted to maintain control over enterprises by buying up shares in their companies; they were forced to use company money because they had no other source and thus they created a shortage of working capital. Tolling helped them in this task. More importantly, tolling did not bleed the companies dry because the benefit for TWG was tax and duties, which it and the aluminium plants did not need to pay.

In 1999 the Russian aluminium industry underwent a new redistribution of property, which resulted in TWG withdrawing from the Russian aluminium market. The bulk of TWG shares were sold to companies belonging to Roman Abramovich and Boris Berezovsky.

Borisov (2003) supposes that, during the crisis, the Reuben brothers saved Russian nonferrous metallurgy from collapse in the manner of giving a dying patient an oxygen source. However, they forget to say that the oxygen source was taken from the national tax budget.

Despite the opposition of the Ministry of Finance and the Russian Audit Chamber, tolling was actively used until the mid-2000s because it was lobbied for by MPs who were close to the Russian aluminium companies. The proportion of tolling was relatively high; for example, in 2002 Russia produced about 2 million tonnes of aluminium by tolling when total production was 3.34 million tonnes.

Moreover, in 2004 the Russian Audit Chamber found that some companies were breaking the law by using external tolling schemes to cover internal tolling. The Chamber found irregularities in the implementation of Norilsk Nickel transactions related to the processing of raw material from Norway. Norilsk Nickel underpaid customs duty, according to the auditors, by about $4 million. The subsidiary of Norilsk Nickel, Kola Peninsula MMC, according to the tolling agreement had to use raw material from a foreign supplier, but instead it used own nickel concentrate thereby reducing taxes (Ryabkov 2005).

Conclusion

A transfer price is a cost at which goods or services are relocated between related units within international corporations without transitions through the independent market. These internal prices do not signify actual market prices, and frequently transfer pricing specifies sham operations between related companies in order to adjust business income or profit.

Transfer pricing between geographical subsidiaries can be employed to arbitrage fiscal variations between one region and another, reducing the firm's effective tax rate and lowering the cost of capital. The company's profit is transferred to an area that proposes exceptional conditions for business, which permits the firm to use a reduced corporate tax rate or authorise additional acceptable expenses against income, such as higher depreciation rates and the carrying forward of business losses of the company.

Also, the profit is shifted to a region where tax avoidance is easier due to tax administration being fragile and having less strict enforcement of fiscal laws, and a region with high corruption, where tax can be reduced to zero.

Domestic transfer pricing creates profit centres in regions where the profit was not actually created: this results in unfair distribution of revenue among different regions, creating tensions between regions and demotivating sustainable development. Widespread use of offshore zones in Russia did not provide an impetus for the development of regions where offshore companies were registered.

Conclusion

This conclusion presents my judgment about the results of the use of arbitrage in Russian business over the past twenty years. It reveals arbitrage as a corporate strategy, where different asymmetries, exploited by company managers to raise earnings capacity, were important elements of the transformation of Russia and the creation of the market economy. This book investigates innovative perspectives on arbitrage as a part of corporate strategy where the scope for arbitrage is the dissimilarities that exist between Russian regions. In addition, it tries to find answers to the questions: How can arbitrage strategies be employed in the economy of Russia? How can opportunities for arbitrage be generated, and who are the main beneficiaries of this strategy?

This book reveals that there are other generic strategies apart from cost leadership and differentiation. Arbitrage as strategy can be put into practice by companies in different industries or markets to boost their performance. It has universal applicability and it does not depend on the company. It is possible to utilise arbitrage as a strategy at the corporate, business and functional levels; moreover, in one company this strategy could be used at only one level or simultaneously at different levels.

Historical examples from Soviet times disclose that arbitrage as an element of business practice is not a new phenomenon; it was inherent within the Soviet system and functioned as a significant controller of economic life. However, in the Soviet Union the opportunity for arbitrage was minimal, and in many cases arbitrage as a business operation was forbidden and was being carried out illegally. After the start of Soviet *perestroika*, with expanding political fluctuations and reduction of state regulation in society, there was exponential growth in opportunities for arbitrage.

It has been shown that arbitrage is possible when there are two conditions: the same asset does not trade at the same price on all markets, and there is a technical opportunity for realisation of arbitrage. As a result, it is feasible to create a matrix of opportunity and price differentiation. This matrix discloses four potential options for arbitrage as well as a diverse strategy for executives. Option 1 describes a position where the opportunity exists for the execution of operations required for arbitrage, but there are few price asymmetries to exploit. Option 2 is the classic case of arbitrage when an opportunity for implementation of operations required for arbitrage exists and there are strong price asymmetries. Option 3 cannot support arbitrage as neither asymmetries nor opportunity exist. Option 4 is the case of robust price asymmetries but feeble opportunity for arbitrage; this option is the characteristic case that determines state and regional regulation, bureaucratic obstacles and limitation of infrastructure of the region.

The book reveals that distance between two regions that have different cultural, economic or administrative dimensions is a significant factor in business. The enormous size of Russia and comparatively undeveloped transportation and communication links generate discrepancies between regions and shape geographical distance between them. Russian cities play an exceptional role as centres for the development and maintenance of the surrounding area. The cities' availability and their network concentration are particularly vital for the national economy. Nevertheless, the small number of cities and the large distances between them reduce population mobility.

The degree of difference of one region from another depends on how the authorities use regional advantages and how effectively they compensate for disadvantages through their own initiatives. A region's business culture reveals a number of examples of social norms and values that create distance between regions. Moreover, cultural distance increases when there is a lack of connective ethnic or social networks; a growth of national self-consciousness in the Russian autonomies forms larger cultural distance among regions.

Russia has inter-regional ties which mostly depend upon geographical distance between regions; on the other hand there is inter-regional antagonism due to regions competing with each other for resources, trade quotas and preferences of local participants. A regional authority desires to protect local industries, which often increases administrative distance. Regional governments try to build special conditions for loyal, regional businesses and to raise barriers against external companies.

Modern spatial patterns of Russian socio-economic development have become extremely mosaic: earlier-developed industrial regions, newly developed resource-extraction areas and the southern agro-industrial regions can be divided into open regions and those closed to the global economy.

The differences between the subjects of the Russian Federation and the size of social spending from the national budget have increased, which leads to an increase in regional disparities in the provision of social benefits, services, education, health, culture and art. There are considerable differences in socio-economic development of the regions and in the living conditions of the population, as well as differences in turnover and gross regional product per capita, in the level of poverty and the unemployment rate, in innovation, and in domestic expenditure on research and development.

Economic distance is maintained by a weak flow of population between regions. Immobility of the population makes migration as a response to changes in regional conditions impossible. A large, low-income population creates an excessive concentration of low-cost jobs. Instability, strong fluctuations in the regional economy, and overdependence of a region on the performance of an individual industry or business correspondingly increase distance.

The book attempts to investigate price asymmetries and opportunities for arbitrage as well as the causes of price asymmetries and how purposeful human activity creates opportunities for arbitrage. It reveals causes that establish price differences and specific opportunities for realisation of arbitrage. In many of the cases presented, prices on dissimilar markets are not a result of the independence of market forces, but rather the result of purposeful activity of a narrow group of participants who are key beneficiaries of such purposeful arbitrage operations. However, there are opportunities to slip into the narrow hole of arbitrage for other participants: firstly, for firms able to make a corresponding market analysis and decisions more quickly than others; and secondly, for firms that are able to find legal loopholes.

Analysis of cases from the agro and food industries reveals that Russian companies together with regional authorities regularly create conditions for arbitrage by generating trade barriers for regional export and import operations. Bureaucracy employs nonmarket prices for agrarian products and limits the export of subsidised products outside their regions. This policy led to an increase in supply and to discounted procurement prices for agricultural products.

Authorities widely utilise a range of approaches for creating and ensuring arbitrage conditions, for instance employing police, and phytosanitary and veterinary controls. In addition, the subsidies paid to farmers are eventually obtained by large agricultural processing companies that are under the direct or indirect control of the authorities; consequently peasants' subsidies are transformed to arbitrage profit of members of the modern aristocracy.

Frequently, a relationship with a regional leader is a central factor because the law has less influence than a ruler's decree. Successful arbitrageurs have access to confidential information, creating possibilities that are unavailable to other participants in the market. For those who are not included in the list of successful arbitrageurs, there are prohibitively high costs of access to information and a lack of access to regulators. The effective arbitrageur has a considerably greater ability to sell services than their opponents due to the proximity of the winner to power and exceptional conditions which set him apart from other participants. For the lucky ones, authorities generate conditions that block unwanted market participants, physically preventing their activity in a given region. Also, barriers can be created by numerous state regulators in the sphere of technical standards and regulations. As a result, beneficial conditions for arbitrage are built for companies that manage to develop a confident interaction with state regulators.

An ability to create conditions for arbitrage is an important resource of a company. A holder of a resource is able to maintain a relative advantage with regard to other companies, on condition that they act rationally. In these situations the holder is protected by a resource position barrier that is, to some extent, equivalent to entry barriers and gives competitive advantage. An ability to create conditions for arbitrage is a valuable and comparatively exceptional resource.

In the context of arbitrage there is an opportunity to realise a complementary generic strategy – anti-arbitrage. This primarily attempts the destruction of price differentiation and opportunities for arbitrage of competitors. However, the cases show that there is limited scope of employing anti-arbitrage strategy if it is employed independently from alternative strategies and if it is not supported by other elements of corporate management.

Geographical differences and administrative barriers create conditions for price asymmetries that give opportunities for product arbitrage. Goods arbitrage as transactions of purchase and sale can be realised with money or in the form of barter operations. Barter was carried out extensively during the initial accumulation of capital in Russia; it was well incorporated into the shadow economy and gave good opportunities for arbitrage.

The Russian economy gives opportunities for arbitrage of commodities employing differences between prices which arise at different times, provided the cost of money for a particular company is lower than the difference between prices. For companies affiliated with authority, the market risk of adverse price changes in assets trading could be hedged by the state due to a close relationship between business and authorities. Specific post-Soviet Russian institutions and substandard work of bailiffs created conditions for postponement of payment. Incidentally, such delays in payment under conditions of high inflation can be considered a sort of arbitrage.

Russian Gazprom uses product arbitrage widely. The company restricted the access of independent gas producers to the Gazprom distribution network; as a result, reducing gas prices allowing further resale of gas by Gazprom and, consequently, the accumulation of profits in the accounts of arbitrage firms. The company limits the access of independent companies to information and participation in tenders, allowing the establishment of large gaps between the market price and the tenders' prices. Also, Gazprom creates conditions for arbitrage by supporting artificial quotas for gas consumers, encouraging them to buy gas at market prices from their subsidiaries, which appear here as arbitrageurs.

This book shows that in Russia there is inadequate valuation of state assets such as land, properties and business. Moreover, private companies using inside information have bought undervalued assets with subsequent resale to a state company.

This account reveals how Russian companies are arbitraging labour costs, transferring operations into low-labour-cost regions to take the benefit of inter-regional differences in working hours and wages. The period of reforms was characterised by a large differentiation in living standards and wages between Russia and the CIS countries as well as between Russian regions. These factors formed and maintained price asymmetries and opportunities for different types of arbitrage.

There are various routes in which higher-wage labour can be substituted for low-wage labour: the transfer of production processes to deprived regions where there are low salaries; the transfer of the workforce from deprived Russian regions as well as from former Soviet Republics; and the use of special closed zones where it is possible to establish special conditions for work and have lower labour expenditure.

There are complementary advantages for companies moving to regions with low wages: emerging markets and asymmetries between high and low levels of labour safety cost, labour law cost, environmental pollution cost and knowledge cost to boost earning capacity. Many Russian regions have a low-cost labour force. However, they often have poor infrastructure and an unfavourable business climate, and so the cheaper labour force is not a sufficient incentive to warrant investment.

Migration gives innovative impetus to Russian corruption and illegality. Companies prefer to employ migrants due to the absence of formal agreements; frequently *gastarbeiter* are not registered in the Russian tax system and do not pay appropriate tax.

The dominant idea of labour arbitrage in Russia is an increase in surplus value by dramatically cutting wages and reducing the qualification requirements of the workforce by replacing the national labour force with foreigners. In contrast to current trends, in which entrepreneurs increase income by substituting the labour force with new equipment and technologies, Russian entrepreneurs substitute expensive labour with cheap labour.

The economic impacts of an influx of cheap labour are an increase in the revenues of companies that employ migrant workers and a consequent increase of unemployment among Russians, a significant reduction of wages in the Russian economy, deficits in the pension and medical insurance funds, and cash outflow from the Russian economy.

This book investigates diverse methods of personnel outsourcing that provide Russian companies with opportunities to optimise their business. However, using outsourcing generates a lack of involvement in the firm's business by external workers and inattention of external staff to the reputation of their temporary employer. Moreover, outstaffing distances workers from the products of their labour and alienates them from other workers. The important factors contributing to the development of outsourcing are optimisation of the costs of the company, changes in the technology of management and the growth of competition.

Outsourcing companies often are brought into conflict with various government organisations; however, outsourcing companies can reduce the risk of strikes and pass responsibility for employees working in hazardous industries to providers. Outsourcing of personnel is a prevalent semi-legal form of work, for which Russian legislation is not comprehensive.

Tolling is a specific case of outsourcing and often represents the processing of raw materials imported into the country using tax-free treatments. The main reasons for the fulfilment of tolling are the desire of companies to reduce their production costs by transferring the production process to countries with lower salary costs, and the lack of the technology or capacity to produce the required product in the country of the customer.

This book examines a mechanism of transfer pricing which operates as an instrument for the distribution of costs and profits between different corporate units and does not represent real market prices. It has been shown that transfer pricing between geographical subsidiaries can be employed to arbitrage fiscal variations between one region and another, reducing the firm's effective tax rate and lowering the cost of capital. The company's profit is transferred to an area that proposes unique conditions for business, which permits the firm to utilise a reduced corporate tax rate or authorise additional acceptable expenses against income such as higher depreciation rates and the carrying forward of business losses of the company.

Also, the profit is shifted to a region where tax avoidance is easier due to tax administration being fragile, with less strict enforcement of fiscal laws; or to a region with high corruption, where tax can be reduced to zero.

Domestic transfer pricing creates profit centres in regions where the profit was not actually created, which results in unfair distribution of revenue between regions creating tensions and demotivating sustainable development. Widespread use of offshore zones in Russia did not provide the impetus for the development of regions where the offshore companies were registered.

In Russia there are different types of transaction and institutional costs that relate to arbitrage. These costs depend on the degree of embeddedness of a company; at high embeddedness, relative costs may be lower. Moreover, for companies that are in close alliance or have family relations with the regional authorities, these costs can be practically zero. Conversely, for beginners without connections to the authorities, the costs are often prohibitively high.

Arbitrage uses a fundamental *modus operandi* in the establishment of strategy and can be implemented by firms in any industry or market. It has universal applicability and so does not depend on the company, and fulfils the criterion of describing strategic positions at an uncomplicated and comprehensive level. Consequently, the firm's relative position in the market is set by its choice of generic strategy: cost leadership, differentiation, arbitrage or symbiosis and the choice of competitive opportunity.

Numerous examples from this book show that arbitrage has become commonplace in business and has progressed from a technical element to the dominant strategy. Arbitrage has become a sustainable norm because it was unprofitable to deviate from it. The stability of arbitrage as a strategy and as a norm of firms' behaviour is ensured by a stabilising mechanism with negative feedback. Moreover, the creation of conditions for arbitrage adjusts, suspends and affects existing law and regulations that impact on the institutional environment. The level of change associated with institutions is directly correlated with the scale of arbitrage.

Arbitrage is embedded in the system of rules, and a refusal to follow these rules may result in a chain of other changes; therefore a company's exit from arbitrage strategy is associated with high costs of transformation. Domination of arbitrage as a strategy generates a particular configuration of the organisational structure of a company and its functionally oriented departments.

The ability of Russian state institutions to regulate the behaviour of large arbitrageurs became increasingly weaker as the financially powerful elite became stronger. Russian institutions created an opportunity for the development of large arbitrageurs. However, it has not been a one-way track: arbitrageurs, together with authorities, have also impacted upon the process of transformation of Russian institutions.

A feature of modern Russia is the relative weakness of central government, despite the brutality of its leaders, which is demonstrated by the failure of federal laws and orders; regions and large corporations often carry out activities independently of Moscow. The weakness and inefficiency of the federal government determines the high level of corruption, crime and unreliability of private property rights. A weak state leads to weakness of private property institutions and as a result to the possibility for certain groups to redistribute property by using state institutions

Considerable socio-economic differences between the regions, and between less developed regions and the centre, generate the conditions for arbitrage. In order to reduce this disparity, and from political considerations, the federal government allocates subsidies to the regions and with some simple arbitrage operations these subsidies are privatised; as a result, the distance is maintained to form a vicious circle of arbitrage.

Arbitrage was the driver of a transition process from state-owned assets to private ownership and a cornerstone of the market ideology. The analysis carried out on the cases in this book gives clear evidence of the importance of arbitrage in wealth accumulation. Arbitrage thus concentrated wealth in the hands of a few owners, generally wealth accumulators and cash extractors, and this slowed the rate at which new technologies and productive systems were renewed to strengthen firms' positions in a competitive global market. Moreover, arbitrage as a core strategy can present a threat to these firms and act as a brake on robust transformation.

There are clear, consistent patterns: firms that are successful are able to create opportunities for arbitrage and benefit from differences between prices. This group of Russian firms have also managed to maintain strong financials and liquidity, helping them to leverage additional lending for investment in their business as well as relatively new technologies. However, it is worrying that these firms are also dominated by a close relationship with authorities where there is also a high level of lobbying, tax arbitrage and wealth extraction, which may damage the long-term condition of these companies.

Usually arbitrage exists in virtue of connections with the authorities; however, it should not be associated only with corruption and dysfunctional bureaucracy. Arbitrage operation profits from corruption, but correspondingly restricts it with its internal channels of balances. The elasticity of Russian regulations and uncertainty of restrictions are at the centre of the functioning of arbitrage.

Arbitrage as a sort of institution is predictable and relatively rational; it helps to glue different businesses, as well as society, together. It allocates incomes, contributes to stability and ensures its own reproduction. Current arbitrage stimulates business to work, offers real and acceptable motivation, but does so in a duplicitous way: its encouragements prioritise short-term achievement at the expense of long-term sustainability.

The scope of this book does not extend to arbitrage in the context of international economic relations and policy. For example, the sanctions applied against businesses and officials from Russia and reciprocal Russian sanctions in 2014 created remarkable arbitrage opportunities for those not included in the sanctions regime. Also, military action in Ukraine favoured some oligarchs in transforming political power into successful arbitrage. Most people hate the war, whilst some like fishing in troubled waters where it can be turned to their advantage.

While the relationship between politics and arbitrage lies outside our focus, it offers a good opportunity for future research into arbitrage as a strategy, not only from a utilitarian and narrowly economic point of view, but also from a wider socio-philosophical perspective. It is my intention that this book will open up discussion about new approaches to strategy and the business environment. The detailed information supplied about the events of the past twenty-five years should lead to better solutions and results.

Bibliography

Academic Dictionary (2009) *Legal nihilism* (*Pravovoj nigilizm*). www.dic.academic.ru, accessed 17 January 2010 (in Russian).

Accounts Chamber (2002) *Report on the audit of Sibneft in 2002* (*Otchet Schetnoy palaty o rezul'tatakh proverki Sibnefti 2002*). Accounts Chamber of the Russian Federation, Moscow. www.compromat.ru/page_14024.htm, accessed 17 January 2011 (in Russian).

Accounts Chamber (2008) *The Materials Produced by JSC AK Transneft on Request of the Accounts Chamber* (*Materialy poluchennyye OAO AK Transneft' po zaprosu Schetnoy palaty*), N ZI-11-03-69/11-03. www.compromat.ru/files/35431.pdf, accessed 28 February 2011 (in Russian).

Accounts Chamber (2009) *Abstracts for the Presentation of SV Stepashin at the Plenary Session of the State Duma, About the Accounts Chamber in 2009* (*Tezisy dlya prezentatsii S.V. Stepashina na plenarnom zasedanii Gosudarstvennoy Dumy, o Schetnoy palate v 2009*). Accounts Chamber of the Russian Federation, Moscow. www.ach.gov.ru/ru/chairman/?id=763, accessed 28 February 2014 (in Russian).

Actual Comment (2010) Garbage – in Jails! (*Musor – v tyur'my!*) *Actual Comment*, 16 July. http://actualcomment.ru/idea/500/, accessed 28 February 2014 (in Russian).

Afanasev, M. (2000) *Clientelism and the Russian Statehood*, 2nd edn. Moscow Public Science Foundation, Moscow (in Russian).

Amit, R. and Schoemaker, P. (1993) Strategic assets and organizational rent. *Strategic Management Journal* 14(1), pp. 33–46.

Anderson, S. and Platzer, M. (2012) *American Made: The Impact of Immigrant Entrepreneurs and Professionals on U.S. Competitiveness*. National Venture Capital Association, Arlington, VA. www.nvca.org, accessed 27 January 2013.

Andreyeva, Y. (2006) The trendy concept of outsourcing continues to confuse. *The St. Petersburg Times*, 24 October (1215). www.sptimes.ru/index.php?action_id=2&story_id=19407, accessed 27 January 2013 (no longer available online).

Ariew, R. (1976) *Ockham's Razor: A Historical and Philosophical Analysis of Ockham's Principle of Parsimony*. University of Illinois, Champaign-Urbana, IL.

Aristotle (1953 [350 BCE]) *Metaphysics*, translated by W.D. Ross. Greek text with commentary. 2 vols. Clarendon Press, Oxford. http://classics.mit.edu/Aristotle/metaphysics.html, accessed 17 January 2014.

Aron, L. (2008) *21st-Century Sultanate*. American Enterprise Institute, 14 November. www.american.com/archive/2008/november-december-magazine/21st-century-sultanate/, accessed 17 January 2010.

ASM (1995) *Car Industry of Russia.* ASM-Holding, Moscow. www.asm-holding.ru, accessed 17 January 2013 (in Russian).

ASM (1997) *Car Industry of Russia.* ASM-Holding, Moscow. www.asm-holding.ru, accessed 17 January 2013 (in Russian).

ASM (2007) *Car Industry of Russia.* ASM-Holding, Moscow. www.asm-holding.ru, accessed 17 January 2013 (in Russian).

Åslund, A. (2007) *Russia's Capitalist Revolution.* Peterson Institute for International Economics, Washington, DC.

AssiDomän (1998) AssiDomän to withdraw from Segezha. *AssiDomän Corporate Communications,* 12 February. http://news.cision.com/sveaskog/r/assidoman-to-with draw-from-segezha,c2481, accessed 10 November 2015.

Astakhova, V. (2005) *Labour Relations in the Modern World: Features and Prospects* (*Trudovyye otnosheniya v sovremennom mire: osobennosti i perspektivy*). International Relations, Moscow (in Russian).

Avdasheva, S. (2001) *Tolling in Russian Industry: Causes and Results of Using* (*Daval'chestvo v rossiyskoy promyshlennosti prichiny i rezul'taty ispol'zovaniya*). Voprosy Ekonomiki, Moscow (in Russian).

Avdasheva, S. and Dementev, V. (2000) Shareholder and non-property mechanisms of integration in the Russian business-groups. *Russian Economic Journal* 1, pp. 13–27.

Avdasheva, S., Rozanov, N. and Popovskaya, E. (1997) Competitive interactions in the economy of Russia: the market of sugar. *Economic Journal of the Higher School of Economics* 2, pp. 67–77.

AvtoVAZ (1996). *Annual Reports 1996.* AvtoVAZ, Togliatti. www.lada-auto.ru, accessed 15 March 2010 (in Russian).

AvtoVAZ (1998). *Annual Reports 1998.* AvtoVAZ, Togliatti. www.lada-auto.ru, accessed 15 March 2010 (in Russian).

Auto-sourcing (2013) *What is Outsourcing and Outstaffing? Auto-sourcing.* www.auto-sorcing.ru/chto-takoe-autstaffing/, accessed 17 January 2014 (in Russian).

Autostat (2010) *Assembly and Localization of Foreign Cars in Russia* (*Sborka i lokalizatsiya inomarok v Rossii*). Autostat, Togliatti, 20 December (in Russian).

Avtotor (2013) *History of Avtotor.* Avtotor, Moscow. www.avtotor.ru/index.php?op tion=com_content&view=article&id=70&Itemid=476, accessed 17 January 2014 (in Russian).

Back-in-USSR (2012) *How Are Prices for Vodka* (*Kak menyalis ceny na vodku*). http:// back-in-ussr.com/2015/01/kak-menyalis-ceny-na-vodku.html, accessed 17 January 2014 (in Russian).

Baker, R. (2005) *Capitalism's Achilles Heel.* John Wiley, Hoboken, NJ.

Barney, J. (1991) Firm resources and sustained competitive advantage. *Journal of Management* 17, pp. 99–120.

Behar, R. (2000) Capitalism in a cold climate. *Fortune,* 12 June.

Belchenko, V. (2011) Hello, barter! *Sterligoff,* 27 April. http://kommersant.ru/doc/2301897, accessed 10 November 2015 (in Russian).

Belkovsky, S. and Golishev, V. (2006) Business of Vladimir Putin. *Modernlib.* http://m odernlib.ru/books/belkovskiy_stanislav/biznes_vladimira_putina/read/, accessed 27 January 2013 (in Russian).

Belkovsky, S., Golishev, V., Karev, R., Krichevsky, N. and Remizov, M. (2006) Cash-ing of authority: the final strategy of the Russian ruling class. In *Russian Sunset and Draft New State – Civilization,* Club 'Red Square', p. 4. www.intelros.org/club/texts/sbornik_2_club.pdf, accessed 27 January 2013 (in Russian).

Belova, I. (2000) Tolling as an economic phenomenon. *Management in Russia and Abroad* 3. www.cfin.ru/press/management/2000-3/14.shtml, accessed 28 February 2014 (in Russian).

Berezkin, Y. (2006) *Problems and Organization of Finance* (*Problemy i sposoby organizatsii finansov*). BGUEP, Irkutsk (in Russian).

Berres, L. and Levin, K. (1995) Prosecutor General's Office could not secure a partner for Mobil Oil. *Kommersant* 177(895). www.kommersant.ru/doc/118302, accessed 28 February 2014.

Bibliofond (2013) Outsourcing: in search of competitive advantage. *Bibliofond*. www.bibliofond.ru/view.aspx?id=560549#1, accessed 28 February 2014 (in Russian).

Bikmuhametov, R. (2010) Higher export duties on Russian round wood again postponed (Povysheniye eksportnykh poshlin na rossiyskiy kruglyak snova otlozheno). *Economics and Life*, 22 January. www.eg-online.ru/article/88960, accessed 28 February 2014 (in Russian).

Blinnikov, M. (2011) *A Geography of Russia and its Neighbors*. Guilford Press, New York.

Bogdanov, S. (2010) *Economic Crime in the USSR 1945–1990. Reproduction Factors and Main Indicators Features of Public Counter* (*Khozyaystvenno – korystnaya prestupnost' v SSSR 1945–1990: faktory vosproizvodstva, osnovnyye pokazateli, osobennosti gosudarstvennogo protivodeystviya*). Abstract thesis for the degree of Doctor of Historical Sciences, 1 June. Gubkin Institute, Gubkin (in Russian).

Boisot, M. and Meyer, M. (2008) Which way through the open door? Reflections on the internationalization of Chinese firms. *Management and Organization Review* 4(3), p. 349.

Borisov, Y. (2003) Aluminium saga (1993–2003) (Alyuminiyevaya saga (1993–2003)). *Sliyaniya i pogloshcheniya* 3. www.ma-journal.ru/archive/3/2003/, accessed 28 February 2014 (in Russian) (no longer available online).

Bratersky, A. (2013 [1762]) New bill to hit businesses hard Wednesday. *The St. Petersburg Times*, 5 June.

Bronfenbrenner, K. and Luce, S. (2004) *The Changing Nature of Corporate Global Restructuring: The Impact of Production Shifts on Jobs in the U.S., China and Around the Globe*. US–China Economic and Security Review Commission, Washington, DC.

Business Petersburg (2010) Sterligov traded of barter for gold (Sterligov promenyal barter na zoloto). *Business Petersburg*. www.dp.ru/a/2010/01/20/Sterligov_promenja l_barter/, accessed 17 January 2014 (in Russian).

Brinkerhoff, W. and Goldsmith, A. (2002) *Clientelism, Patrimonialism and Democratic Governance: An Overview and Framework for Assessment and Programming*. Abt Associates Inc., Bethesda, MD.

Burkov, A. (2001) Tolling: an economic analysis (Tolling: Ekonomicheskiy analiz). *Problems of Forecasting* 2. www.ecfor.ru/fp/index.php?pid=archive/2001_2, accessed 28 February 2014 (in Russian).

Bushueva, J. (2001) How can we liberalize Gazprom? (Kak nam liberalizovat' Gazprom?). *Vedomosti*, 21 May (in Russian).

Call Center Guru (2012) Sberbank creates Omsk Contact Centre on 2500 workspaces. *Call Center Guru*, 6 July. www.callcenterguru.ru/news/1339, accessed 28 February 2014 (in Russian).

Carter, C. and Harding, A. (2013) *Special Economic Zones in Asian Market Economies*. Routledge, London and New York.

Census (2010) *The Results of the National Population Census*. Federal State Statistics Service, Moscow. www.perepis-2010.ru/results_of_the_census, accessed 27 January 2013.

Cheberko, I. and Rozhkova, M. (1997) Karelia issued an ultimatum concern re AssiDoman (Kareliya vydvinula ul'timatum kontsernu AssiDoman), *Kommersant* 107(1289). www.kommersant.ru/doc/180752, accessed 17 January 2014 (in Russian).

Chechen Republic (2001) The ban on the export of commodity grain outside the Chechen Republic, *Order of the Government of the Chechen Republic*, 10 August, N 257-p. www.zakonprost.ru/content/regional/77/308570, accessed 17 January 2013 (in Russian).

Chelischeva, V. (2013) Gazprom: dreams of investigation coming true (Gazprom: Mechty sledstviya sbyvayutsya). *Novaya gazeta* 48, 6 May. www.novayagazeta.ru/inquests/57849.html, accessed 28 February 2014 (in Russian).

CIA (2012) *Russia*. Central Intelligence Agency, Langley, VA. www.cia.gov/library/publications/the-world-factbook/geos/rs.html, accessed 17 January 2014.

CIS (2005) *The Commonwealth of Independent States in 2005*. Commonwealth of Independent States, Moscow (in Russian).

Coase, R. (1937) The nature of the firm. *Economica, New Series* 4(16), pp. 386–405.

Collis, D. and Montgomery, C. (2005) *Corporate Strategy: A Resource-Based Approach*, 2nd edn. McGraw-Hill/Irwin, Boston, MA.

Constitution (2013) *The Constitution of the Russian Federation*. www.constitution.ru/en/10003000-04.htm, accessed 17 January 2014.

Constitutional Law (2013) *Constitutional Law*. Academic, Moscow.

Couto, V., Lewin, A., Mani, M., Manning, S., Sehgal, V. and Russell, J. (2007) *Offshoring 2.0: Contracting Knowledge and Innovation to Expand Global Capabilities Companies Seeking Intellectual Talent Beyond their Borders*. Offshoring Research Network, Centre for International Business Education and Research, Duke University, Fuqua School of Business. www.offshoring.fuqua.duke.edu/pdfs/, accessed 27 January 2013 (no longer available online).

Criminal Code (1960) *Criminal Code of the RSFSR from 27.10.1960, Article 154, 'Speculation'*. http://arhiv.inpravo.ru/texts3/document3053/page4.htm, accessed 17 January 2014 (in Russian).

Csaki, C., Matusevich, V., Nash, J. and Kray, H. (2002) *Food and Agricultural Policy in Russia. Progress to Date and the Road Forward*. Technical Paper N 523. World Bank, Washington, DC.

CUPVSTO (2013) *Pipeline System Eastern Siberia–Pacific Ocean*. CUPVSTO, Angarsk. http://en.cupvsto.transneft.ru/about/, accessed 10 November 2015.

Danilova, S. (2012) Banks, confectioners, tobacco manufacturers, telecom operators already transferred to the province of its back-office (Banki, konditery, proizvoditeli tabaka, operatory svyazi uzhe pereveli v provintsiyu svoi bek-ofisy). *Vedomosti*, 17 May (in Russian).

Decree (1961) Decree of the Presidium of the Supreme Soviet of the USSR from July 1, 1961 'On strengthening the criminal liability for violation of the rules on foreign currency transactions'. *Bulletin of the Supreme Soviet of the USSR* 27, p. 26 (in Russian).

Decree (1985) Decree of the USSR Supreme Soviet Presidium 'On the Increased Struggle Against Hard Drinking and Alcoholism', in *Sobriety – The Law of Our Lives*. Political Literature Publishing House, Moscow (in Russian).

Deloitte (2005) *Calling a Change in the Outsourcing Market. The Realities for the World's Largest Organizations*. Deloitte Development LLC.

Demsetz, H. (2008) *From Economic Man to Economic System: Essays on Human Behavior and the Institutions of Capitalism.* Cambridge University Press, Cambridge.

Derbilova, C. and Reznik, I. (2004) Gazprom will block the pipe independent gas producers (Gazprom perekroyet trubu nezavisimym proizvoditelyam gaza). *Vedomosti*, 1 July (in Russian).

Dmitrienko, D. (2012) Vekselberg commented on the Hungarian case (Veksel'berg prokommentiroval vengerskoye delo). *Vedomosti*, 24 February (in Russian).

Dni (2009) In Noginsk police rescue children from slavery (V Noginske militsiya spasla detey iz rabstva). *Dni*, 28 December. www.dni.ru/incidents/2009/12/28/182510.html, accessed 27 January 2014 (in Russian).

Dni (2010a) In the Moscow regions 30 Vietnamese slaves were rescued (V Podmosko-v'ye spasli 30 rabov iz V'yetnama). *Dni*, 26 March. www.dni.ru/society/2010/3/26/188326.html, accessed 17 January 2014 (in Russian).

Dni (2010b) Gucci and Armani sewn in Zelenograd (Gucci i Armani shili v Zelenograde). *Dni*, 20 April. www.dni.ru/incidents/2010/4/20/190091.html, accessed 17 January 2014 (in Russian).

Dufy, C. (2005) Barter and transactions between companies: normalization of calculations after the 1998 crisis. *Problems of Forecasting* 1.

Dyck, A. (2002) *The Hermitage Fund: Media and Corporate Governance in Russia*, Case Study N2-703-010. Harvard Business School, Cambridge, MA. http://hermitagefund.com/Harvard%20Business%20School.pdf, accessed 17 January 2014 (no longer available online).

Egorova, T. (2005) In Tyumen – allowed, TNK-BP use of transfer prices (V Tyumeni – pozvoleno TNK-BP ispol'zuyet transfertnyye tseny). *Vedomosti*, 4 August. www.compromat.ru/page_17193.htm, accessed 28 February 2014 (in Russian).

Egorova, T. and Grozovskiy, B. (2005) Sibneft pay off (Sibneft otkupilas'). *Vedomosti*, 18 April, 68(1349). http://old.vedomosti.ru/newspaper/opinions.shtml?2005/04/18/90919, accessed 17 January 2014 (in Russian).

Eggertsson, T. (1990). *Economic Behavior and Institutions.* Cambridge University Press, New York.

Ermoshina, E. (2005) Outsourcing: legal basis, accounting and tax accounting (Autsorsing: Pravovyye osnovy, bukhgalterskiy i nalogovyy ucheta). *Actual Issues of Accounting and Taxation* 7 (in Russian).

ERTA (2007) *Proposals for the Organization of Access to the Gas Transportation System of JSC Gazprom* (*Predlozheniya po organizatsii dostupa k gazotransportnoy sisteme OAO Gazprom*). Group ERTA. http://gasforum.ru/obzory-i-issledovaniya/1605/, accessed 28 February 2014 (in Russian).

Expert (2012) *Regions Ranking.* Expert, Moscow. www.expert.ru, accessed 7 January 2014 (in Russian).

FAO (2001) Paper and paperboard in the Russian Federation, in *ECE/FAO Forest Products Annual Market Review.* Food and Agriculture Organization, Rome, p. 11.

FAS (2013) Decision of case number 111/109-12, July 15. Commission of the Federal Antimonopoly Service, Moscow. www.fas.gov.ru/netcat_files/234/186/h_ccf8bcc9853a6a79751d412f2f11fb52, accessed 28 February 2014 (in Russian).

FBI (2014) Hewlett-Packard Russia agrees to plead guilty to foreign bribery viola-tions. *US FBI/Department of Justice*, 9 April. www.fbi.gov/washingtondc/press-releases/2014/hewlett-packard-russia-agrees-to-plead-guilty-to-foreign-bribery-violations, accessed 28 June 2014.

Federal Law (1991) *The RSFSR Law of 26 June 1991, N 1488-I, 'On Investment Activity in the RSFSR' (with amendments)*. Garant-Service, Moscow. http://base.garant.ru/10105703/, accessed 28 February 2014 (in Russian).

Federal Law (1996) *Federal Law of 22 January 1996 N 13-FZ 'About the Special Economic Zone in the Kaliningrad Region'*. Consultant Plus. http://base.consultant.ru/cons/cgi/online.cgi?req=doc&base=LAW&n=57728, accessed 28 February 2014 (in Russian).

Federal Law (1999) *The Federal Law of 31 March, 1999, N 69-FZ 'On Gas Supply in the Russian Federation'*. Garant-Service, Moscow. http://base.garant.ru/180285/, accessed 28 February 2014 (in Russian).

Federal Law (2005) The Federal Law of 22 July 2005, N 116-FZ 'On special economic zones in the Russian Federation'. *Rossiyskaya Gazeta*, Federal Issue 3831 (in Russian).

Federal Law (2006) *The Federal Law of 26 July 2006, N 135-FZ 'On Protection of Competition'*. Base Garant. http://base.garant.ru/12148517/, accessed 28 February 2014 (in Russian).

Federal Law (2010) *The Federal Law of 28 September 2010, N 244-FZ 'On the Innovation Centre Skolkovo'*. Russian Presidential Executive Office. www.rg.ru/2010/09/30/skolkovo-dok.html, accessed 10 November 2015 (in Russian).

Federal Law (2011) The Federal Law of 18 July 2011, N 223-FZ 'On procurement of goods, works and services certain types of legal entities'. *Rossiyskaya Gazeta*, 22 July, No. 5535. www.rg.ru/2011/07/22/zakupki-dok.html, accessed 28 February 2014 (in Russian).

Federal Law (2013) *The Federal Law of 2 November 2013, N 296-FZ 'On Amending Article 12 of the Federal Law on State Regulation of Production and Turnover of Ethyl Spirit, Alcohol and Alcohol Products and About Limiting Consumption (Drinking) of Alcohol Products'*. Russian Presidential Executive Office. www.kremlin.ru/acts/17297, accessed 28 February 2014 (in Russian).

Fedoseev, S. (1997) *Execution is Not Retroactive (Rasstrel obratnoy sily ne imeyet)*. Federal Security Service of the Russian Federation. www.fsb.ru/fsb/history/author/single.htm!id%3D10318003@fsbPublication.html, accessed 28 February 2014 (in Russian).

Fish Alliance (2013) *About the Association*. Fish Alliance, Moscow. www.fish-alliance.ru/ru, accessed 10 November 2015 (in Russian).

Forbes (2013) Viktor Vekselberg. The World's Billionaires #73. *Forbes*. www.forbes.com/profile/viktor-vekselberg/, accessed 28 February 2014.

FSIN (2013) *Feature*. Federal Penitentiary Service of Russia, Moscow. www.fsin.su/eng/feature/, accessed 17 January 2014.

Fukunari, K. (2001) *Subcontracting and the Performance of Small and Medium Firms in Japan*. International Bank for Reconstruction and Development, The World Bank, Washington, DC.

Gasnikova, V. (2013) Anti-monopolists against arbitrage (Antimonopol'shchiki protiv arbitrazha). *Kommersant-Petersburg* 16(5047). www.kommersant.ru/doc/2116009, accessed 28 February 2014 (in Russian).

Gavshina, O. and Reznik, I. (2010) Billions from pipes (Milliardy iz truby). *Vedomosti*, 17 November. www.compromat.ru/page_30101.htm, accessed 28 February 2014 (in Russian).

Gazeta (2013) The visa regime survival. *Gazeta*, 9 April. www.gazeta.ru/comments/2013/04/09_a_5248613.shtml, accessed 17 January 2011 (in Russian).

Gazprom (2013) *About Gazprom*. Gazprom, Moscow. www.gazprom.ru/about/, accessed 17 January 2014.

Gelpern, A. (2014) Russia's contract arbitrage. *Capital Markets Law Journal* 9(3), pp. 308–326.

Gereffi, G. (2005) *The New Offshoring of Jobs and Global Development*, ILO Social Policy Lectures. ILO Publications, Geneva.

Gessen, M. (2011) William Browder: in Russia there is no state. *Snob*, 25 May, www.snob.ru/thread/71, accessed 28 February 2014.

Ghemawat, P. (2003) The forgotten strategy. *Harvard Business Review* 81(11), pp. 76–84.

Ghemawat, P. (2007) *Redefining Global Strategy: Crossing Borders in a World Where Differences Still Matter*. Harvard Business School Press, Boston, MA.

GKS (2003) *Education in Russia 2003*. Federal State Statistics Service, Moscow. www.gks.ru/bgd/regl/b03_33/IssWWW.exe/Stg/d010/i010630r.htm, accessed 27 January 2013.

Global Wage Report (2013) *Global Wage Report 2012/2013: Wages and Equitable Growth*. International Labour Office, Geneva.

Golden Telecom (2013) *Call Centre*. Golden Telecom. www.goldentele.com/rus/data_center.php, accessed 27 January 2013 (in Russian).

Golikova, V., Karhunen, P. and Kosonen, R. (2013) *Internationalization of Russian Firms as Institutional Arbitrage: The Case of Finland*. National Research University Higher School of Economics, Institute for Industrial and Market Studies, Moscow. www-sre.wu.ac.at/ersa/ersaconfs/ersa13/ERSA2013_paper_01144.pdf, accessed 8 February 2015.

Golubovic, A. (2005) 'Yukos affair' – a show trial or pay for mistakes? ('Delo YUKOSa'- pokazatel'nyy protsess ili plata za oshibki?). *Expert*, 5 December. www.expert.ru/printissues/expert/2005/46/46ex-yukos, accessed 28 February 2014 (in Russian) (no longer available online).

Gordon, I., Haslam, C., McCann, P. and Scott-Quinn, B. (2005) *Off-Shoring and the City of London*. International Capital Market Association (ICMA) Centre, University of Reading, Reading.

GOST (1976) *Petroleum for Oil-Processing Plants* (*Neft' dlya neftepererabatyvayushchikh zavodov*), Specifications, GOST 9965–9976. Date of introduction 01/01/77, Interstate Standard (in Russian).

Gorshkova, E. (2012) Bully of the Saratov assembly is salvation of ZiL (Bychok saratovskoy sborki – spaseniye ZiLa). *Cargofon*, 23 April. http://cargofon.ru/corporate-news/bychok-saratovskoj-sborki-spasenie-zila.html, accessed 28 February 2014 (in Russian).

Government Decree (1992) *Russian Federation Government Decree 11.03.92 N 465-P, 'On Maintenance Company Sheet Cold Steel'*. http://russia.bestpravo.ru/fed1992/data03/tex14622.htm, accessed 28 February 2014 (in Russian).

Government Decree (1997) *Government Decree of 14 July 1997, N 858, 'On Providing Independent Access to the Gas Transmission System of Open Joint-Stock Company Gazprom' (With Amendments)*. Garant-Service, 2013. http://base.garant.ru/11900753, accessed 17 January 2014 (in Russian).

Government Decree (2001) *Government Decree from 11.10.2001, N 717, 'On the Federal Target Program to Reduce the Sisparities in Socio-Economic Development of Russian Regions (2002–2010 and until 2015)'*. http://base.garant.ru/183843/, accessed 17 January 2011 (in Russian).

Government Resolution (1995) *Russian Government Resolution from September 1, 1995, N 864, 'On Improving the Structure of Stock Company Oil Company Yukos'*.

http://old.lawru.info/base29/part7/d29ru7791.htm, accessed 28 February 2014 (in Russian).

Government Resolution (1996) *Russian Government Resolution from April 23, 1996, N 524, 'On Measures of State Support of Production Assembly of Modern Cars in Kaliningrad Region'*. www.alppp.ru/law/finansy/nalogi-i-sbory/8/postanovlenie-pra vitelstva-rf-ot-23-04-1996-524.html, accessed 28 February 2014 (in Russian).

Government Resolution (2007) Resolution of the Government of the Russian Federation from February 3, 2007, N 70, 'On the establishment of the Krasnodar Territory of the special economic zone of tourist-recreational type'. *Collected Legislation of the Russian Federation, Moscow* 7, Art. 891 (in Russian).

Government Resolution (2010) *About Early Termination of a Special Economic Zone of Tourist-Recreational Type in the Krasnodar Territory.* Government Resolution of 24 September, N 752 (in Russian).

Granberg, A. S. (2006) *Movement of Russian Regions to the Innovative Economy (Dvizheniye regionov Rossii k innovatsionnoy ekonomike)*. Institute of Economics, RAS, Nauka, Moscow (in Russian).

Grigoriev, S., Zubarevich, N. and Urozhaeva, Y. (2008) Scylla and Charybdis of regional policy (Stsilla i Kharibda regional'noy politiki). *Voprosy ekonomiki* 2, p. 83 (in Russian).

Grivach, A. (2004) Antitrust in action. FAS is looking for dirt on Gazprom (Antimonopoliya v deystvii. FAS ishchet kompromat na Gazprom). *News Time*, 10 August. http://gasforum.ru/news/2004/10-110804_gp-nort.shtml, accessed 17 January 2014 (in Russian).

Gross, A. (2013) Refusing impunity for the killers of Sergei Magnitsky. *Parliamentary Assembly, Committee on Legal Affairs and Human Rights*, 24 June. www.assembly. coe.int/nw/xml/XRef/X2H-Xref-ViewPDF.asp?FileID=20084&lang=en, accessed 10 November 2015.

Gubskiy, A. and Shtanov, V. (2012) Vladimir Shcherbakov: 'Cars are not wine, over the years do not become better' (Vladimir Shcherbakov: 'Avtomobili ne vino, s godami luchshe ne stanovyatsya'). *Vedomosti*, 4 June. www.vedomosti.ru/library/ news/1812472, accessed 27 January 2013 (in Russian) (no longer available online).

Gusev, A. (2011) Trading threat to the territorial integrity of Russia (Torgovaya ugroza territorial'noy tselostnosti Rossii). *Kapital strany*, 11 November. www.kapital-rus. ru/articles/article/194876, accessed 20 February 2014 (in Russian).

Hambrick, D. and Fredrickson, J. (2001) Are you sure you have a strategy? *Academy of Management Executive* 15, pp. 48–59.

Hardy, J., Currie, F. and Zhen, Y. (2005) Cultural and political embeddedness, foreign investment and locality in transforming economies: the case of ABB in Poland and China. *Competition and Change* 9(3), pp. 277–297.

Haslam, C., Andersson, T., Tsitsianis, N. and Yin, Y. (2012) *Redefining Business Models: Strategies for a Financialized World*. Routledge, London, New York.

Hitt, M., Ireland, R. and Hoskisson, R. (2007) *Strategic Management: Competitiveness and Globalization*, 7th edn. Thomson South-Western, Mason, OH.

Hodgson, G. (2006) What are institutions? *Journal of Economic Issues* 40(1), pp. 1–25.

Honoré, T. (1987) *Making Law Bind*, repr. 2002. Oxford University Press, Oxford.

Hopkin, J. (2006) Clientelism and party politics, in Katz, R. and Crotty, W. (eds), *Handbook of Party Politics*. Sage, London, pp. 406–412.

Horngren, C., Bhimani, A., Foster, G. and Datar, S. (2002) *Management and Cost Accounting*. Financial Times/Prentice Hall, Harlow.

HR-Portal (2011) Outstaffing: the controversy continues (Autstaffing spory pro-dolzhayutsya). *HR-Portal*, 12 July. www.hr-portal.ru/news/autstaffing-spory-prodolzha yutsya, accessed 17 January 2014 (in Russian).

Huang, Y. (2003) *Selling China: Foreign Direct Investment during the Reform Era.* Cambridge University Press, Cambridge.

Human Rights Watch (1996) *Russia. The Ingush-Ossetian Conflict in the Prigorodnyi Region.* Human Rights Watch, Helsinki. www.hrw.org/reports/1996/Russia.htm, accessed 17 January 2014.

Human Rights Watch (2009) *Are You Happy to Cheat Us?* Human Rights Watch, Moscow. www.hrw.org/en/reports/2009/02/09/are-you-happy-cheat-us, accessed 17 January 2013.

Ignatov, V. (2009) Asymmetry of the socio-economic development of the Russian Federation regions (Asimmetriya sotsial'no-ekonomicheskogo razvitiya regionov Rossiyskoy Federatsii). *Terra Economicus* (*Ekonomichesky Journal of the Rostov State University*) 7(2), pp. 132–137 (in Russian).

Ignatova, M. (2004) The fate of the exporter (Sudba-eksportera). *Forbes.ru*, 2 November. www.forbes.ru/forbes/issue/2004-11/21838-sudba-eksportera, accessed 28 February 2014 (in Russian).

IFS (2002) *Evaluation of the Tax Burden on Russian Major Oil Companies in 2000–2001 (Otsenka nalogovoy nagruzki na rossiyskiye VINK v 2000–2001 godakh).* Institute for Financial Studies, 23 November. www.ifs.ru/upload/otb-1002.pdf, accessed 27 January 2013 (in Russian).

ILO (2006) *Export Processing Zones.* International Labour Organization, Geneva. www.ilo.org/public/english/dialogue/sector/themes/epz.htm, accessed 11 September 2013.

INDEM (2004) Typology of subjects of the Russian Federation, in Satarov, G. (ed.), *Regional Policy of Russia: Adapting to Diversity.* INDEM, Moscow, pp. 48–83.

Ionov, A. and Sapozhnikov, P. (1998) Swedes leave the Russian (Shvedy ukhodyat iz Rossii). *Kommersant* 50(1453), 24 March. www.kommersant.ru/doc/195013, accessed 17 January 2011 (in Russian).

Ivakhnenko, G. (2013) Health of migrant workers in Russia (Zdorov'ye trudovykh migrantov v Rossii). *Sociology of Medicine* 2.

Ivanov, V. and Matirko, V. (2001) *Russian Science Cities: From Methodology to Practice (Naukogrady Rossii: ot metodologii k praktike).* Scanrus, Moscow (in Russian).

Izvestia (2013) We are not the best but not the worst situation in the labour market. *Izvestia*, 3 April. http://izvestia.ru/news/547957, accessed 28 February 2014 (in Russian).

Japan Special Economic Zones (2009) *Japan Special Economic Zones*, 1st edn. World Strategic and Business Information Library, International Business Publications, Washington, DC.

Johnson, G., Whittington, R., Scholes, K., Angwin, D. and Regnér, P. (2013) *Exploring Strategy Text & Cases.* Pearson, Harlow.

Judgement (2005) *The Judgement of the Meshchansky District Court (Postanovleniye Meshchanskogo rayonnogo suda).* Khodorkovsky Mikhail Borisovich. The Meshchansky District Court of the City of Moscow, 16 May (in Russian).

Kallioma, L. (2009) Jobs for local residents regions replace the guest workers (Vakansii dlya mestnykh Zhiteli regionov zamenyat gastarbayterov). *RGRU* 69531, March. www.rg.ru/2009/03/31/rossiya.html, accessed 27 January 2014 (in Russian).

Kalyuzhny, A. and Anohin, S. (2000) The redistribution of property: bankruptcy mechanism in action (Peredel sobstvennosti: mekhanizm bankrotstva v deystvii).

Sodeystviye 3/4. http://referat.tver.ru/cat9/referat9584/T, accessed 28 February 2014 (in Russian) (no longer available online).

Kashina, A. (2011) In Perm – 'accounting boom' (V Permi – 'bukhgalterskiy bum'). *59.RU*, 25 February. www.audit-it.ru/news/account/296493.html, accessed 10 November 2015 (in Russian).

Katargin, D., Idiyatullin, A. and Tretyakov, A. (2012) RF Ministry of Agriculture Marat Akhmetov blamed for the collapse of Russia. *Business Online* (*Business-gazeta*), 10 August. www.business-gazeta.ru/article/64450, accessed 17 January 2014 (in Russian).

Katsik, D., Smirnov, A. and Panichev, V. (2008). The impact of finance of large companies into social and economic development of Krasnoyarsk Region (Vliyaniye finansovykh potokov krupnykh korporatsiy na sotsial'no-ekonomicheskoye razvitiye regionana primere Krasnoyarskogo kraya). *Problems of Forecasting* 3. Institute of Economic Forecasting (Ecfor), Krasnoyarsk, Russia (in Russian).

Kertzer, D. (1988). *Politics and Power.* Yale University Press, New Haven, CT and London.

Kharitonova, V. (2010) Types of client's groups in the public service of the Russian Federation (Vidy kliyentarnykh grupp v gosudarstvennoy sluzhbe RF). *Vlast'* 12 (Institute of Sociology, RAN) (in Russian).

Khlebnikov, P. (2003) The case of Yukos: a milestone on the way to the rule of law. *Vedomosti* 45(234).

Khodakovskaya, E. (2011) GR in the Russian on the examples of lobbying campaigns 2008–2010 (GR v Rossii na primerakh lobbistskikh kampaniy 2008–2010). *Pandia.* www.pandia.ru/text/77/212/94242.php, accessed 28 February 2014 (in Russian).

Khodorkovsky, M. (2010) Testimony of M. B. Khodorkovsky (Svidetel'skiye pokazaniya Khodorkovskogo M.B.). *Vedomosti*, 12 April. www.vedomosti.ru/cgi-bin/get_ document.cgi/vedomosti_.pdf?file=///0_1757374236, accessed 10 November 2015 (in Russian).

Kim, W. and Mauborgne, R. (2005) *Blue Ocean Strategy.* Harvard Business School Press, Cambridge, MA.

Klevtsova, A. (2012) In the gas capital of Russia restricted entry. *Radio Azattyk*, 6 December. http://rus.azattyq.org/content/restrict-entry-into-new-urengoy-gas-capita l-of-russia/24790582.html, accessed 28 February 2014 (in Russian).

Komisar, L. (2005) Yukos kingpin on trial. *Corporate Watch*, 10 May. www.corpwa tch.org/article.php?id=12236, accessed 28 February 2014.

Kodeks (2012) *Russian Federation Federal Law 'On the status of Russian Science City'* ('*O statuse naukograda Rossiyskoy Federatsii*'), amended 27 December 2009. JSC Code. www.docs.cntd.ru/document/901730261, accessed 28 February 2014 (in Russian).

Kononenko, B. (2003) *The Big Dictionary Of Cultural Studies.* Veche, Moscow.

Kostenko, N. and Malkova, I. (2010) Torch for $1.3 billion (Fakel na $1 mlrd). *Vedomosti* 49(2567), 22 March. www.vedomosti.ru/newspaper/article/2010/03/22/ 228707, accessed 27 January 2014 (in Russian) (no longer available online).

Kozichev, E. (2009) History of duties on foreign cars in Russia (Istoriya poshlin na inomarki v Rossii). *Kommersant Vlast* 4(808), 2 February. www.kommersant.ru/ Doc/1111783, accessed 27 January 2013 (in Russian).

Kozlova, N. (2008) Ghost town (Gorod prizrakov). *RG*, 28 October. www.rg.ru/2008/ 10/28/fantomi, accessed 27 January 2014 (in Russian) (no longer available online).

Kozyrev, M. (2011) The main mystery of Gazprom are brokers (Glavnaya tayna 'Gazproma' – posredniki). *Russian Forbes*, 15 February. www.forbes.ru/ekonomika/

kompanii/63306-gaz-bez-otkaza-no-cherez-posrednikov, accessed 27 June 2014 (in Russian).

Krajewski, A. and Viswanatha, A. (2014) HP pays $108 million to settle foreign bribery probes. *Reuters*, 9 April. www.reuters.com/article/2014/04/09/us-poland-hp-idUSBREA380EZ20140409, accessed 27 June 2014.

Krasavin, A. and Makeev, N. (2006) The 'gray schemes' of Mezhregiongaz (Seryye skhemy Mezhregiongaza). *Kompaniya*, 25 August. www.kompromat.ru/2006/08/25/quot-serye-nbsp-sxemy-quot-nbsp-mezhregiongaza-nbsp, accessed 28 February 2014 (in Russian) (no longer available online).

Kreknina, A. (2013) Conspiracy of veterinarians (Zagovor veterinarov). *Vedomosti* 128(3390), 19 July. www.vedomosti.ru/companies/news/14358551/zagovor-veterinarov, accessed 28 February 2014 (in Russian).

Kremlin (2010) *Verbatim Record of the Meeting of the Commission for Modernisation and Technological Development of Russia*. Administration of the President of the Russian Federation, Obninsk. www.kremlin.ru/transcripts/7585, accessed 27 January 2013 (in Russian).

Krylov, A. and Rogoza, A. (2012) Vietnamese who died in a factory Yegorievsk were locked from the outside (V'yetnamtsy, pogibshiye na fabrike v Yegor'yevske, byli zaperty snaruzhi). *Komsomolskaya Pravda*, 12 September. www.km.ru/v-rossii/2012/09/12/mchs-rf/692051, accessed 27 January 2014 (in Russian) (no longer available online).

Kudinov, V. and Nikolsky, A. (2013) MVD accuses Browder in the purchase of shares of 'Gazprom' on the grey schemes (MVD obvinyayet Braudera v skupke aktsiy 'Gazproma' po serym skhemam). *Vedomosti* 38(3300), 6 March. www.vedomosti.ru/politics/news/9795161, accessed 28 February 2014 (in Russian) (no longer available online).

Kuvalin, D. (1995) Around 'Raspadskaya' (Vokrug 'Raspadskoy'). *Problems of Forecasting* 1 (in Russian).

Kuvalin, D. (2009) *Economic Policy and the Behaviour of Companies: Mechanisms of Mutual Influence (Ekonomicheskaya politika i povedeniye predpriyatiy: mekhanizmy vzaimnogo vliyaniya)*. MAKS, Moscow (in Russian).

Kuznetsov, A. (2002) Oligarchs leave in the open space. Baikonur as an offshore zone (Oligarkhi Vyshli v Otkrytyy Kosmos. Baykonur kak offshornaya zona). *Novaya Gazeta*, 18 March (in Russian).

Kyoto Convention (1973) *International Convention on the Simplification and Harmonization of Customs Procedures*, 1st edn. World Customs Organization, Kyoto.

Lapin, N. (1998) Russian regional elites: Who rules the field? *Russia and the Modern World* 1(18), pp. 98–120 (in Russian).

Law of Kalmykia (1995) *Law of the Republic of Kalmykia from 28.01.1995 N 7-I-Z 'The Granting of Tax Benefits to Certain Categories of Taxpayers'* (O predostavlenii nalogovykh l'got otdel'noy kategorii platel'shchikov). www.rusouth.info/territory9/pack9p/paper-hfowbd.htm, accessed 28 February 2014 (in Russian).

Law of Kalmykia (1999) *Law of the Republic of Kalmykia March 12, 1999 N 12-II-Z, 'About Tax Preferences for Companies to Invest in the Economy of Kalmykia'* (O nalogovykh l'gotakh predpriyatiyam, osushchestvlyayushchim investitsii v ekonomiku respubliki kalmykiya). http://docs.cntd.ru/document/802000048, accessed 28 February 2014 (in Russian).

Ledyaeva, S., Karhunen, P. and Whalley, J. (2013) *If Foreign Investment is Not Foreign: Round-Trip Versus Genuine Foreign Investment in Russia*. CEPII, Paris. www.cepii.fr/PDF_PUB/wp/2013/wp2013-05.pdf, accessed 26 February 2014.

LinkedIn (2013) *Outstaffing*. www.linkedin.com/company/hrc-recruitment-company/ outstaffing-738177/product, accessed 28 February 2014 (in Russian).

Lopez-Claros, A. (2006) *The Global Competitiveness Report 2006–2007*. Palgrave Macmillan, Basingstoke.

Lotman, Y. (1992) The phenomenon of culture (Fenomen kul'tury), in Lotman, Y., Featured articles in three volumes. V.1, *Articles About Topology and Semiotics of Culture*. Alexander, Tallinn (in Russian).

Lubnin, K. (1997) The new land fleet of Russia – Kia (Novyy sukhoputnyy flot Rossii – Kia). *Kommersant Money* 19(127), p. 5. www.kommersant.ru/doc/20375, accessed 27 January 2013 (in Russian).

Lukoil (2013) *LUKOIL*. www.lukoil.com, accessed 27 January 2013.

Makarkin, A. (1999) Murder of Felix Lvov (Ubiystvo Feliksa L'vova). *Segodnya*, 18 November. www.compromat.ru/page_26962.htm, accessed 28 February 2014 (in Russian).

Makeev, N. and Romanova, L. (2004) The most recent warning by Roman Abramovich (Samoye posledneye preduprezhdeniye Romanu Abramovichu). *Gazeta*, 4 March. www.compromat.ru/page_14541.htm, accessed 28 February 2014 (in Russian).

Markov, A. (2013) The extermination of pigs by governor Gordeev (Svinotsid gubernatora Gordeyeva). *The Moscow Post*, 30 September. www.compromat.ru/page_ 33817.htm, accessed 28 February 2014 (in Russian).

Mazneva, E. and Nikolsky, A. (2008) Gas arithmetic (Arifmetika gaza). *Vedomosti*, 24 December. www.compromat.ru/page_23780.htm, accessed 28 February 2014 (in Russian).

Mazneva, E., and Peretolchina, A. (2009) Unusual order (Strannyi zakaz). *Vedomosti*, 15 October. www.compromat.ru/page_28400.htm, accessed 28 February 2014 (in Russian).

MAPSSSR (2013) *Buran*. Ministry of the Aviation Industry of the USSR (MAPSSSR). www.mapsssr.ru/korol.html, accessed 27 January 2013 (in Russian).

MCPR (2013) *Can Russia Be Out of the World Prison Leader Race at the Beginning of the XXI Century?* Moscow Centre for Prison Reform (MCPR). www.prison.org/ english/ps_leader.htm, accessed 27 January 2014 (no longer available online).

Makarov, V. and Kleiner, G. (1996) *Barter in the Russian Economy: Trends and Characteristics of Transition (Barter v rossiyskoy ekonomike: osobennosti i tendentsii perekhodnogo perioda)*. CEMI, Moscow. www.cemi.rssi.ru/publication/preprint/wp 96006t.php, accessed 10 November 2015 (in Russian).

Marine Harvest (2012) *Salmon Farming Industry Handbook 2012*. Marine Harvest, Bergen, Norway. www.cfwp.be/uploads/contenu/2012%20Salmon%20Handbook% 2018.juli_hy%20tl.pdf, accessed 10 November 2015.

Melnik, O. (2009) Outsourcing: from dream to reality (Autsorsing: ot mechty k real'nosti). *Open Systems* 4(54), 29 September. www.crn.ru/numbers/spec-numbers/detail.php?ID= 31888, accessed 10 November 2015 (in Russian).

Merton, R. (1968) *Social Theory and Social Structure*. The Press, New York.

Milberg, W. and Winkler, D. (2008) *Financialization and the Dynamics of Offshoring*. Department of Economics, New School for Social Research, New York.

Mintzberg, H. (1988) Generic strategies: toward a comprehensive framework, in *Advances in Strategic Management*, Vol. 5. JAI Press, Greenwich, CT, pp. 1–67.

Minregion (2010) *Typology of Regions in Socio-Economic Status (Tipologiya regionov po urovnyu sotsial'no-ekonomicheskogo statusa)*. Ministry of Regional Development of the Russian Federation, Moscow. www.minregion.ru/activities/monitor/region_ dev_monitor/, accessed 27 January 2013 (in Russian) (no longer available online).

Mitrokhin, S. (2013) How and who Sobyanin planted (Kak i kogo ozelenyayet Sobyanin). *Yabloko*, 15 July. www.yabloko.ru/blog/2013/07/15, accessed 10 November 2015 (in Russian).

Miyazaki, H., (2007) Between arbitrage and speculation: an economy of belief and doubt. *Economy and Society* 36(3): 397–416.

Miyazaki, H. (2013) *Arbitraging Japan. Dreams of Capitalism at the End of Finance.* University of California Press, Oakland, CA.

Morzharetto, I. (2011) AVTOTOR: 240,000 per year (AVTOTOR: 240,000 v god). *Za rulem*, 24 October. www.zr.ru/content/articles/372794-avtotor_240_000_v_god/print/, accessed 27 January 2013 (in Russian).

Moscow News (2009) Oleg Soskovets. *The Moscow News*, 24, 1 September, www.comp romat.ru/page_10094.htm, accessed 28 February 2014 (in Russian).

Moscow Police (2013) In the north-west of the capital raided 'illegal immigrants'. *Moscow Department of the Russian Ministry of Interior Affairs*, 30 May. http://p etrovka38.ru/news/item/6018590/, accessed 10 November 2015 (in Russian).

MRG (2013) Gazprom Mezhregiongaz today. *Mezhregiongaz*. http://mrg.gazprom.ru/a bout/, accessed 10 November 2015 (in Russian).

Mulyukov, S. (1997) Market reforms in the oil sector of Russia: problems of pricing, in Kashirin, V. (ed.), *Establishment of a Market Economy in Russia*. Moscow Public Science Foundation Series, 'A New Perspective', Vol. X. http://ecsocman.hse.ru»da ta/758/646SEIFULx60MULYUKOV.pdf, accessed 28 February 2014 (in Russian) (no longer available online).

Nafeev, A., Tihonov, V., Asanov, B., Bulgakov, S. and Magomedov, M. (2013) Epidemiological risk factors due to labour migration (Faktory epidemiolo-gicheskogo riska v svyazi s trudovoy migratsiyey). *Problems of Social Hygiene, Health and Medical History* 5, pp. 10–12.

Natural Gas (2014) Natural gas – from wellhead to burner tip. *Natural Gas*. www.na turalgas.org/naturalgas/storage.asp, accessed 28 February 2014.

Navalny, A. (2008) How sawing in Gazprom. *Navalny LiveJournal*, 24 December. www.compromat.ru/page_23780.htm, accessed 10 November 2015 (in Russian).

Navalny, A. (2009) As Gazprom bought turbine (Kak Gazprom kupil turbinu). *Navalny LiveJournal*, 15 October. www.compromat.ru/page_28400.htm, accessed 28 February 2014 (in Russian).

Navalny, A. (2011) When Putin will leave (Kogda uĭdet Putin). *svoboda.org*, 11 April. www.svoboda.org/content/article/3550209.html, accessed 10 November 2015 (in Russian).

Navalny, A. (2013) Natusik wants BMW 750Li xDrive (Natusik khochet BMW 750 Li xDrive). *Navalny LiveJournal*, 26 May. http://navalny.livejournal.com/802291.html, accessed 28 February 2014 (in Russian).

Nekrasov, K. (2009) Kalmykia, good bye! Plan UK shareholders led by Robert Dudley to withdraw TNK-BP from the Kalmyk offshore. *Solomin*, 23 October. www.compromat.ru/page_28438.htm, accessed 28 February 2014 (in Russian).

Nemtsov, B. and Milov, V. (2008a) *Putin and Gazprom* (*Putin i Gazprom*). Moscow. www.democrat-info.ru/2008/09/17/doklad-bnemtsova-i-vmilova-putin-i-gazprom/, accessed 10 November 2015 (in Russian).

Nemtsov, B. and Milov, V. (2008b) *Independent Expert Report 'Putin. Results'* (*Nezavisimyi ekspertnyi doklad 'Putin. Itogi'*). Novaya Gazeta, Moscow (in Russian).

News Tula (2012) In the Penal Colony number 6 opens manufacturing facility for the production of secondary polymer pellets. *News Tula*. http://newstula.ru/news/

53203/v-ispravitelnoj-kolonii-no6-novomoskovska-otkroetsa-proizvodstvennyj-ceh-p o-vypusku-vtoricnyh-polimernyh-granul, accessed 10 November 2015 (in Russian).

Newspark (2011) Dagestan slavery – the story of an entrepreneur (Dagestanskoye rabstvo – istoriya odnogo predprinimatelya). *Newspark*, 8 July. http://newspark.net.ua/ zhizn/dagestanskoe-rabstvo-istoriya-odnogo-predprinimatelya/, accessed 28 February 2014 (in Russian).

NGFR (2008a) YUKOS. *NGFR (Oil, Gas and Stock Market)*. www.ngfr.ru/library. html?yukos, accessed 28 February 2014 (in Russian).

NGFR (2008b) Sibneft. NGFR (*Oil, Gas and Stock Market*). www.ngfr.ru/library.htm l?sibneft, accessed 28 February 2014 (in Russian).

Nguyen (2010) Secret world of Vietnamese workers in Russia. *BBC Vietnamese*, Moscow, 4 April. http://news.bbc.co.uk/1/hi/world/asia-pacific/8482466.stm, accessed 28 February 2014.

Nocera, J. (2009) Propping up a house of cards. *The New York Times*, 27 February. www.nytimes.com/2009/02/28/business/28nocera.html?dbk, accessed 28 February 2014.

Norilsk Nickel (2003) *Annual Report 2003*. Norilsk Nickel, Moscow. www.nornickel. ru, accessed 17 January 2008.

North, D. (1992) *Institutions, Institutional Change and Economic Performance*. Cambridge University Press, Cambridge.

North, D. (1989) *Institutions and Economic Growth: An Historical Introduction*. Elsevier, Amsterdam.

Novaya Gazeta (2004) Just give the tower (Tol'ko dayte vyshku). *Novaya Gazeta* 67, 13 September. www.novayagazeta.ru/economy/22798.html, accessed 28 February 2014 (in Russian).

Olma (2004) *Sibneft*. Olma, Moscow. www.olma.ru/analytic/Sibneft_rus.pdf, accessed 27 January 2014 (in Russian) (no longer available online).

Oreanda (2009) Vladimir Putin has threatened oil companies to huge fines (Vladimir Putin prigrozil neftyanym kompaniyam ogromnymi shtrafami). *Oreanda-News*, 10 November. http://burneft.ru/news/main/1, accessed 28 February 2014 (in Russian).

Overchenko, M. and Dmitrienko, D. (2011) Abramovich admitted that the auction of "Sibneft" was a fake (Abramovich priznal, chto auktsion po «Sibnefti» byl fikt-siyey) *Vedomosti*, 2 November. www.vedomosti.ru/politics/news/1410605/, accessed 27 January 2013 (in Russian) (no longer available online).

Pakhomov, A. and Burlakov, S. (2012) Situation analysis: business relations in the sugar industry. *Lerc Bulletin* 40, p. 10, www.lerc.ru/?part=bulletin&art=40&page= 10, accessed 28 February 2014 (in Russian).

Pasmi (2013) The country is low self-esteem (Pervoye antikorruptsionnoye SMI). *Pasmi*, www.imperia-a.ru/news/id/4983, accessed 10 November 2015.

Perm neft (2012) Lord of the numbers (Poveliteli tsifr). *Perm Oil* 24(348), 4 December. www.permneft.lukoil-perm.ru/index.html?num=348, accessed 17 June 2013 (in Russian).

Petrov, D. (2009) Useless labour of prisoners (Bespoleznyy trud zaklyuchennykh). *Trud* 26, 13 February. www.trud.ru/article/13-02-2009/138101_bespoleznyj_trud_ zakljuchennyx.html, accessed 27 January 2014 (in Russian).

Petrov, N. and Titkov, A. (2012) *Social Atlas of Russian Regions*. Moscow Carnegie Centre, Independent Institute for Social Policy, Moscow. http://atlas.socpol.ru/ overviews/econ_condition/index.shtml, accessed 10 November 2015.

Polterovich, V. (1999) *Institutional Traps and Transition*. Central Economics and Mathematics Institute, New Economic School, Moscow. http://mathecon.cemi.rssi.ru/vm_polterovich/files/ep99003.pdf, accessed 27 January 2013.

Popov, I. (2013) From the Central Committee of the CPSU in the billionaires: how Vladimir Shcherbakov builds 'Russian Detroit'. *Forbes.ru*, 7 February, www.forbes.ru/milliardery/potrebitelskii-rynok/233968-iz-tsk-kpss-v-milliardery-kak-vladimir-shcherbakov-stroit-ru, accessed 27 January 2013 (in Russian).

Porter, M. (1980) *Competitive Strategy: Techniques for Analysing Industries*. Free Press, New York.

Porter, M. (1985) *Competitive Advantage*. Free Press, New York.

Porter, M. (1990) The competitive advantage of nations. *Harvard Business Review* 68, pp. 73–93.

Porter, M. (1996) What is strategy? *Harvard Business Review* 74(6), 61–78.

Pravosudov, S. (2013) Oil fields of Transneft. *Russian Focus*, 1 December, www.compromat.ru/page_25243.htm, accessed 28 February 2014 (in Russian).

Presidential Decree (1992) *Presidential Decree of November 5, 1992 N 1333, 'On the Transformation of the State Gas Company Gazprom in Russian Joint-Stock Company Gazprom (With Amendments)'* (*O preobrazovanii Gosudarstvennogo gazovogo kontserna 'Gazprom' v Rossiyskoye aktsionernoye obshchestvo 'Gazprom'*). Garant-Service, 2013. http://base.garant.ru/104727/, accessed 28 February 2014 (in Russian).

Presidential Decree (1995) Presidential Decree of 24.08.95 N 872, 'The Establishment of Joint Stock Company "Siberian Oil Company"' (Ob uchrezhdenii otkrytogo aktsionernogo obshchestva "Sibirskaya neftyanaya kompaniya). *Law Russia*. www.lawrussia.ru/texts/legal_185/doc185a379x272.htm, accessed 28 February 2014 (in Russian).

Presidential Decree (1997) Presidential Decree, May 28, 1997 N 529, 'About the Order of Circulation of Shares of Russian Joint-Stock Company "Gazprom" for a Period of Fixing in the State-Owned Shares' (*O poryadke obrashcheniya aktsiy Rossiyskogo aktsionernogo obshchestva 'Gazprom' na period zakrepleniya v federal'noy sobstvennosti aktsiy Rossiyskogo aktsionernogo obshchestva 'Gazprom'*). Base Consultant. http://base.consultant.ru/cons/cgi/online.cgi?req=doc;base=LAW;n=14604, accessed 28 February 2014 (in Russian).

Prihodko, S., Volovyk, N., Hecht, A., Sharpe, B. and Mandres, M. (2007) *Special Economic Zones*. Consortium for Applied Economic Research, Canadian International Development Agency, Moscow. www.iep.ru/files/text/cepra/oez.pdf, accessed 28 February 2014.

Pronin, S. (2007) The wellbore fluid (Skvazhinnaya zhidkost'). *Neft', gaz i fondovyy rynok*, 22 June. www.ngfr.ru/article.html?032, accessed 28 February 2014 (in Russian).

Properm (2010) Beeline will open the call-centre at the plant Dzerzhinsky (Bilayn otkroyet call-tsentr na territorii zavoda Dzerzhinskogo). *City Portal of Perm*, 27 July. http://properm.ru/news/business/18718/, accessed 28 February 2014 (in Russian).

Pushkarev, V. (2005) Last Trade Minister of USSR (Posledniy Ministr Torgovli SSSR). *businesspress.ru* 87/88(281/282), 5 December. www.businesspress.ru/newspaper/article_mId_21962_aId_362860.html, accessed 27 January 2013 (in Russian).

Putin, V. (2012) *Economic Tasks*. Government of the Russian Federation, Moscow. http://archive.premier.gov.ru/eng/events/news/17888/, accessed 10 November 2015.

Quong, N. (2012) *The Second Stage of the Formation of the Vietnamese Diaspora. Imports of Vietnamese Workers in the USSR in the Early 80s*. Nguyễn Huy Cường,

Hanoi University, 2 June. http://web.hanu.vn/ru/mod/forum/discuss.php?d=134, accessed 27 January 2013.

Radaev, V. (2000) Return of the crowds and rationality of action: a history of Russian 'financial bubbles' in the mid-1990s. *European Societies* 2(3), pp. 271–294.

Rappaport, R. (1999). *Ritual and Religion in the Making of Humanity*. Cambridge University Press, New York.

Rawls, J. (1971) *A Theory of Justice*, 1st edn. Belknap Press, Cambridge, MA.

Regnum (2004) In Khabarovsk is found a clandestine plant for the production of plastic windows (V Khabarovske vyyavlen podpol'nyy tsekh po proizvodstvu plastikovykh okon). *regnum.ru*, 6 August. www.regnum.ru/news/304057.html, accessed 27 January 2013 (in Russian).

Regnum (2010) In Primorye a clandestine Chinese factory was revealed that produced dangerous shoes (V Primor'ye vyyavlena podpol'naya kitayskaya fabrika, proizvodivshaya opasnuyu obuv'). *regnum.ru*, 21 April. www.regnum.ru/news/1275957.htm l, accessed 27 January 2013 (in Russian).

Resolution (1987) *Resolution of the Council of Ministers, Council of Trade Unions and the Komsomol N 321, March 13, 1987, 'About Formation of All-Union Coordination Council of Scientific and Technical Creative of Youth and Wage of Members of Creative Youth Collective and Full-Time Employees of the Centre Scientific and Technical Creative of Youth'*. Consultant Plus. http://base.consultant.ru/cons/cgi/online.cgi?req=doc;base=ESU;n=28158, accessed 10 November 2015 (in Russian).

Resolution (1993) *Resolution of the Council of Ministers, 'On the Establishment of Open Joint Stock Company "Oil Company YUKOS"'* 15 April 1993, N 354. http://gaidar-arc.ru/databasedocuments/theme/details/1885, accessed 10 November 2015 (in Russian).

RIA Novosti (2010) Transneft: test of ESPO was initiated by the new management of the company. *RIA Novosti*. http://ria.ru/economy/20101116/297067950.html, accessed 28 February 2014 (in Russian).

RIA Rating (2013) *Regions Ranking*. Expert, Moscow. http://riarating.ru/regions_ra nkings/20120702/610227349.html, accessed 17 January 2010 (in Russian).

Roach, S. (2003). *Outsourcing, Protectionism, and the Global Labor Arbitrage*, Special Economic Study. Morgan Stanley, London.

Roberts, P. (2004) Global labour arbitrage. Dismantling America. *VDARE.COM*, 28 July. www.vdare.com/articles/global-labor-arbitrage-dismantling-america, accessed 10 November 2015.

Rosen, S. (2000) *Nihilism: A Philosophical Essay*, 2nd edn. St Augustine's Press, South Bend, IN.

Ruehl, C. and Schaffer, M. (2004) Transfer pricing and calculating GDP. *The Moscow Times*, 19 February. www.themoscowtimes.com/opinion/article/transfer-pricing-a nd-calculating-gdp/232777.html, accessed 17 January 2013.

Rupor (2009) Semyon Weinstock taken $2 billion from Transneft (Semen Vaynshtok vyvel $2 mlrd iz Transnefti). *Ruporinfo*, 10 April. www.compromat.ru/page_11073. htm, 28 February 2014 (in Russian).

Russia in Figures (1997) *Russia in Figures. Statistical Handbook*. Goscomstat of Russia, Moscow.

Rustabak (2013) In the centre of Moscow is closed tobacco factory, the owner sells the property to a billion roubles (V tsentre Moskvy zakryta tabachnaya fabrika, vladelets rasprodayet imushchestvo na milliard rubley). *Russian Tobacco*, 2 April. www.rustabak. ru/articles/detail.php?ID=49281, accessed 17 June 2013 (in Russian).

Ryabkov, E. (2005) Tolling: to be continued. Metal supply and sales. *lobbying.ru*, 18 January. http://beer.lobbying.ru/print.php?article_id=2074, accessed 27 January 2013 (in Russian).

Rybalchenko, I. (2009) Gazprom stifles independent producers (Gazprom dushit nezavisimykh proizvoditeley gaza). *Georgia Online*, Tbilisi, Georgia, 29 May. www.apsny.ge/2009/eco/1243636650.php, accessed 17 January 2013 (in Russian).

Rybin, J. (2009) Construction sites of Dagestan supplied the slave system (Stroyki Dagestana snabzhal rabovladel'cheskiy story). *Kommersant* 192(4247), 15 October. www.kommersant.ru/doc/1255909, accessed 17 January 2013 (in Russian).

Samykina, E., Samykina, L., Bogdanova, R., Samykina, S. and Skazkina, O. (2013) Evaluation of the dangers of air in the production of plastics (Otsenka opasnostey vozdukha v proizvodstve plastmass), in Ilyinskikh, N. (ed.), *Topical Problems of Modern Science, X. Anniversary International Teleconferencing, Vol. 2, No. 1.* Samara State Medical University, Regional Hospital (in Russian).

SCBK (2012) *History of Segezha Pulp and Paper Mill*. SCBK. www.scbk.ru/portal/content/view/29/51/, accessed 28 February 2014 (in Russian).

Serbina, T. and Perova, A. (2010) The Russian government has closed the first special economic zone, 'New Anapa' in Krasnodar region. *Kommersant, Rostov* 182(4480), 1 October (in Russian).

Serova, E. (2000) Effect of inter-regional trade barriers in the development of the agro-food markets in Russia, in *Inter-regional Barriers in the Russian Federation, The Socio-Economic Consequences and Ways to Overcome: European Experience and Lessons for Russia.* IET, Moscow, pp. 257–260. http://fadr.msu.ru/iet/barrier.htm, accessed 28 February 2014 (in Russian).

Sharpe, W., Alexander, G. and Bailey, J. (1998) *Investments*, 6th edn. Prentice-Hall, Englewood Cliffs, NJ.

Shelburne, R. and Palacin, J. (2007) *Remittances in the CIS: Their Economic Implications and a New Estimation Procedure.* Discussion Paper Series No. 5. United Nations Economic Commission for Europe. www.unece.org/fileadmin/DAM/oes/disc_papers/ECE_DP_2007-5.pdf, accessed 17 January 2014.

Shleinov, R. (2008) Back streets of Gazprom (Zakoulki Gazproma). *Novaya Gazeta*, 24 December. www.compromat.ru/page_23780.htm, accessed 28 February 2014 (in Russian).

Shokoladka (2013) Inspired by the chocolate. Life after the death of Soviet confectionery brands (Vdokhnovlennyye shokoladom. Zhizn' posle smerti sovetskikh konditerskikh marok). *Shokoladka*, 19 November. www.shokoladka.ru/news.php?n_id=3484, accessed 17 January 2014 (in Russian).

Sichkar, O. and Granik, I. (2010) Silicon Valley have registered in Skolkovo (Kremniyevuyu dolinu propisali v Skolkovo). *Kommersant* 47(4347), 19 March. www.kommersant.ru/doc/1338990, accessed 17 January 2013 (in Russian).

Shulga, I. (1996) Gazprom remained without a stabilizer (Gazprom ostalsya bez stabilizatora). *Kommersant Vlast* 17(176), p. 31, 14 May. www.kommersant.ru/doc/12463, accessed 28 February 2014 (in Russian).

Sikka, P. and Willmott, H. (2010) The dark side of transfer pricing: its role in tax avoidance and wealth retentiveness. *Critical Perspectives on Accounting* 21(4), pp. 342–356.

Sinjaeva, J. (2013) Senators want to resolve Russian Far East live by their own rules (Senatory khotyat razreshit' Dal'nemu Vostoku zhit' po sobstvennym pravilam). *RBC Daily*, 24 January. http://rbcdaily.ru/economy/562949985577302, accessed 27 January 2014 (in Russian).

Sitnikova, M. (2006) *Outstaffing in Russia*. Alinga Consulting Group, Woodside, CA. www.acg.ru/outstaffing_in_russia, accessed 10 November 2015.

Sreda (2012) *Atlas of Religions and Nationalities of the Russian*. Sreda, Moscow. http://sreda.org/en/arena, accessed 10 November 2015.

Stabus (2013) Standard accounting services (Standart bukhgalterskikh uslug). *Stabus*. www.stabus.ru/, accessed 27 January 2014 (in Russian).

Stiglitz, J. (1999). Whither Reform? Ten Years of theTransition. Paper presented at the World Bank Annual Bank Conference on Development Economics, 28–29 April 1999, Washington, DC.

Stranagordeev (2013) Plague and the son of the governor of the Voronezh region ruin of peasants (Chuma i syn gubernatora Voronezhskoy oblasti razoryayut krest'yan). *Stranagordeev*, 19 July. www.stranagordeev.ru/content/, accessed 28 February 2014 (in Russian).

Tache, I. and Lixandroiu, D. (2006) Rent seeking behaviour in transition countries: the case of Romania. *International Advances in Economic Research* 12(3), pp. 395–407. http://link.springer.com/article/10.1007%2Fs11294-006-9027-1, accessed 10 November 2015.

Tarusin, M. (2010) How many Orthodox in Russia? (Skol'ko pravoslavnykh v Rossii?) *Pravoslaviye i mir*, 3 April. www.pravmir.ru/skolko-pravoslavnyx-v-rossii/, accessed 17 January 2014 (in Russian).

TASS (2015) Russia to decide on Ukraine's $3 bln bond repayment in nearest future – PM. *ITAR-TASS News Agency*, Moscow. http://itar-tass.com/en/economy/771088, accessed 17 January 2014.

TGC-1 (2013) Company. *TGC-1*. www.tgc1.ru/en/company, accessed 28 February 2014.

Thompson, A. and Strickland, A. (2003) *Strategic Management Concepts and Cases*, 13th edn. McGraw-Hill/Irvin, Boston, MA.

Tolokonnikova, N. (2013) You are now always being punished ('Vy teper' vsegda budete nakazany'). Letter of Nadezhda Tolokonnikova. *Lenta*, 23 September. http://lenta.ru/articles/2013/09/23/tolokonnikova/, accessed 26 February 2014 (in Russian).

Tolstykh, P. and Puzyrev, D. (2012) Vodka market – a huge market of shadow cache for regional elites (Rynok vodki – eto ogromnyy rynok tenevogo kesha dlya regional'nykh elit). *RBC Daily*, 26 March. http://rbcdaily.ru/market/562949983360637, accessed 17 January 2014 (in Russian).

Transneft (2014) *Transneft*. Moscow. www.en.transneft.ru/about/, accessed 17 January 2014.

Treacy, M. and Wiersema, F. (1995) *The Discipline of Market Leaders: Choose Your Customers, Narrow Your Focus, Dominate Your Market*. Addison-Wesley, Boston, MA.

Trushin, A. (2009) Head of Rosstandart Elkin approved the corrupt state standards of Institute of Concrete and Reinforced Concrete (Rukovoditel' Rostekhregulirovaniya El'kin utverdil korruptsionnyye GOSTy NII Betona i Zhelezobetona). *Solomin*, 28 October. www.compromat.ru/page_28456.htm, accessed 20 February 2014 (in Russian).

Tsvetkova, N. (2009) The governors impose restrictions on the importation of alcoholic beverages. *Denga*, 27 April. http://denga.ru/reviews/4145/, accessed 28 February 2014 (in Russian) (no longer available online).

Tulskiy, M. (2004) Capitalism with a badge of the Komsomol (Kapitalizm so znachkom vlksm). *Versiya*, 15 November. www.compromat.ru/page_15825.htm, accessed 10 November 2015 (in Russian).

Turovsky, R. (2006) *Political Regionalism*. Publishing House of the HSE, Moscow (in Russian).

Ukolov, R. (2008) Shokhin, Rutberg and machine guns behind the fence (Shokhin, Rutberg i pulemety za zaborom). *Nezavisimaya Gazeta*, 27 March. www.flb.ru/info/43294, accessed 17 January 2013 (in Russian) (no longer available online).

Uniconf (2013) *United Confectioners*. www.uniconf.ru/ru/about/, accessed 27 January 2014.

Vahonicheva, O. (2007) Outstaffing, outsourcing and other methods of deception (Autstaffing, autsorsing i drugiye sposoby obmana). *HR-Portal*. www.hr-portal.ru, 2007-05-20, accessed 27 January 2013 (in Russian).

Vasiliev, S. (2006) Special economic zones along the Chinese model (Osobyye ekonomicheskiye zony po kitayskomu obraztsu). *Business Lawyer* 8. www.center-bereg.ru/g1012.html, accessed 10 November 2015 (in Russian).

VCIOM (2010) *Do We Believe in God?* (*Verim li my v boga?*). Russian Public Opinion Research Center (VCIOM), Moscow. http://wciom.ru/index.php?id=268&uid=13365, accessed 27 January 2014 (in Russian).

Veblen, T. (1994 [1899]) *The Theory of the Leisure Class*. Penguin Books, New York.

Vokrug novostey (2007) Oil and corruption: some specific features of state-owned businesses, 'Transneft' (Neft' i korruptsiya: O nekotorykh spetsificheskikh osobennostyakh biznesa goskompanii 'Transneft'). *Vokrug novostey*, 14 May. www.compromat.ru/page_20710.htm, accessed 28 February 2014 (in Russian).

Vozhdaeva, O. (2012) Vietnam workers kept like slaves at factory in Russia. *BBC Russian.com*, 10 August. www.bbc.co.uk/news/world-europe-19197095, accessed 27 January 2014.

Weber, M. (1947) *The Theory of Social and Economic Organization*. Free Press, New York.

Wernerfelt, B. (1984) A resource-based view of the firm. *Strategic Management Journal* 5(2), pp. 171–180.

World Bank (2008) *Migration and Remittances, Factbook 2008*. World Bank, Washington, DC. http://econ.worldbank.org/wbsite/external/extdec/extdecprospects/0,contentMDK: 21352016, accessed 27 January 2014 (no longer available online).

Williamson, O. (1985) *The Economic Institutions of Capitalism*. Free Press, New York.

Wit, B. and Meyer, R. (2010) *Strategy Process, Content, Context*, 4th edn. Cengage Learning, Andover.

Yin, R. (2003) *Case Study Research: Design and Methods*. Sage, Thousand Oaks, CA.

Yukos (2006) About us. *Yukos Oil Company*. www.ngfr.ru/library.html?yukos, accessed 10 November 2015.

Yuzhnyy, M. (2013) Slaves in Dagestan lured by tickets for the matches Anji (Rabov v Dagestan zamanivayut biletami na matchi Anzhi). *Komsomolskaya Pravda*, 15 May. www.kp.ru/daily/26075/2981401, accessed 17 January 2014 (in Russian).

Zubarevich, N. (2008) Socio-economic development of regions: the myths and realities of the alignment (Sotsial'no-ekonomicheskoye razvitiye regionov: mify i realii vyravnivaniya). *SPERO* 9, pp. 7–22. http://spero.socpol.ru/docs/N9_2008_01.pdf, accessed 17 January 2014 (in Russian).

Zubarevich, N. (2011) Four Russians (Chetyre Rossii). *Vedomosti*, 30 December. www.vedomosti.ru/opinion/news/1467059/chetyre_rossii, accessed 17 January 2014 (in Russian).

Index

For Product Safety Concerns and Information please contact our EU
representative GPSR@taylorandfrancis.com
Taylor & Francis Verlag GmbH, Kaufingerstraße 24, 80331 München, Germany

www.ingramcontent.com/pod-product-compliance
Lightning Source LLC
Chambersburg PA
CBHW050438280326
41932CB00013BA/2163